PROFESSIONAL
FUNCTIONAL PROGRAMMING

D1031265

Continues

PROFESSIONAL

Functional Programming in C#

CLASSIC PROGRAMMING TECHNIQUES
FOR MODERN PROJECTS

Oliver Sturm

RETIRÉ DE LA COLLECTION UNIVERSELLE
Bibliothèque et Archives nationales du Québec

WILEY

Wiley Publishing, Inc.

Professional Functional Programming in C#: Classic Programming Techniques for Modern Projects

This edition first published 2011

©2011 John Wiley & Sons, Ltd

Registered office

John Wiley & Sons Ltd, The Atrium, Southern Gate, Chichester, West Sussex, PO19 8SQ, United Kingdom

For details of our global editorial offices, for customer services and for information about how to apply for permission to reuse the copyright material in this book please see our website at www.wiley.com.

The right of the author to be identified as the author of this work has been asserted in accordance with the Copyright, Designs and Patents Act 1988.

All rights reserved. No part of this publication may be reproduced, stored in a retrieval system, or transmitted, in any form or by any means, electronic, mechanical, photocopying, recording or otherwise, except as permitted by the UK Copyright, Designs and Patents Act 1988, without the prior permission of the publisher.

Wiley also publishes its books in a variety of electronic formats. Some content that appears in print may not be available in electronic books.

Designations used by companies to distinguish their products are often claimed as trademarks. All brand names and product names used in this book are trade names, service marks, trademarks or registered trademarks of their respective owners. The publisher is not associated with any product or vendor mentioned in this book. This publication is designed to provide accurate and authoritative information in regard to the subject matter covered. It is sold on the understanding that the publisher is not engaged in rendering professional services. If professional advice or other expert assistance is required, the services of a competent professional should be sought.

978-0-470-74458-1
978-0-470-97028-7 (ebk)
978-0-470-97110-9 (ebk)
978-0-470-97109-3 (ebk)

A catalogue record for this book is available from the British Library.

ABOUT THE AUTHOR

OLIVER STURM has over 20 years experience developing professional software. He is a well-known expert in various areas of application architecture, programming languages and the third party .NET tools made by DevExpress. His main focus has been on the .NET platform since 2002. Oliver has spoken at many international conferences and has written more than 20 training classes and more than 100 magazine articles in English as well as German. He has also taught classes on topics around computer programming for more than 15 years. For his contributions to the .NET community, he has been awarded the C# MVP Award by Microsoft United Kingdom for several years now.

Based in Scotland, UK, Oliver works as a freelance consultant and trainer, and he is an associate at thinktecture, an international consultancy firm. You can find his blog at www.sturmnet.org/blog and his commercial website at www.oliversturm.com. His e-mail address is oliver@oliversturm.com.

CREDITS

VP CONSUMER AND TECHNOLOGY PUBLISHING DIRECTOR
Michelle Leete

ASSOCIATE DIRECTOR—BOOK CONTENT MANAGEMENT
Martin Tribe

ASSOCIATE PUBLISHER
Chris Webb

PUBLISHING ASSISTANT
Ellie Scott

ASSOCIATE MARKETING DIRECTOR
Louise Breinholt

MARKETING EXECUTIVE
Kate Parrett

EDITORIAL MANAGER
Jodi Jensen

SENIOR PROJECT EDITOR
Sara Shlaer

PROJECT EDITOR
Brian Herrmann

TECHNICAL EDITORS
Michael Giagnocavo
Matthew Podwysocki

SENIOR PRODUCTION EDITOR
Debra Banninger

COPY EDITOR
Maryann Steinhart

PROOFREADER
Sheilah Ledwidge, Word One

INDEXER
Robert Swanson

COVER DESIGNER
Mike Trent

COVER IMAGE
© Oleg Kruglov/istockphoto.com

CONTENTS

INTRODUCTION

FUNCTIONAL PROGRAMMING is an important paradigm of programming that looks back on a long history. The subject has always been very relevant to people who teach others how to program — the clean and logical concepts of functional programming lend themselves especially well to teaching. Certain industries that use computers and self-written programs heavily have also found functional programming to be the most productive approach for their purposes. However, for many of the "mainstream" software manufacturers, functional programming has long held an air of the academic and they widely chose to use approaches with an imperative heritage, like object orientation.

In recent years, more and more functional elements have been included in imperative languages on the .NET platform, and with Visual Studio 2010, F# has been included — the first hybrid functional language in the box with Microsoft's mainstream development platform. Even more than the functional features that have been introduced to C# and VB.NET, this shows a commitment on Microsoft's side.

WHO THIS BOOK IS FOR

The topic of functional programming in C# can be seen from two different angles. On the .NET platform there are many experienced developers and development teams, who have been using C# or VB.NET, or in some cases C++, to create software for the platform. If you have that sort of experience, there are lots of reasons you should be looking into functional programming: it's a clean and easily maintainable style, it's an important basis of programming as we know it today, and certain specific current concerns, like parallelization, can be targeted successfully with the help of functional programming ideas.

On the other hand, perhaps you're not a .NET programmer at all. Instead, you have experience in one or more "traditional" functional programming languages. You need to work with people who use C#, or you want to use the language yourself. This book will help you understand how you can use the approaches you're familiar with in C#, and it may give you valuable starting points when it comes to explaining these ideas to team members without your functional background.

The book assumes a basic level of understanding of C# language constructs, at least up to version 3.0 of the language. However, Part II is written to explain a few particular features of the language that are especially important, rather complex or often misunderstood. From experience, I recommend you give Part II a good look even if you're quite fluent in C# — there are usually some little-known intricacies about the features that have been selected for this part, which may lead to misunderstandings later.

WHAT THIS BOOK COVERS

The language of the vast majority of examples in this book is C# 4.0, running on Microsoft .NET. There are a few examples in other languages, but they are for illustrative purposes only. If you want to try out the examples for yourself, but you're not on C# 4.0 or Visual Studio 2010 yet, you may still have success using C# 3.0 and Visual Studio 2008 — there aren't many new features in C# 4.0 specifically, and none of them have been exploited in the examples. However, a few examples utilize .NET Framework features like Parallel Extensions, which are available only in .NET 4.0.

The book introduces you to concepts of functional programming and describes how these can be used with the C# language. An effort has been made to provide samples with a practical background, but most of them still focus mostly on language level considerations. Functional programming is a technique for code, algorithm and program structure — as opposed to, for instance, application architecture. Of course it needs to fit in with application architecture . . . you get the point: it's sometimes hard to find the perfect compromise between being too theoretical and going off-focus, but I've tried my best.

While I wrote this book, I developed a library of functionally oriented helpers, called FCSlib (that's "Functional CSharp Library"). You can use this library in your own projects as you like, but please note that it doesn't come with any warranty. The downloadable file containing the library code (more information about downloads in the upcoming section "Source Code") includes a copy of the LGPL license text, which applies to the FCSlib code.

HOW THIS BOOK IS STRUCTURED

This book has four parts. The first part provides an overview of functional programming, both from a historical and a current point of view. Part II proceeds to give you the C# background you'll need to understand the more complex examples that follow later. Again, reading this is recommended even if you know C# — it does have a few pretty basic items, but generally it's not meant to be a language introduction for newbies.

Part III is the most important one. Its 10 chapters describe a variety of functional programming topics from a C# point of view, showing lots of examples and code snippets. The code library that accompanies this book, FCSlib, is built on the ideas described in this part.

Finally, Part IV gives you an overview of practical concerns of using functional programming in C#. I picked a few specific scenarios, and there are descriptions of functional programming ideas in existing products and technologies that you may be familiar with.

WHAT YOU NEED TO USE THIS BOOK

All code in this book has been tested with Visual Studio 2010, C# 4.0 and .NET 4.0. Much of it has been originally developed on C# 3.0, so you should have good success running the code on .NET 3.5. Going back further than that would mean major rewrites in many areas — the concepts may translate even to C# 2.0 in many cases, but the language features that make them reasonably easy to use are just not available in that version.

I have made several attempts to build the code on the Mono platform, but unfortunately I stumbled upon compiler bugs every time. Your mileage may vary if you try to use Mono — after all, it changes all the time.

CONVENTIONS

To help you get the most from the text and keep track of what's happening, we've used a number of conventions throughout the book.

> *The pencil icon indicates notes, tips, hints, tricks, and asides to the current discussion.*

As for styles in the text:

➤ We *italicize* new terms and important words when we introduce them.

➤ We show keyboard strokes like this: Ctrl+A.

➤ We show file names, URLs, and code within the text like so: `persistence.properties`.

➤ We present code in two different ways:

```
We use a monofont type with no highlighting for most code examples.
We use bold to emphasize code that is particularly important in the present
context or to show changes from a previous code snippet.
```

SOURCE CODE

As you work through the examples in this book, you may choose either to type in all the code manually, or to use the source code files that accompany the book. All the source code used in this book is available for download at `www.wrox.com`. When at the site, simply locate the book's title (use the Search box or one of the title lists) and click the Download Code link on the book's detail page to obtain all the source code for the book. Code that is included on the website is highlighted by the following icon:

Available for
download on
Wrox.com

Listings include the filename in the title. If it is just a code snippet, you'll find the filename in a code note such as this:

Code snippet filename

 Because many books have similar titles, you may find it easiest to search by ISBN; this book's ISBN is 978-0-470-74458-1.

Once you download the code, just decompress it with your favorite compression tool. Alternately, you can go to the main Wrox code download page at www.wrox.com/dynamic/books/download .aspx to see the code available for this book and all other Wrox books.

ERRATA

We make every effort to ensure that there are no errors in the text or in the code. However, no one is perfect, and mistakes do occur. If you find an error in one of our books, like a spelling mistake or faulty piece of code, we would be very grateful for your feedback. By sending in errata, you may save another reader hours of frustration, and at the same time, you will be helping us provide even higher quality information.

To find the errata page for this book, go to www.wrox.com and locate the title using the Search box or one of the title lists. Then, on the book details page, click the Book Errata link. On this page, you can view all errata that has been submitted for this book and posted by Wrox editors. A complete book list, including links to each book's errata, is also available at www.wrox.com/misc-pages/ booklist.shtml.

If you don't spot "your" error on the Book Errata page, go to www.wrox.com/contact/ techsupport.shtml and complete the form there to send us the error you have found. We'll check the information and, if appropriate, post a message to the book's errata page and fix the problem in subsequent editions of the book.

P2P.WROX.COM

For author and peer discussion, join the P2P forums at p2p.wrox.com. The forums are a Web-based system for you to post messages relating to Wrox books and related technologies and interact with other readers and technology users. The forums offer a subscription feature to e-mail you topics of interest of your choosing when new posts are made to the forums. Wrox authors, editors, other industry experts, and your fellow readers are present on these forums.

At p2p.wrox.com, you will find a number of different forums that will help you, not only as you read this book, but also as you develop your own applications. To join the forums, just follow these steps:

1. Go to p2p.wrox.com and click the Register link.

2. Read the terms of use and click Agree.

3. Complete the required information to join, as well as any optional information you wish to provide, and click Submit.

4. You will receive an e-mail with information describing how to verify your account and complete the joining process.

 You can read messages in the forums without joining P2P, but in order to post your own messages, you must join.

Once you join, you can post new messages and respond to messages other users post. You can read messages at any time on the Web. If you would like to have new messages from a particular forum e-mailed to you, click the Subscribe to this Forum icon by the forum name in the forum listing.

For more information about how to use the Wrox P2P, be sure to read the P2P FAQs for answers to questions about how the forum software works, as well as many common questions specific to P2P and Wrox books. To read the FAQs, click the FAQ link on any P2P page.

PART I
Introduction to Functional Programming

1

A Look at Functional Programming History

WHAT'S IN THIS CHAPTER?

➤ An explanation functional programming

➤ A look at some functional languages

➤ The relationship to object oriented programming

Functional programming has been around for a very long time. Many regard the advent of the language LISP, in 1958, as the starting point of functional programming. On the other hand, LISP was based on existing concepts, perhaps most importantly those defined by Alonzo Church in his lambda calculus during the 1930s and 1940s. That sounds highly mathematical, and it was — the ideas of mathematics were easy to model in LISP, which made it the obvious language of choice in the academic sector. LISP introduced many other concepts that are still important to programming languages today.

WHAT IS FUNCTIONAL PROGRAMMING?

In spite of the close coupling to LISP in its early days, functional programming is generally regarded a paradigm of programming that can be applied in many languages — even those that were not originally intended to be used with that paradigm. Like the name implies, it focuses on the application of functions. Functional programmers use functions as building blocks to create new functions — that's not to say that there are no other language elements available to them, but the function is the main construct that architecture is built from.

Referential transparency is an important idea in the realm of functional programming. A function that is referentially transparent returns values that depend only on the input parameters that are passed. This is in contrast to the basic ideas of imperative programming, where program state often influences return values of functions. Both functional and imperative programming use the term *function*, but the mathematical meaning of the referentially transparent function is the one used in functional programming. Such functions are also referred to as pure functions, and are described as having no side effects.

It's often impossible to define whether a given programming language is a functional language or not. On the other hand, it is possible to find out the extent to which a language supports approaches commonly used in the functional programming paradigm — recursion, for example. Most programming languages generally support recursion in the sense that programmers can call into a particular function, procedure, or method from its own code. But if the compilers and/or runtime environments associated with the language use stack-based tracking of return addresses on jumps like many imperative languages do, and there are no optimizations generally available to help prevent stack overflow issues, then recursion may be severely restricted in its applications. In imperative languages, there are often specialized syntax structures to implement loops, and more advanced support for recursion is ignored by the language or compiler designers.

Higher order functions are also important in functional programming. Higher order functions are those that take other functions as parameters or return other functions as their results. Many programming languages have some support for this capability. Even C has a syntax to define a type of a function or, in C terms, to refer to the function through a function pointer. Obviously this enables C programmers to pass around such function pointers or to return them from other functions. Many C libraries contain functions, such as those for searching and sorting, that are implemented as higher order functions, taking the essential data-specific comparison functions as parameters. Then again, C doesn't have any support for anonymous functions — that is, functions created on-the-fly, in-line, like lambda expressions, or for related concepts such as closures.

Other examples of language capabilities that help define functional programming are explored in the following chapters in this book.

For some programmers, functional programming is a natural way of telling the computer what it should do, by describing the properties of a given problem in a concise language. You might have heard the saying that functional programming is more about telling computers what the problem is they should be solving, and not so much about specifying the precise steps of the solution. This saying is a result of the high level of abstraction that functional programming provides. Referential transparency means that the only responsibility of the programmer is the specification of functions to describe and solve a given set of problems. On the basis of that specification, the computer can then decide on the best evaluation order, potential parallelization opportunities, or even whether a certain function needs to be evaluated at all.

For some other programmers, functional programming is not the starting point. They come from a procedural, imperative, or perhaps object oriented background. There's much anecdotal evidence of such programmers analyzing their day-to-day problems, both the ones they are meant to solve by writing programs, and the ones they encounter while writing those programs, and gravitating toward solutions from the functional realm by themselves. The ideas of functional programming often provide very natural solutions, and the fact that you can arrive there from different directions reinforces that point.

FUNCTIONAL LANGUAGES

Functional programming is not language specific. However, certain languages have been around in that space for a long time, influencing the evolution of functional programming approaches just as much as they were themselves influenced by those approaches to begin with. The largest parts of this book contain examples only in C#, but it can be useful to have at least an impression of the languages that have been used traditionally for functional programming, or which have evolved since the early days with functional programming as a primary focus.

Here are two simple functions written in LISP:

```lisp
(defun calcLine (ch col line maxp)
  (let
    ((tch (if (= col (- maxp line)) (cons ch nil) (cons 46 nil))))
    (if (= col maxp) tch (append (append tch (calcLine ch (+ col 1) line maxp)) tch))
    )
  )

(defun calcLines (line maxp)
  (let*
    ((ch (+ line (char-int #\A)))
      (l (append (calcLine ch 0 line maxp) (cons 10 nil)))
      )
    (if (= line maxp) l (append (append l (calcLines (+ line 1) maxp)) l))
    )
  )
```

The dialect used here is Common Lisp, one of the main dialects of LISP. It is not important to understand precisely what this code snippet does. A much more interesting aspect of the LISP family of dialects is the structure and the syntactic simplicity exhibited. Arguably, LISP's Scheme dialects enforce this notion further than Common Lisp, Scheme being an extremely simple language with very strong extensibility features. But the general ideas become clear immediately: a minimum of syntax, few keywords and operators, and obvious blocks. Many of the elements you may regard as keywords or other built-in structures — such as defun or append — are actually macros, functions, or procedures. They may indeed come out of the box with your LISP system of choice, but they are not compiler magic. You can write your own or replace the existing implementations. Many programmers do not agree that the exclusive use of standard round parentheses makes code more readable, but it is nevertheless easy to admire the elegance of such a basic system.

The following code snippet shows an implementation of the same two functions, the same algorithm, in the much newer language Haskell:

```haskell
calcLine :: Int -> Int -> Int -> Int -> String
calcLine ch col line maxp =
  let tch = if maxp - line == col then [chr ch] else "." in
  if col == maxp
    then tch
```

```
        else tch' ++ (calcLine ch (col+1) line maxp) ++ tch

calcLines :: Int -> Int -> String
calcLines line maxp =
  let ch = (ord 'A') + line in
  let l = (calcLine ch 0 line maxp) ++ "\n" in
  if line == maxp
    then l
    else l ++ (calcLines (line+1) maxp) ++ l
```

There is a very different style to the structure of the Haskell code. Different types of brackets are used to create a list comprehension. The if...then...else construct is a built-in, and the ++ operator does the job of appending lists. The type signatures of the functions are a common practice in Haskell, although they are not strictly required. One very important distinction can't readily be seen: Haskell is a strongly typed language, whereas LISP is dynamically typed. Because Haskell has extremely strong type inference, it is usually unnecessary to tell the compiler about types explicitly; they are known at compile time. There are many other invisible differences between Haskell and LISP, but that's not the focus of this book.

Finally, here's an example in the language Erlang, chosen for certain Erlang specific elements:

```
add(A, B) ->
    Calc = whereis(calcservice),
    Calc ! {self(), add, A, B},
    receive
        {Calc, Result} -> Result
    end.

mult(A, B) ->
    Calc = whereis(calcservice),
    Calc ! {self(), mult, A, B},
    receive
        {Calc, Result} -> Result
    end.


loop() ->
    receive
        {Sender, add, A, B} ->
            Result = A + B,
            io:format("adding: ~p~n", [Result]),
            Sender ! {self(), Result},
            loop();
        {Sender, mult, A, B} ->
            Result = A * B,
            io:format("multiplying: ~p~n", [Result]),
            Sender ! {self(), Result},
            loop();
        Other ->
            io:format("I don't know how to do ~p~n", [Other]),
            loop()
    end.
```

This is a very simple learning sample of Erlang code. However, it uses constructs pointing at the Actor model based parallelization support provided by the language and its runtime system. Erlang is not a very strict functional language — mixing in the types of side effects provided by `io:format` wouldn't be possible this way in Haskell. But in many industrial applications, Erlang has an important role today for its stability and the particular feature set it provides.

As you can see, functional languages, like imperative ones, can take many different shapes. From the very simplistic approach of LISP to the advanced syntax of Haskell or the specific feature set of Erlang, with many steps in between, there's a great spectrum of languages available to programmers who want to choose a language for its functional origins. All three language families are available today, with strong runtime systems, even for .NET in the case of the LISP dialect Clojure. Some of the ideas shown by those languages will be discussed further in the upcoming chapters.

THE RELATIONSHIP TO OBJECT ORIENTED PROGRAMMING

It is a common assumption that the ideas of functional programming are incompatible with those of other schools of programming. In reality, most languages available today are hybrid in the sense that they don't focus exclusively on one programming technique. There's no reason why they should, either, because different techniques can often complement one another.

Object oriented programming brings a number of interesting aspects to the table. One of them is a strong focus on encapsulation, combining data and behavior into classes and objects, and defining interfaces for their interaction. These ideas help object oriented languages promote modularization and a certain kind of reuse on the basis of the modules programmers create. An aspect that's responsible for the wide adoption object oriented programming languages have seen in mainstream programming is the way they allow modeling of real-world scenarios in computer programs. Many business application scenarios are focused on data storage, and the data in question is often related to physical items, which have properties and are often defined and distinguished by the way they interact with other items in their environments. As a result, object oriented mechanisms are not just widely applicable, but they are also easy to grasp.

When looking at a complicated industrial machine, for example, many programmers immediately come up with a way of modeling it in code as a collection of the wheels and cogs and other parts. Perhaps they consider viewing it as an abstract system that takes some raw materials and creates an end product. For certain applications, however, it may be interesting to deal with what the machine does on a rather abstract level. There may be measurements to read and analyze, and if the machine is complex enough, mathematical considerations might be behind the decisions for the parts to combine and the paths to take in the manufacturing process. This example can be abstractly extended toward any non-physical apparatus capable of generating output from input.

In reality, both the physical and the abstract viewpoints are important. Programming doesn't have a golden bullet, and programmers need to understand the different techniques at their disposal and make the decision for and against them on the basis of any problem with which they are confronted. Most programs have parts where data modeling is important, and they also have parts where algorithms are important. And of course they have many parts where there's no clear distinction, where both data modeling and algorithms and a wide variety of other aspects are important. That's why so many modern programming languages are hybrid. This is not a new idea either — the first object oriented programming language standardized by ANSI was Common Lisp.

SUMMARY

Today's .NET platform provides one of the best possible constellations for hybrid software development. Originally a strong, modern and newly developed object oriented platform, .NET has taken major steps for years now in the functional direction. Microsoft F# is a fully supported hybrid language on the .NET platform, the development of which has influenced platform decisions since 2002. At the other end of the spectrum, albeit not all too far away, there's C#, a newly developed language strongly based in object orientation, that has been equally influenced by functional ideas almost from its invention. At the core of any program written in either language there's the .NET Framework itself, arguably the strongest set of underlying libraries that has ever been available for application development.

2

Putting Functional Programming into a Modern Context

WHAT'S IN THIS CHAPTER?

➤ Managing side effects

➤ Agile programming methodologies

➤ Declarative programming

➤ Functional programming as a mindset

➤ The feasibility of functional programming in C#

There have always been groups of programmers more interested in functional programming than in other schools of programming, and certain niches of the industry have provided a platform for those well versed in functional approaches and the underlying theory. At the same time, however, the mainstream of business application programming — the bread and butter of most programmers on platforms made by Microsoft and others — has evolved in a different direction. Object orientation and other forms of imperative programming have become the most widely used paradigms in this space of programming, to the extent that programmers have been neglecting other schools of thought more and more. For many, the realization that solutions to certain problems can be found by looking back to something "old" is initially a surprise.

One of the main reasons programmers become interested in functional programming today is the need for concurrency programming models. This need, in turn, comes from the evolution of the hardware toward multicore and multiprocessor setups. Programs no longer benefit very much from advances in technology like they did when increases in MHz were a main measurable reference point. Instead, programs need to be parallelized to take advantage of more than one CPU, or CPU core, available in a machine. Programmers are finding that parallelization is no longer a mere luxury, but rather a requirement if they don't want to see their codebase, their architecture, and their algorithms left behind gradually.

One area of the parallelization problem is increasingly being covered by standard tools of the platform, and that's the technical side of dealing with parallelization. For a long time, programmers had to work with the underlying structures of the Windows operating system itself: processes and threads, mainly. This was true even for the managed .NET environment. In 2010, Microsoft released a new library called the Parallel Extensions to the .NET Framework, formerly identified as Parallel FX or just PFX. This library, packaged with .NET 4.0, revolutionizes the technical side of concurrency programming for the .NET programmer, providing task objects instead of threads, which are coordinated intelligently by the framework. It also allows for some advanced interaction between these units so that certain problems are now much easier to solve — no need to write your own scheduler to control the number of parallel execution units, no complex structures to retrieve results from background processes, and so on.

Unfortunately there's still a structural problem because an application that has been written in a normal imperative style, based on the sharing and changing of state information, is often not easy to parallelize due to all the data exchange/shared access challenges. Imperative and object oriented programming almost make it a rule to store data in places where it can be accessed (for reads as well as writes) by more than just a single method or function. While the Parallel Extensions library provides handy utility functions to replace standard single-threaded ones readily, the functions are not that easy to use in reality because the rest of the code hasn't been written with parallelization in mind. For instance, there is a `Parallel.ForEach` function that does vaguely the same thing as the standard C# `foreach` statement except it parallelizes its execution — but this will only work if the code that is in the loop has been structured so that there are no data access collisions.

MANAGING SIDE EFFECTS

In spite of the help provided by libraries such as Parallel Extensions, you still need to do a lot of potentially complex structural work on your codebase in order to parallelize it. In functional programming, the kind of data access where multiple methods or functions in a program have shared access to the same data — most importantly write access to that data — is called a side effect. One of the main ideas of functional programming is to manage such side effects. This may mean to prevent them, and it is certainly a target to reduce these side effects to begin with, because that makes the remaining ones easier to manage. It is an illusion, however, that a computer program could do anything useful without having side effects in the technical sense — whenever something is seen on screen, data is stored in a file or a database, or something is sent over a network, that is, on some level, a side effect.

The imperative reaction to the problem of shared data access is typically to impose restrictions, with the technical term being synchronization. This is often summarized as mutual exclusion, which describes the idea very well: while one execution thread accesses a particular piece of information to make a change, others can't do so at the same time. It's a simple and efficient concept, but quite hard to get right. As soon as there are many pieces of information, as there are bound to be in imperative applications, the individual critical sections tend to overlap and nest, and it becomes difficult to keep track of all the possible interaction scenarios, resulting in all sorts of locking issues.

There are other solutions to many of these, such as specialized lock types or other synchronization structures like queues or flags.

In functional programming, programmers have learned to deal with the management of side effects in a different way because the structure and background of their languages required this to a higher degree. It would be wrong to say that functional programming has all the answers to the parallelization problems, but there's definitely a large pool of knowledge there on the topic of programming without side effects, which in turn means easy parallelization. Taking those strategies into account is what makes functional programming interesting to so many these days, whether or not their languages were meant to be functional by their inventors. Parts of this book describe the application of functional techniques specifically with parallelization in mind.

AGILE PROGRAMMING METHODOLOGIES

After parallelization, a second interesting consideration is that of functional modularization — that is, modularization on the level of individual functions. In object oriented languages, there are typically classes and methods within classes. There are languages that allow the nesting of methods, but many do not — in C#, for instance, methods can't be nested. But the use of anonymous methods and lambda expressions allow the creation of functions that are local to methods, which opens the door to modularization on the algorithm level.

This notion fits in very well with the application of modern software development methodologies like Agile. One of the main ideas in this space is an evolutionary approach in which programmers work along simple requirement specifications and, in a nutshell, do only what's necessary in each step to satisfy these requirements. Refactoring becomes an important part of the concept, and modularization, with the implied reuse resulting from it, can be very useful as a technique on a method or function level when the introduction of new methods on the class level seems like too large a step to take. Just like in the area of techniques for parallelization, functional programming doesn't offer a magical solution here, but there's a lot to learn from functional techniques that have employed functions as reusable building blocks for a long time.

DECLARATIVE PROGRAMMING

Functional programming is generally regarded as a style of declarative programming. The target of declarative programming is to specify the goal, the logic of what a program, or a part of a program, should do, without describing the steps necessary to achieve that goal. In other words, it is about leaving choices to the computer when it comes to the details of executing a program, instead of requiring the programmer to specify these. Many types of declarative programming have been accepted into the mainstream over the years.

Domain-specific languages are one example. HTML, XML, and XAML can be regarded as languages that describe documents and data as well as execution instructions. Regular expressions describe complex input and their engines effectively parse and manipulate data. Querying languages such as SQL and the in-code querying functionality of LINQ are variations of declarative programming, as are the code contracts available in .NET 4.0. Functional programming is a less specific type of declarative programming, compared to these examples, but it is still just an extension of ideas that are already quite common today.

FUNCTIONAL PROGRAMMING IS A MINDSET

In the end, functional programming is a mindset. If you are willing to think in a certain way, it can offer you interesting solutions or at least food for thought, with a relevance to many practical aspects of programming today. You can do it in any programming language you want — well, almost. It should make your life easier and reduce the amount of code you need to write as well as the time to market for your next project and the maintenance efforts that come later.

Something that's sometimes criticized about functional programming is the fact that the approaches are not bound to the most performative ones you could use to solve any given problem. This may or may not be true for any given algorithm–language combination — it is, of course, hard to make a general statement about this. It's also difficult to judge given that an application of functional principles may enable you to utilize the processing resources provided by your machine more efficiently. The reality is that if a qualified person sat down and optimized each algorithm by hand, on a low level, using C code or assembler instructions, then he could certainly make everything run more efficiently. But at some point in the past the majority of programmers started moving away from such approaches and using higher level languages for most of the programming work they needed to do. They started looking at the time to market, the programmer's efficiency, as a higher priority than the creation of the perfect algorithm from a machine utilization point of view.

Of course these steps were made gradually. Perhaps somebody went from C to C++ first, assuming that the compiler would be almost as efficient for C++ as it was for C. Maybe they moved on to Java or .NET at some later point in time, where a virtual machine is the platform to program against, and just-in-time (JIT) compilers do the — hopefully efficient — job of translating to the native CPU code. The world gets more complicated then because while there's a potential performance loss in the additional translation work required, new possibilities are created at the same time, including those to translate an intermediate code binary file intelligently toward the precise processor and machine architecture used at runtime and applying any number of clever optimizations in the process.

Any kind of declarative programming is a logical next step in that sequence. You gain efficiency because the declarative languages allow you to specify the problems you're trying to solve, and the computer can help more with the solutions than it's allowed to in purely imperative programming scenarios. The quality of that help is eventually what decides the performance of the final result. But in today's complex world of hardware, multicore CPUs in machines and even on graphics cards, and different versions and architectures of CPUs with many important distinctions, it isn't hard to imagine that in the vast majority of cases a computer will make better choices — and much more quickly and efficiently than humans. For those edge cases where statistics fail, and for those perfectionists and control freaks among us, there's still the possibility of interfacing with code written directly in a low-level language.

The first priority today is to program efficiently. The second priority, however closely it may follow, is to write efficient programs.

IS FUNCTIONAL PROGRAMMING IN C# A GOOD IDEA?

When all you have is a hammer, everything looks like a nail. Should programming languages be seen as general problem solving devices that can be applied to any problem and, as a consequence, to any solution strategy? Or should they be viewed as tools that are good for particular tasks, and less good or even useless for others? Practical understanding of different programming languages, the driving factors that define their priorities, and the consequences of the design decisions seems to point quite clearly toward the "tool" understanding of programming languages. Functional programming is a good example to document this statement. Let's face it: if you want to write some purely functional code, you'll have a much easier time doing it with the help of a purely functional language — that is, one that has been created with the precise techniques in mind that you are going to employ. No surprise there, really.

In reality, it's all about finding the best compromise. It is certainly a goal to strive for to understanding the specialties of different languages and to be able to make informed decisions about their applicability to a particular problem situation. But in most real-world projects, there are limits to the number of such choices you can reasonably make. Other programmers involved may not be familiar with the same subset of tools that you know. It pays in the long term to have some consistency across projects, because it keeps down maintenance effort. It also makes it easier to hire new people to support existing code bases. At the same time, programmers who restrict themselves to just one language will often miss important opportunities offered elsewhere. And they will never be seen by their bosses or clients as the final point of reference in what should be their area of expertise.

Knowing the pros and cons of using particular tools and approaches is important. You can have any number of reasons for a decision to make a move or to stay where you are, but if you find that a choice is right in front you and you aren't thinking about a decision, you are probably missing out.

SUMMARY

Picking up functional programming while staying with C# as a language is a strategy that should be based on practical considerations. This book is not telling you that C# can do everything functional just as easily as LISP, or Haskell, or even F# on the same .NET platform. It can't. Yes, you can do most things, but they are harder, more syntactically complex, and perhaps even more difficult to understand as a consequence. This book shows you how it works, what you can and cannot do, and where the limits are.

If you are a C# programmer and you have reasons why the adoption of a different or an additional programming language is not an option for yourself or your team, this book is for you. If you want to learn about functional programming on the basis of a language you're already familiar with, this book is for you. And if you know functional programming and you're wondering how you can go about explaining it to your imperative programmer friends, this book is also for you.

Does it make sense to program functionally in C#? Yes, for all sorts of reasons, it does. Read on.

PART II
C# Foundations of Functional Programming

3

Functions, Delegates, and Lambda Expressions

WHAT'S IN THIS CHAPTER?

➤ Functions and methods

➤ Considerations for reuse

➤ Anonymous functions and lambda expressions

➤ Extension methods

➤ Referential transparency

Almost all programming languages have a means of defining blocks of code and of declaring certain execution sequences as belonging together, usually for the purpose of reusability as well as for structural and maintenance reasons. The details of these mechanisms vary considerably between languages.

FUNCTIONS AND METHODS

C# is an object oriented language. Not just that, it's a comparatively pure object oriented language. The degree of object orientation can't really be measured, but different programming languages adhere to the ideas of certain programming philosophies to a certain extent, and rarely do they go all the way. In this case the interesting point is that C# doesn't allow any functions outside of classes. This is a big difference compared to C++ — the first object oriented programming language for many "mainstream" programmers — which allows functions to live outside of classes, mainly for backward compatibility with C code. It can be argued that since C# supports classes with static members, and even fully static classes are supported since version 3.0, imperative code is simply hidden behind object oriented terminology as needed. However, looking at the understanding of C# evident with the majority of programmers, the C# design team succeeded in creating a perception of an almost purely object oriented language.

Because functions in C# can only exist within classes, they are typically called methods. Methods can accept a number of parameters, and they can have a return value. Some people might argue that they always have a return value, but the return value can be of type void, which basically means that the method doesn't return anything. Just in case you haven't ever seen a C# method before, here's one:

```
class MyClass {
  int Square(int x) {
    return x * x;
  }
}
```

There are a few common elements missing from this simple class (accessibility specifiers for one thing), but there are also a few things in there that might not be entirely intuitive if you haven't used C# before. Unfortunately, this book isn't a general C# introduction. These introductory chapters point out and explain those C# features that are important in the following parts of the book. If you need a general introduction to the language, or to object oriented programming (although the latter isn't very important in the rest of the book), you should probably start with a different book, such as *Beginning C# 3.0: An Introduction to Object Oriented Programming* (Wrox, ISBN 978-0-470-26129-3).

As is the case in many object oriented languages, methods in C# classes can be instance or class methods. Instances are created from classes, which goes a long way to explaining the difference. There can be many instances of the same class, and a class method works on the level of the class, while an instance method works on the level of the instance. That is a bit abstract until you start thinking about other types of members a class can have, such as variables and fields. Variables store information, and they also live either on the class level or on the instance level. A class field exists once per class (so that's exactly once, from the point of view of any given application) and an instance field exists once per instance. Class methods can access information in class fields only, whereas instance methods can access information in the instance fields of their own instance. Instance methods can also access class fields, and if they have references to other instances, they can also access instance fields in those other instances. Enough of that — again, those are basics of the C# language and of object oriented programming.

Here's why this is interesting for functional programming: in pure functional programming, there are no classes or instances of classes — there are of course techniques for the storage of data, but they aren't usually called classes and they tend to work differently in many ways. Where all other elements live inside classes and objects ("object" is another word for "instance of a class," by the way) in object oriented environments, all other elements live inside functions in functional programming. There may be data that is local to the function, like variables declared in a method in C#, but there isn't the idea of data, especially data that can be modified during runtime, being anywhere outside the scope of functions. The typical C# instance method, which can access information outside its own scope, is not a function that fits in with the concept of functions that functional programming has.

Nevertheless, functional programming is possible on the basis of the object oriented .NET platform, both using languages that have special support for it and those that don't have such support. F# uses class-level members for global members, and due to the special syntax support, the programmer isn't confronted with the fact that there is a "translation" taking place. Unfortunately it isn't possible to make C# do this automatically, but the solution remains the same. To simulate functions on a global level (or in any other scope), create them as class-level members inside classes. These members use the keyword `static`. Because they are encapsulated in classes, members can have varying visibility. Most functional environments have encapsulation levels — in modules or namespaces, for example — so apart from slightly more complex syntax in C#, there's really no significant difference.

Some functional languages have top-level functions or allow modules or namespaces to be imported so that a qualification of a function call is no longer required. Here's an example:

```
DoSomething "string parameter"
```

In C#, such a call always needs a qualifying class name, unless the function lives in the same class where the call is being written:

```
SomeClass.DoSomething("string parameter");
```

REUSING FUNCTIONS

Reuse is the greatest overall problem in computer programming. The assembly languages understood by processors are fine for the purpose of programming computers to do anything and everything you want — there's nothing that can't be done on this level. The problem is that after a very short time, small and large blocks of functionality start recurring, and programmers start trying to find ways to avoid wasting time by re-implementing code that's already been written. If you think about it, that's why functions in programming languages were invented in the first place: because they provide a common place for a block of code, a piece of functionality, that will presumably be used more than once.

Of course functions are not the end of the line when it comes to reusability. Especially in object oriented programming, the step beyond functions is made very quickly. Classes are used as building blocks together with interfaces and even larger modules. There are some mechanisms that work on the function level and promote reuse, and object oriented programmers have invented a slew of patterns to go along with these, many of which also work on the function level.

As a built-in language feature, C# only supports overloading of functions as a direct means of modularization on a functional level. C# 4.0 has both named and optional parameters so that the overload resolution process becomes quite complex, especially when taking other related mechanisms like inference of generic types for method calls into account. But these elaborate details are not the subject now, so here's just a short, simple example of an overloaded method:

```
int Add(int x, int y) {
  return x + y;
}

int Add(int x, int y, int z) {
  return Add(x, y) + z;
}

double Add(double x, double y) {
  return x + y;
}

double Add(double x, double y, double z) {
  return Add(x, y) + z;
}
```

In this example it becomes obvious why overloading has to do with reuse: it allows programmers to create new functions, similar to existing ones, while potentially making use of functionality that has already been implemented. All the functions have slightly different parameter lists, which allows the compiler to distinguish between them by looking at the types of values that are being passed when a call occurs. If there is any sort of conflict, the compiler shows an error message. All overloads have the same name (they wouldn't be called overloads anymore if they had different names), which makes it easier for other programmers to understand the relationship between a group of functions.

In the context of algorithms, reusability can be quite a bit more complex than this. The idea is that it should be possible to write functionality that can later be used in ways that weren't supported in particular when the code was written. In many of the more obvious cases, at least the general purpose of the function in question will be the same, but there are also algorithms so generic in their definition that they can be used to solve almost arbitrary problems. For example, look at the following implementation of the Bubble Sort algorithm. Some comments included for clarity.

```
public static void Sort(int[] values) {
  bool swapped;

  do {
    swapped = false;
    // iterate over the whole list
    for (int i = 0; i < values.Length - 1; i++) {
      // if the current index value is greater than
      //the one that follows it...
      if (values[i] > values[i + 1]) {
        // then the two are swapped
        int temp = values[i];
        values[i] = values[i + 1];
        values[i + 1] = temp;
        // remember that we did some swapping
        swapped = true;
      }
    }
```

```
      // and restart, as long as there was any swapping done on
      // the last run
      // The whole thing ends when a run is completed without
      // finding anything that needs to be swapped.
    } while (swapped);
  }
```

If you look at the algorithm closely, you will find that there's only one small part in it that is specific to the type it is written for: the comparison of the two values. This is particularly common with sorting algorithms because they always have the requirement of finding which one of two values is greater than the other one. With the exception of the comparison operation, the whole algorithm could be written to work with any type of data. That's a good thing because the sort functions will be easier to reuse; the more flexible the algorithm, the more valuable it is.

Depending on the language you use, there are different ways to replace a specific type with a less specific one. In object oriented languages like C#, there is typically a base class that can be used for the purpose. In older procedural languages like C, you would have used a pointer instead. The problem with these approaches is the same: they lose type information. In other words, the preceding implementation of the algorithm knows that it works with values of type int, but an implementation that uses object (which is the base class of everything in .NET) doesn't know anything about the type. There are things that can be done with int values: add them, output them, and importantly, compare them. Given a bunch of object type values, it is unknown which operations the objects support, and how those operations need to be performed. The core of this problem isn't going to be solved now (look at Chapter 4 for explanations of Generics in C#), but one important step that can be made is to extract parts of the algorithm into separate functions. In this case, the relevant part is the comparison operation.

The idea behind this is that while the sort algorithm doesn't know, or care, what types of objects it finds in the array, there will be other parts of any complete application where this information is available. Specifically, the place where the Sort method is called should have that information. After all, the data in the array must come from somewhere. The array has been populated at some point, and at that point it must have been known which types were being put into it. That's when it would be possible to write a function that compares two values of whatever type. Here are a few functions that take objects as parameters and then perform comparison operations on the data.

```
bool IsAGreaterThanB_Int(object a, object b) {
  return ((int) a) > ((int) b);
}

bool IsAGreaterThanB_String(object a, object b) {
  return ((string) a)[0] > ((string) b)[0];
}

bool IsAGreaterThanB_Customer(object a, object b) {
  return IsAGreaterThanB_String(((Customer) a).Name, ((Customer) b).Name);
}
```

Each of these functions just makes assumptions about the types, which isn't perfect — but again, you'll see the solution to that part of the issue later.

These functions all have the exact same signature (that is, they have the same parameters and the same return type), which makes them exchangeable. It becomes possible to write the sorting algorithm using a placeholder helper function to do the comparison, like this:

```
...
for (int i = 0; i < values.Length - 1; i++) {
  if (IsAGreaterThanB(values[i], values[i + 1])) {
    object temp = values[i];
    values[i] = values[i + 1];
    values[i + 1] = temp;
...
```

Of course the problem that remains is how to specify which function to use for the comparison. It depends on the data in the array, and that is known only at the point where the function is called. So why not simply pass in the correct comparison function together with the data?

```
var sourceObjects = new object[] { 7, 6, 9, 8, 5, 10, 273, 15, 11 };
Bubblesorter.Sort(sourceObjects, IsAGreaterThanB_Int);
foreach (object item in sourceObjects)
  Console.Write("{0} ", item);
Console.WriteLine( );
```

`int` values are being used in the array, and the comparison function that is being passed in is also the one that can deal with `int` values. Great; this should work. But what does the `Sort` function itself look like? After all, it needs to receive a parameter that is a function. This is what it looks like:

```
public delegate bool IsAGreaterThanBDelegate(object a, object b);

public static void Sort(object[] values, IsAGreaterThanBDelegate isAGreaterThanB) {
  bool swapped;

  do {
    swapped = false;
    for (int i = 0; i < values.Length - 1; i++) {
      if (isAGreaterThanB(values[i], values[i + 1])) {
        object temp = values[i];
        values[i] = values[i + 1];
        values[i + 1] = temp;
        swapped = true;
      }
    }
  } while (swapped);
}
```

The `public delegate` line isn't part of the function itself; it could live elsewhere. But it's important, because it specifies the function type that is then accepted by the `Sort` function as a parameter. As you might have guessed from the use of the keyword `delegate`, these types are called *delegate types* (also referred to as *function types*, though). They specify which parameters and what return type a function needs to have to be compatible with the delegate type — two parameters of type `object` and a `bool` return type in this case. The preceding comparison functions are all compatible with this delegate type, and with its help, the `Sort` function can be implemented to work with any arbitrary data type. As long as there's some point in the application where the types are known, you can create a function that performs the necessary comparison action and pass it in together with the data.

A function like this Sort, which takes parameters of delegate types, is called a higher order function. Higher order functions can also return new functions instead of taking them as parameters — read more about that in the next section.

ANONYMOUS FUNCTIONS AND LAMBDA EXPRESSIONS

Not all functions are important enough to have a name. C# has supported anonymous functions since version 2.0, and a second syntactic variation — lambda expressions — was introduced in version 3.0. Generally speaking, these are functions that don't live on the class level and that don't have names. References to such functions are stored in variables, so effectively the function can be called wherever the reference to it is available.

Technically speaking, there are certain restrictions in place on anonymous functions. One is particularly unfortunate, and that's the fact that they can't be generic (more on generics in Chapter 4). They also can't be used to implement iterators (more on iterators in Chapter 5), which is another desirable thing. But apart from that, anonymous functions can do almost everything "normal" methods can do. The term *anonymous functions* is a bit diluted because it can be a general term that encompasses all types of functions that don't have names, but it can also be used as a name for the C# 2.0 feature specifically. The feature was really called *anonymous methods*, but *anonymous functions* is widely used as an exchangeable term.

Here's what one of the earlier comparison functions could look like in C# 2.0 syntax:

```
static void AnonymousMethods( ) {
  Bubblesorter.IsAGreaterThanBDelegate compareInt =
    delegate(object a, object b) {
      return ((int) a) > ((int) b);
    };
}
```

As you can see, the keyword delegate is used in place of a method name. The parameter list and the body of the method looks just like before. A variable is used to store the reference to the method, with the type of the variable being the only slightly confusing thing — the delegate type that was used earlier in this chapter is defined within the class Bubblesorter. At the same time, this example makes it obvious that the anonymous method is fully compatible with the delegate type that was previously used with the Bubblesorter.

The same anonymous method can be written like this, using C# 3.0 lambda expression syntax:

```
Bubblesorter.IsAGreaterThanBDelegate compareInt2 =
  (object a, object b) => { return ((int) a) > ((int) b); }
```

This is shorter, but only because the delegate keyword is missing and the whole body has been formatted on one line. The body in a lambda expression is the part to the right of the "goes-to" operator, which appears as =>. There are several steps that can be taken to shorten the code further. First, you can drop the types of the parameters because these can be inferred by the compiler from the declaration of the delegate type:

```
Bubblesorter.IsAGreaterThanBDelegate compareInt2 =
    (a, b) => { return ((int) a) > ((int) b); }
```

Next, because the function doesn't do anything but return a value, you can convert the body of the function into an expression body and benefit from an implicit return:

```
Bubblesorter.IsAGreaterThanBDelegate compareInt3 =
    (a, b) => ((int) a) > ((int) b);
```

Expression bodies are useful because they allow for a concise implementation of the particular behavior that functional programming asks for in a function: accept parameters, then return a value. Expression bodies can't contain any code that is not related to the computation of the return value (that is, as long as they have a return value; unfortunately it is possible to use expressions without return values in expression bodies).

Since .NET 3.5 and C# 3.0, there is a feature called expression trees. This is a framework feature that allows runtime storage of functions in a non-compiled format, coupled with a language feature that can translate lambda expressions into the storage format. Up to C# version 4.0, only lambda expressions with expression bodies are supported by the translation feature. The C# team has indicated that future language versions may support translation to expression trees more fully, but until that happens, expression bodies are important for certain widely used features of the .NET Framework that are based on expression trees.

 Expression trees are explained in a little more detail in Chapter 7, but are rarely used in this book.

Previous examples in this chapter have included custom delegate types declared for the functions that were stored and passed as parameters. In .NET 3.5, several new standard delegate types were added to the framework, meaning it's no longer necessary to create custom delegates every time a function is used that has an as yet unknown signature, that is, one that hasn't had a delegate created so far. These delegate types are generic — more information on generics in Chapter 4. There is still a point to custom delegates: their explicit names give an indication of their purpose, which may help programmers who use an API you created.

The preceding example could look like this using one of the generic delegate types:

```
Func<object, object, bool> compareInt4 =
    (a, b) => ((int) a) > ((int) b);
```

This delegate takes two object type parameters and returns a bool. It is an additional advantage of the generic delegate types that they make the types easier to see because they are mentioned explicitly in the delegate type and the compiler infers them for the lambda expression.

An important detail to keep in mind when working with lambda expressions is that type inference only works as long as all types are specified, according to several complicated rules. Compilers don't always infer types correctly, so if all types are specified, the compiler is satisfied:

```
Func<int, int, int> add = (x, y) => x + y;
```

You cannot use the `var` keyword with this lambda expression. In C#, the compiler must be able to infer the types at the point of declaration, which is impossible with a statement like this:

```
var add = (x, y) => x + y;
```

The functional language Haskell has a construct called type classes, where a type can define things like "this is an element that can be added to another element." In the preceding case, Haskell would be able to infer the types of x and y by simply assuming they belong to the type class that allows elements to be added — a bit like an interface, but not quite the same thing. Other functional languages support other mechanisms to resolve this situation, but in C# it just renders a compiler error.

Look at this statement:

```
var add = (int x, int y) => x + y;
```

You would think this could work, but it doesn't. The reasoning on the side of the language team was that it's because the compiler can't decide whether add is going to be a `Func<int, int, int>` or perhaps an `Expression<Func<int, int, int>>` (this nested generic type would be used to support expression trees). There is also the problem that delegate types with the same signature are not compatible. For instance, the following code doesn't compile:

```
private static void DeclaringLambdas( ) {
  Func<int, int, int> add = (x, y) => x + y;

  // Failure here, because the delegate types are incompatible
  TakeMethod((IntIntIntDelegate) add);
}

delegate int IntIntIntDelegate(int x, int y);

private static void TakeMethod(IntIntIntDelegate del) {
}
```

Some C# programmers regard it as unfortunate that the language has been designed with the requirement for this degree of explicitness in all type inference scenarios. They argue it would have been possible to pick meaningful defaults in many of the cases, which would cover a large enough portion of use cases to save developers considerable time. It remains a fact that when you're trying to work with constructs like the preceding and they don't appear to work as they should, it's possible that you are simply failing to explain yourself well enough to the compiler.

EXTENSION METHODS

In C# 3.0, Microsoft introduced a new feature called extension methods. .NET 3.5, which became available at the same time, includes LINQ as a new feature, which makes heavy use of extension methods.

Extension methods are static methods in static classes that are marked up specially. Here is an example:

```
namespace CompanyWideTools {
  public static class StringHelpers {
    public static string Concat(this string[] strings, string separator) {
      bool first = true;
      var builder = new StringBuilder( );
      foreach (var s in strings) {
        if (!first)
          builder.Append(separator);
        else
          first = false;
        builder.Append(s);
      }

      return builder.ToString( );
    }
  }
}
```

The markup that makes Concat an extension method is the little keyword this used in front of the parameter strings in the parameter list of the method. This keyword is specific to C#, and it instructs the compiler to add the ExtensionMethodAttribute to the method. Other .NET languages may or may not have a similar keyword, but as long as they support attributes, they are able to utilize extension methods.

The extension method can be called just like any other static method:

```
string[] strings = new[] {
  "to", "be", "or", "not", "to", "be"
};

Console.WriteLine(StringHelpers.Concat(strings, " "));
```

However, because it is an extension method, it can also be called like this:

```
Console.WriteLine(strings.Concat(" "));
```

The syntax of the call is more concise when taking advantage of the extension method. Discoverability of the helper function Concat is increased, because Visual Studio IntelliSense shows the method Concat in the popup list in the editor as soon as you type the dot after strings. You don't have to know that there is a StringHelpers class, instead Visual Studio helps you find the functionality. The one thing that is required for the compiler (and Visual Studio) to find the method is a using statement for the namespace in which the class with the extension method lives:

```
using CompanyWideTools;
```

Every extension method has a specific type that it extends: the type of the first parameter, the one that gets marked with `this`. This is only allowed for the first parameter, not for any of the others. The type in the previous example is `string[]`, so the extension method is available for `string[]` as well as all types derived therefrom (of which there are none, because it is impossible to derive from `string[]`).

You can write extension methods where the first parameter is of a base class type, or an interface, or even `System.Object`. Extension methods can also be generic, and they can extend generic types (more details on those in Chapter 4). Here are a few additional examples of creating and using extension methods:

```
public static class OtherHelpers {
  public static void PrintType(this object thing) {
    Console.WriteLine(thing.GetType( ).FullName);
  }

  public static int Square(this int x) {
    return x * x;
  }

  public static T SecondElement<T>(this IList<T> collection) {
    return collection[1];
  }
}

...

"String".PrintType( );
var intVal = 42;
intVal.PrintType( );

Console.WriteLine(52.Square( ));
int[] ints = new[] { 10, 20, 30, 40, 50 };
Console.WriteLine(ints.SecondElement( ));
```

You can see that it is possible to call an extension method on literals of a supported type just as well as on variables of that type. The method `SecondElement` even extends a generic interface type, which is implemented by the `int` array that is passed in in the example code — but the same interface is implemented by many other collection types, making the function widely applicable. Using a parameter type that opens a function for a wide group of types is just good practice, but with extension methods such a helper becomes readily, and obviously, available.

In later chapters of this book, you will see further interesting details of how extension methods form the basis of standard .NET mechanisms, and many standard extension methods will be mentioned and explained.

REFERENTIAL TRANSPARENCY

In imperative programming, writing a computer program means to define a sequence of steps that need to be taken to achieve a goal. In that sequence, states are defined together with state transitions — how to get from A to B, what A and B are precisely, and when getting from A to B is even an option. That's what people mean when they say imperative programming is all about state.

Theoretically, a sequential program could be written line by line, the execution running from top to bottom and ending there. In reality, of course, even on the CPU level there are tools to make programming a bit more efficient, and programming languages have functions and methods and other blocks that can be used to add levels of abstraction. The basic function of such blocks in imperative programming is to remove code duplication and to break code into functional blocks that are easy to manage. One of the major issues in imperative programming has always been that code blocks tend to grow larger over time, and this is still apparent in many code bases.

Because of the focus on execution sequence, functions and methods in imperative programming tend to be referentially opaque. This means that even if they are called with the same (or no) input parameters, they are not guaranteed to return the same result every time. Implementations of the functions often use variables in a larger scope (class level fields for instance), which is generally referred to as global state. Just like the code in the earlier hypothetical example of the endless sequence of single lines, the extracted functions and methods are meant to be used in a particular order, so that the state on the outside of them is compatible with their algorithms.

Referential transparency is the opposite of this. The term can be applied to any expression, and it means that the expression could be replaced with its value without changing the program, that is, without changing the results rendered by the algorithm in which the hypothetical replacement happens.

In mathematics, expressions are always referentially transparent, so it is easy to find examples there. For instance, the expression "3 + 2" can be replaced by "5" in any mathematical context, without changing anything about the meaning. Unfortunately things aren't quite so simple in computer programming.

Some expressions or functions can never be referentially transparent because it is their purpose to return values that change, or to return a different value every time. .NET examples of this would be `DateTime.Now`, `File.ReadByte()` or `Console.Read()`. In C#, functions that have a return type of `void` can't be used as an expression, so they are referentially opaque as well.

One of the most important concepts in functional programming is the avoidance of side effects in the implementation of functions. This topic is very close to that of referential transparency. A pure function is one that does not have any side effects, one that just calculates a return value from a set of parameters. The function can call other functions as part of its algorithm, and it can access values from outside its own scope, provided these are referentially transparent and never change. Imagine an algorithm that uses `Math.PI` — that's allowed because it's a constant value being accessed.

The general description of pure functions and side effects leaves out the perspective of the call site, from which a pure function can also be defined by saying that a call into a pure function is expected to be referentially transparent. This description may not be as precise in certain circumstances, where minor side effects can exist that don't influence referential transparency — think of debug output, for example.

To write pure functions, use only your input parameters and return a value at the end. To access things outside your scope, structure your code so that you end up calling other pure functions in order to do so. To access actual data elements, make sure they are constant. Everything you do that doesn't fit this description is a side effect, which you generally don't want.

Some programming languages simply make side effects impossible through their syntax and semantics. If you've given the matter some thought, you will find that it seems impossible to ever get anything really useful done without side effects. Display something on screen? Save or load a file? These are side effects according to the preceding definition. Obviously computer programs wouldn't be very powerful if programmers didn't have a way to do these things.

As a result, there's an even more important goal than the one of avoiding side effects: managing side effects. Depending on the language you use, this can be easy or hard. Pure functional languages that enforce the use of pure functions most of the time typically have a way of breaking out of that world temporarily, in certain places in code, to invoke the side effects the program requires. In Haskell, for example, monads allow you to do this. There are other ways in other languages, but that's not important here — unfortunately, C# doesn't have any such special support in the language, which makes the avoidance of side effects a discipline and the management of them an architectural and structural task.

A final word should be said about the reasoning behind the targets of pure function, avoiding and managing side effects, and referential transparency. One of the consequences of writing code this way is that the evaluation order of expressions, as well as the call order of functions, doesn't really matter. The programmer defines how various functions form a network of dependencies — function A performs a calculation and calls function B in the process, so the result of function A depends on function B — but it can be left to the compiler and/or the runtime environment to determine the optimal evaluation order. This makes optimizations possible, duplicate expressions can be extracted automatically, caches applied, logical parts executed in parallel. The list of possibilities is endless, and many pure functional environments automate a number of these approaches. Enough theory — chapters later in this book show to what extent these ideas can be used in C# and what the benefits are.

 In .NET 4.0 and Visual Studio 2010, Microsoft introduced the feature of code contracts. You might not be aware of this yet, because the tools required to utilize the feature are still a separate download. Code contracts are certainly worth a recommendation, but they aren't particularly relevant to the content of this book. There is one feature, however, that seems to deal with function purity and therefore looks like an important addition to the toolset of the functional C# programmer.

The feature is visible through an attribute called PureAttribute, *which can be applied to methods as well as types. It shows the programmer's intention for functional purity of the member, but unfortunately code contracts don't do anything to check that assumption. The reason it has been included is currently the opposite: members that have been marked* Pure *can be used in contract definitions.*

SUMMARY

You have seen how C# interprets functions and methods, named and unnamed, how they can be created, stored, referred to, and passed around. Type safety coupled with the need for ease of use makes for interesting discussions in C#, with its type inference support useful only in some situations. Programming for function purity and referential transparency is a discipline in C# that doesn't enjoy specific support from the compiler, but that enables you to utilize many functional approaches described in the following chapters.

4

Flexible Typing with Generics

WHAT'S IN THIS CHAPTER?

➤ Generic functions, classes, and other elements

➤ Constraints

➤ Covariance and contravariance

The .NET type system has a feature called generics. With the help of this feature, certain pieces of type information can be extended by type parameters. In .NET, classes, methods, interfaces, and delegates can be generic.

One of the common examples of the use of generics is a container class, like a list. In an object oriented language, you can either write a List class to work with elements of a particular type (perhaps you create a `ListElement` for the purpose) or use a base class that is so general purpose that it allows users of the List type to add elements of arbitrary types (in .NET, `System.Object` comes to mind). Both of these approaches have disadvantages. Using the all-purpose base class allows the addition of potentially incompatible elements to the list, and using a particular special purpose class for the elements only defers the problem because the actual type must be encapsulated in the end.

Generics provide a solution to this issue. The List class is created to have a type parameter, and when instances are created, the type parameter is resolved so that any actual instance of the List class works with a particular type (and those derived from it).

Generally, a generic type G is written to work with one or more other types — O1, O2, and so on — but the idea is that the implementation of G doesn't actually need to know very much about Ox. The earlier list example shows that the typing happens for the benefit of the user of G, not for G itself. Constraints on the types Ox allow G to know a bit more about what their respective properties are, but be aware this is not always desirable. The statement holds that in a typical generics use case, G doesn't care much about Ox.

This chapter introduces generics to the extent that you understand the notation used in C# and how to use classes and other elements written with generics. Creating your own architecture based on generics is a complex topic in its own right, but it isn't of great relevance in the rest of the book, so it isn't discussed in detail.

GENERIC FUNCTIONS

Any method can be made generic by adding one or more type parameters to the method signature like this:

```
static void OutputThing<T>(T thing) {
  Console.WriteLine("Thing: {0}", thing);
}
```

T is the type variable in this example, and it is listed in angle brackets right after the method name. Once it has been declared that way, it can be used in place of a type in the parameter list and also within the method body. In the example, thing is simply passed in to the Console.WriteLine method, which accepts parameters of any type and calls their ToString method in order to format them for output. As mentioned before, the method doesn't actually care about the element thing or its type; it just passes the value on to some other method to deal with.

Here's a call to this function with a explicit type parameters:

```
OutputThing<string>("A string");
OutputThing<int>(42);
```

Using explicit type parameters means that the type is checked by both Visual Studio IntelliSense and the C# compiler. A call like the following would elicit an error message at compile time:

```
OutputThing<double>("Hello world");
```

Although the example is extremely simple, it demonstrates one of the purposes of generics: instead of using a parameter of type object, the type is mentioned explicitly in these calls, which enables strict checking.

At the same time, many programmers regard it as too much of a hassle to actually specify the type explicitly. The OutputThing method can also be called like this:

```
OutputThing("A different string");
OutputThing(52);
```

Type inference is used here to deduce the type from the literal value. This is not an untyped call; there's still a type variable T on the OutputThing method, and it is equal to string and int, respectively, in these two calls, as in the preceding examples. But the compiler does the work of inserting these types for the programmer.

When you need to decide whether to specify types explicitly on generic method calls or not, you should keep in mind that a reader of your code will have to go through the same type inference steps as the compiler in order to fully understand how the method is called. Complex scenarios involving a large number of generic type parameters as well as generic and non-generic method overloads, this can be complicated and it may be a better strategy to mention types explicitly. Many programmers also view type inference in C# as a feature they use only when needs dictate it, not as a general tool to be used whenever possible. So make sure that your strategy of mentioning or leaving out types is understood and accepted by your team members.

Here is a slightly more complex (as well as useful) example of a generic method:

```
static void Apply<T>(IEnumerable<T> sequence, Action<T> action) {
  foreach (T item in sequence) {
    action(item);
  }
}
```

Again, there's a type parameter called T, but this time it's used in both parameters of the method. There's a connection being established: the first parameter is a sequence of "things", and the second parameter is a delegate that has a parameter of the same "thing" type that is in the sequence. This is where generics prove really powerful because there's no way to express the same thing without them and still keep the method flexible to work with different types.

The method Apply is another good example of the statement that generic elements don't really care about the types themselves. In this case, Apply provides a useful abstraction of a certain algorithm: iterating over a list and applying a function to each element. But given the right parameters, the method itself isn't actually interested in the types it's working with. The benefit is there for the consumer of the method, in the strict type checking the compiler can perform.

Here's a call to Apply:

```
var values = new List<int> { 10, 20, 35 };
Apply(values, v => Console.WriteLine("Value: {0}", v));
```

Take a moment to look at all the interesting things happening in this example. values is a list of int values, as the generic parameter to the List class declares explicitly. Apply is called, but the generic parameter is left out. The compiler needs to infer the type of T for the Apply call, and it does this by looking at the parameters. It finds the values parameter, of type List<int>, which implements IEnumerable<int> — so the type T from the point of view of the method Apply must be int.

Moving on, the compiler also performs type inference for the lambda expression that's passed as the second parameter. The parameter v must be an int, because the type for Apply has been inferred as being an int already. The compiler checks whether the code in the body of the lambda is compatible with v being an int, which is the case here.

There are numerous potential issues that could be found right away by the compiler, due to the typing provided by generics. If you're interested, play around in Visual Studio a bit and find ways of breaking the code based on the types — the compiler should catch them all.

GENERIC CLASSES

It is also possible to add type information to classes. The scope of the type parameter is the entire class in this case, but it is used exactly the same way: in the place of a type. Here is an example of an (incomplete) linked list implementation:

```
public class ListItem<T> {
  public ListItem(T value) {
    this.value = value;
  }

  private ListItem(T value, ListItem<T> next) : this(value) {
    this.next = next;
  }

  private readonly T value;
  public T Value {
    get {
      return value;
    }
  }

  private ListItem<T> next;

  public ListItem<T> Prepend(T value) {
    return new ListItem<T>(value, this);
  }
}
```

The class `ListItem` has a generic type parameter `T`. This is the type encapsulated in the `ListItem` container, and it is used throughout the class in a variety of places where an explicit type could also be mentioned. The use of the generic type makes the `ListItem` more flexible, allowing it to encapsulate information of any other kind.

At the same time, the generic type system makes checking of types at compile time more powerful. For instance, the `Prepend` method is written in such a way that only values of type `T` will be accepted. From the perspective of any one instance of the `ListItem` class, `T` is fixed — in other words, the new value will always need to be of the same type as that of the current instance. Look at this code that uses the class:

```
private static void ListTest( ) {
  var intItem = new ListItem<int>(10);

  // Prepending further int values is possible
  var secondItem = intItem.Prepend(20);

  // Prepending other types is caught by the compiler
  //var thirdItem = secondItem.Prepend("string");
}
```

The syntax is simple: a type parameter is added to the name of the class when it is used with the `new` keyword. The instance that is stored in the `intItem` variable is now typed to contain values of type int. As a result, the Prepend method is expected to take a parameter of type int — for this instance, T is now equal to int. The commented line, where an attempt is made to pass a string value to the method, doesn't work and is caught by the compiler because the types don't match.

One final piece of generics syntax is multiple type parameters. In any situation where type parameters can be used, it is possible to have more than one of them. A simple example of that is the following Tuple class, which combines two values in a single container (.NET 4.0 now has its own Tuple classes, so this example is for illustration only).

```
public class Tuple<T1, T2> {
  private Tuple(T1 val1, T2 val2) {
    this.val1 = val1;
    this.val2 = val2;
  }

  private readonly T1 val1;
  public T1 Val1 {
    get {
      return val1;
    }
  }

  private readonly T2 val2;
  public T2 Val2 {
    get {
      return val2;
    }
  }
}
```

There's really nothing special to say about the capability to have many parameters; it's just important to realize that this is possible. A final point: type parameters in classes and those in methods can be used at the same time, and you must ensure that they don't collide. The class Tuple with its two parameters T1 and T2 could have a method with its own type parameter T, for instance, but calling the method parameter(s) T1 or T2 is not a good idea for obvious reasons. It is technically possible to "override" type parameters by using the same names on class and method levels, but since this is rarely intended, the compiler issues a warning if you do so.

CONSTRAINING TYPES

Wherever generic type parameters are used, they can also be constrained through the use of a where clause. Here's an example using a method:

```
static void OutputValue<T>(T value) where T : ListItem<string> {
  Console.WriteLine("String list value: {0}", value.Value);
}
```

The declaration of the constraint is straightforward in this example: the type T has to be compatible with ListItem<string>. It is tempting to say "T needs to be derived from ListItem<string>," which the colon seems to signify, but that wouldn't be correct because `ListItem<string>` itself is a valid type in this example. The generic type constraint `T : X` means that `T` may be equal to `X`, derived from `X`, or implementing `X` (if `X` is an interface). In other words, if you had an instance of type `T` called `t`, you would be able to assign a variable like this:

```
X x = t;
```

Constraints can mention specific types, like the preceding example, and in these cases the types can't be sealed. There are several special keywords that can be used instead of or in addition to a type specifier. The keyword `class` can specify that the type has to be a reference type, while `struct` denotes that it has to be a value type. In combination with `class` or with any specific type, the `new()` keyword (which must include the parentheses) can be used to require a default constructor on the type (that's a constructor without any parameters).

The final use of a constraint is to define a relationship between two type parameters. For instance, if there are parameters `T` and `U`, a constraint `T : U` would specify that `T` must be compatible with `U` (as described earlier).

Here are a few more examples of generic constraints, to demonstrate these slightly abstract explanations. Some of them demonstrate a few minor details of the syntax, such as the use of more than one `where` clause on a single generic type and more than one element in a `where` clause:

```
public class Factory<T> where T : new( ) {
  //...
}

public class KeyedList<K, V>
  where K : IComparable
  where V : class {
  // ...

  public void Add(K key, V value) {
  }

  public void Add<KA, VA>(KeyedList<KA, VA> addList)
    where KA : K
    where VA : class, V {
    // adding the content of addList to this list
    // is now completely type safe
  }

  // ...
}
```

The last example is, admittedly, a rather complicated one of combining class level and method level type parameters with complex constraints. It is nevertheless entirely practical and a good summary of several of the features that have been discussed in this chapter.

When using constraints, there is one important consideration to keep in mind: the basic purpose of generics is to offer a type-safe way to write code that can easily work with different types. The more constraints are used, the more this idea is diluted, because flexibility is taken away by the constraints. On one end of the spectrum of possible generic use cases, the generic type or method is entirely ignorant of the details of the types it works with. This is where generics provide the most value over other typing mechanisms.

On the other end, the type is restricted as much as possible, for example to one single base class or interface. In cases of extreme type restriction you should consider the alternative of writing a non-generic method to work with the base class or the interface. On the other hand, sometimes generics can still make sense because constraints can be applied to an entire class or interface at once.

To summarize, an important criterion to distinguish use cases that make sense from those that don't is the "orientation" of functionality written in generic code. Code that cares too much about the types it works with is an indication that generics may not be the right solution anymore. Because the construction of large generic APIs is not a focus of this background chapter, that shall suffice as a guideline.

OTHER GENERIC TYPES

In addition to methods and classes, structs, delegates, and interfaces can also have type parameters. Structs and interfaces are obvious; the syntax looks much like that of classes:

```
public struct MyPoint<T> where T : struct {
  public MyPoint(T x, T y) {
    this.x = x;
    this.y = y;
  }

  private readonly T x;
  public T X {
    get { return x; }
  }

  private readonly T y;
  public T Y {
    get { return y; }
  }
}

public interface IListItem<T> {
  T Value { get; }
  ListItem<T> Prepend(T value);
}
```

Even with delegates there's nothing surprising about the syntax. Following is an example of an alternative Factory implementation called `ParameterFactory` that uses a creation delegate instead of relying on the `new()` constraint and using a default constructor:

```
public delegate R CreateDelegate<T, R>(T param);

public class ParameterFactory<T, R> {
  CreateDelegate<T, R> createDelegate;
```

```
public ParameterFactory(CreateDelegate<T, R> createDelegate) {
  this.createDelegate = createDelegate;
}

// ...
}
```

This includes the declaration of the `CreateDelegate`, which represents a function that takes a parameter of type `T` and returns a value of type `R`.

 This is a good example of a statement that was made in Chapter 3, where the standard delegate types `Func<...>` *were introduced. The* `ParameterFactory` *works with its own delegate type* `CreateDelegate` *instead of using* `Func<T, R>`, *because this gives an indication about the intended use of the function this is passed in.* `Func<T, R>` *says that the function will take a* `T` *and return an* `R`, *but in addition to that,* `CreateDelegate` *indicates that something is being created on the way. This is certainly not a replacement for a well designed API, or for code documentation, but it helps make your code just a little bit more readable.*

The use of generics in delegates is very powerful, and since .NET 2.0, lots of generic delegates have been introduced into the .NET Framework. Many of these will be discussed in detail later in the book, but the `Func` delegates deserve another mention right here:

```
public delegate TResult Func<T1, T2, T3, T4, TResult>(T1 arg1, T2 arg2,
    T3 arg3, T4 arg4);
```

Using generics, these delegates can be used to represent almost arbitrary functions. `Func` delegates come with the .NET Framework since version 3.5, and the preceding one has placeholders for four parameters of the function it represents, plus one for the return type of that function. There are others included with different numbers of parameters, and it is also possible to create your own. The `Action<...>` delegates complete the picture with their capability to represent methods that don't have a return type.

COVARIANCE AND CONTRAVARIANCE

The topic of variance is complex because it applies to many different code constructs. Designers of programming language make (hopefully conscious) decisions to support variance in a variety of different scenarios, or not to do so.

There is a distinction being made between covariance and contravariance. Very roughly, an operation is covariant if it preserves the ordering of types, and contravariant if it reverses this order. The ordering itself is meant to represent more general types as larger than more specific types.

Here's one example of a situation where C# supports covariance. First, this is an array of objects:

```
object[] objects = new object[3];
objects[0] = new object( );
objects[1] = "Just a string";
objects[2] = 10;
```

Of course it is possible to insert different values into the array because in the end they all derive from `Object` in .NET. In other words, `Object` is a very general or large type. Now here's a spot where covariance is supported: assigning a value of a smaller type to a variable of a larger type.

```
string[] strings = new string[] { "one", "two", "three" };
objects = strings;
```

The variable `objects`, which is of type `object[]`, can store a value that is in fact of type `string[]`. Think about it — to a point, it's what you expect, but then again it isn't. After all, while `string` derives from `object`, `string[]` doesn't derive from `object[]`. The language support for covariance in this example makes the assignment possible anyway, which is something you'll find in many cases. Variance is a feature that makes the language work more intuitively.

The considerations around these topics are extremely complicated. For instance, based on the preceding code, here are two scenarios that will result in errors.

```
// Runtime exception here - the array is still of type string[],
// ints can't be inserted
objects[2] = 10;

// Compiler error here - covariance support in this scenario only
// covers reference types, and int is a value type
int[] ints = new int[] { 1, 2, 3 };
objects = ints;
```

An example for the workings of contravariance is a bit more complicated. Imagine these two classes:

```
public class Person : IPerson {
  public Person( ) {
  }
}

public class Woman : Person {
  public Woman( ) {
  }
}
```

`Woman` is derived from `Person`, obviously. Now consider you have these two functions:

```
static void WorkWithPerson(Person person) {
}

static void WorkWithWoman(Woman woman) {
}
```

One of the functions does something (it doesn't matter what) with a `Woman`, the other is more general and can work with any type of `Person`. On the `Woman` side of things, you now also have these:

```
delegate void AcceptWomanDelegate(Woman person);

static void DoWork(Woman woman, AcceptWomanDelegate acceptWoman) {
  acceptWoman(woman);
}
```

`DoWork` is a function that can take a `Woman` and a reference to a function that also takes a `Woman`, and then it passes the `Woman` instance to the delegate. Consider the size of the elements you have here. `Person` is larger than `Woman`, and `WorkWithPerson` is larger than `WorkWithWoman`. `WorkWithPerson` is also considered larger than `AcceptWomanDelegate` for the purpose of variance.

Finally, you have these three lines of code:

```
Woman woman = new Woman( );
DoWork(woman, WorkWithWoman);
DoWork(woman, WorkWithPerson);
```

A `Woman` instance is created. Then `DoWork` is called, passing in the `Woman` instance as well as a reference to the `WorkWithWoman` method. The latter is obviously compatible with the delegate type `AcceptWomanDelegate` — one `Woman` type parameter, no return type.

The third line is a bit odd, though. The method `WorkWithPerson` takes a `Person` as a parameter, not a `Woman`, as required by `AcceptWomanDelegate`. Nevertheless, `WorkWithPerson` is compatible with the delegate type. Contravariance makes it possible, so in the case of delegates the larger type (`WorkWithPerson`) can be stored in a variable of the smaller type (`AcceptWomanDelegate`). Once more it's the intuitive thing: if `WorkWithPerson` can work with any `Person`, passing in a `Woman` can't be wrong, right?

By now you may be wondering how all this relates to generics. The answer is that variance can be applied to generics as well. The preceding example used object and string arrays. Here the code uses generic lists instead of the arrays:

```
List<object> objectlist = new List<object>( );
List<string> stringlist = new List<string>( );
objectlist = stringlist;
```

If you try this out, you will find that this is not a supported scenario in C#. In C# version 4.0 as well as .NET 4.0, variance support in generics has been cleaned up, and it is now possible to use the new keywords `in` and `out` with generic type parameters. They can define and restrict the direction of data flow for a particular type parameter, allowing variance to work. But in the case of `List<T>`, the data of type `T` flows in both directions — there are methods on the type `List<T>` that return `T` values, and others that receive such values.

The point of these directional restrictions is to allow variance where it makes sense, but to prevent problems like the runtime error mentioned in one of the previous array examples. When type parameters are correctly decorated with `in` or `out`, the compiler can check, and allow or disallow, variance at compile time. Microsoft has gone to the effort of adding these keywords to many standard .NET interfaces, like IEnumerable<T>:

```
public interface IEnumerable<out T> : IEnumerable {
  ...
}
```

For this interface, the data flow of type T objects is clear: they can only ever be retrieved from methods supported by this interface, not passed into them. As a result, it is possible to construct an example similar to the List<T> attempt described previously, but using IEnumerable<T>:

```
IEnumerable<object> objectSequence = new List<object>( );
IEnumerable<string> stringSequence = new List<string>( );
objectSequence = stringSequence;
```

This code is acceptable to the C# compiler since version 4.0 because IEnumerable<T> is covariant due to the out specifier on the type parameter T.

When working with generic types, it is important to be aware of variance and the way the compiler is applying various kinds of trickery in order to make your code work the way you expect it to. There's more to know about variance than is covered in this chapter, but this shall suffice to make all further code understandable.

SUMMARY

Generics are today an important tool in the C# language, and they are widely used in the .NET Framework to construct flexible general purpose APIs. It is important for any C# programmer to have a good understanding of the caller side of generic APIs, although most programmers may never have the requirement of creating their own generic APIs. Familiarity with generic syntax is important for your understanding of code examples in upcoming chapters. Many of these use extensive lists of generic parameters — hopefully this chapter helps make such code less intimidating.

5

Lazy Listing with Iterators

Handling data efficiently is an important task of programming languages and frameworks today. .NET has a well-structured system of collection classes, which are based on simple iteration functionality for sequences of data.

THE MEANING OF LAZINESS

I have always maintained that it is a good thing for a programmer to be lazy. No offense is intended with this statement. The assumption is that a programmer does her job, whether she's lazy or not. Only when she's lazy, she'll spend time thinking about the work she does. She recognizes that there are elements that simply require time to get right, which can't be helped. There are elements that are fun and others that aren't, but all of them need to be completed.

And there are elements that are boring because they are repetitive, and that can be helped by finding out what these elements are exactly, and how they can be done more efficiently. It is frustrating to do something more than once, and being lazy makes a programmer want to figure out how to avoid such situations. There are also things that are done, and then something changes and you find you didn't really have to spend all that time doing those things because the results are no longer needed. For many programmers, this feeling of having wasted time is something they want to avoid at all cost. They are certainly not always successful, but the attitude is a healthy one for a programmer.

Laziness (well, within the terms described here) makes a programmer write better programs. Perhaps surprisingly, computer languages employ laziness themselves to prevent doing things that aren't really required at a particular point in time.

Chapter 9 contains a lot of information on execution strategies, and how laziness can be applied in C# in all kinds of situations. But one particular kind of laziness has been embedded not just in C#, but in the entire .NET Framework from the beginning: it's the idea of lazy enumeration, and it is at the core of .NET collection and sequence classes. Since .NET 3.5 and C# 3.0, with the advent of Language-Integrated Query (LINQ), lazy enumeration has gained even more significance because LINQ to Objects, the in-memory subsystem of LINQ, is based heavily on that approach.

Lazy enumeration is an iteration approach, which has at its core the idea that data should be fetched only when it is actually needed. This allows any algorithm to be as efficient as possible, while retaining the flexibility to retrieve as much data as necessary without any overhead.

ENUMERATING THINGS WITH .NET

The basis of .NET collection types is an interface called IEnumerable. Newer classes (all those introduced since .NET 2.0) are based on the generic IEnumerable<T> instead, but for the purposes of this description, the untyped basic IEnumerable shall suffice. All collection classes implement IEnumerable, but sometimes classes that implement only this interface are called sequences instead of collections. As you will see, IEnumerable only requires extremely basic functionality. Here's the interface declaration itself:

```
public interface IEnumerable {
  IEnumerator GetEnumerator( );
}
```

The only thing the interface IEnumerable actually allows you to do is to query another interface (IEnumerator) from a class. Here's the declaration of IEnumerator:

```
public interface IEnumerator {
  object Current { get; }
  bool MoveNext( );
  void Reset( );
}
```

Imagine a list object that implements IEnumerable. When GetEnumerator is called, the object returns an implementation of IEnumerator. That implementation allows iteration over the elements of the list. Call Reset to get to the start, get to the object in the current position using the Current property, and then call MoveNext and evaluate its return value to see if there are more elements. Extremely simple, really, but very powerful.

As far as this description goes, the system sounds quite clean. Unfortunately the C# compiler muddies the waters a little bit by implementing some trickery, so that a class like the following is in fact the simplest implementation of the iteration pattern declared by `IEnumerable` and `IEnumerator`:

```
public class EndlessListWithoutInterfaces {
  public EndlessListWithoutInterfaces GetEnumerator( ) {
    return this;
  }

  public bool MoveNext( ) {
    return true;
  }

  public object Current {
    get { return "something"; }
  }
}
```

It is possible to use the C# `foreach` construct with the class `EndlessListWithoutInterfaces`:

```
var list = new EndlessListWithoutInterfaces( );
foreach (var item in list)
  Console.WriteLine(item);
```

The implementation is extremely basic and so this will result in an endless loop. But the important thing to point out is that `foreach` does its job even though the `IEnumerable` and `IEnumerator` interfaces aren't "officially" implemented. The `Reset` method is missing entirely. Arguably this "tolerant" behavior of `foreach` isn't a desirable thing, but that's what it has been since .NET and C# 1.0. You are well advised not to rely on this behavior, if only because other .NET languages don't necessarily implement it in the same way as C#.

A full (though only slightly more useful) implementation of the list class looks like this:

```
public class EndlessListWithInterfaces: IEnumerable, IEnumerator {
  public EndlessListWithInterfaces( ) {
  }

  public IEnumerator GetEnumerator( ) {
    return this;
  }

  public object Current {
    get { return "something"; }
  }

  public bool MoveNext( ) {
    return true;
  }

  public void Reset( ) {
  }
}
```

The main issue with this class, apart from infinite looping, is that it returns itself as the IEnumerator implementation every time. An enumerator is expected to have an idea of a position within the collection, that is, the value that is returned by Current when it's called. Assuming that multiple iteration processes are active at the same time, it must be possible to distinguish the positions that these processes are currently at. You don't have to think multiple threads for this; it would be enough that one iteration is started and iterated for a bit, then another one is started, and so on — an implementation like the preceding one breaks as soon as a second iteration is required.

The following implementation of an EndlessList class uses separate classes for IEnumerator and IEnumerable. The classes are nested, although they don't need to be. But in reality, nesting the enumerator implementation within the enumerable is a common pattern. To make things a bit more practical, this implementation also uses integer values instead of returning the same string all the time.

There's still one major difference compared to most real-world implementations: there's no data encapsulated in the outer list implementation. You may wonder why this example wasn't constructed in a more realistic fashion. The answer is that it would have meant either creating some rather complex data structure code, or using an existing data structure, which would have made the example unrealistic in a different way because all the standard data structures already have their own IEnumerable implementation.

```
public class EndlessList : IEnumerable {
  public class Enumerator : IEnumerator {
    int val = -1;

    public object Current {
      get { return val; }
    }

    public bool MoveNext( ) {
      val++;
      return true;
    }

    public void Reset( ) {
      val = -1;
    }
  }

  public IEnumerator GetEnumerator( ) {
    return new Enumerator( );
  }
}
```

This pattern of implementing value sequences is very flexible and quite powerful. In certain circumstances, however, it can be quite hard to implement—for instance, if the data in the list doesn't easily allow sequential and/or random access. Most importantly, though, creating such implementations isn't quick and easy. Sometimes algorithmic problems have easy solutions based on sequences, but on the basis of explicit interface implementation, .NET iterators don't lend themselves well to the creation of ad hoc iterators to solve such problems.

IMPLEMENTING ITERATOR FUNCTIONS

C#'s iterator feature, introduced in C# version 2.0, allows you to create implementations of the IEnumerable/IEnumerator combination without ever implementing either of those interfaces manually. It goes even farther by supporting the generic interfaces in addition to the non-generic ones, and making it possible to implement IEnumerator only.

Typically, it is only necessary to implement a function with a particular return type to use this feature. The second criterion the compiler looks for in order to apply its transformations (more about that in a moment) is the use of at least one of several special keywords within that function. Most common is the yield return statement. For example, the earlier EndlessList example can be implemented as a C# iterator like this (using a generic interface for a change):

```
public static IEnumerable<int> EndlessListFunction( ) {
  int val = 0;
  while (true)
    yield return val++;
}
```

To understand how to work with this, it's easiest to take it literally. The return type of the function is an IEnumerable<int>, so you use it in the same places where you might otherwise use a class instance that implements this interface. Here's some code that iterates through the EndlessListFunction sequence:

```
var list = EndlessListFunction( );
foreach (var item in list)
  Console.WriteLine(item);
```

The C# compiler automatically creates a class that implements the interface IEnumerable<int>. The logic of that class and the corresponding IEnumerator implementation is carefully structured to return the same sequence of values that is generated by the logic in the function implementation.

Here's a simple iterator:

```
public static IEnumerable<int> ThreeNumbers( ) {
  yield return 3;
  yield return 11;
  yield return 27;
}
```

The following contains the class code that the compiler generates for the ThreeNumbers iterator function. The code has been summarized somewhat to show the most important concepts, but you can use the .NET Reflector tool to see for yourself what happens once you compile code using the yield return statement like before:

```
class ThreeNumbersIterator : IEnumerable<int>, IEnumerable,
  IEnumerator<int>, IEnumerator {
  int state;
  int current;
```

```
    int initialThreadId;

    public ThreeNumbersIterator(int state) {
      this.state = state;
      this.initialThreadId = Thread.CurrentThread.ManagedThreadId;
    }

    bool MoveNext() {
      switch (state) {
        case 0:
          this.state = -1;
          this.current = 3;
          this.state = 1;
          return true;

        case 1:
          this.state = -1;
          this.current = 11;
          this.state = 2;
          return true;

        case 2:
          this.state = -1;
          this.current = 27;
          this.state = 3;
          return true;

        case 3:
          this.state = -1;
          break;
      }
      return false;
    }

    IEnumerator<int> GetEnumerator() {
      if ((Thread.CurrentThread.ManagedThreadId == this.initialThreadId) &&
          (this.state == -2)) {
        state = 0;
        return this;
      }
      return new ThreeNumbersIterator(0);
    }

    int Current {
      get {
        return current;
      }
    }
  }
}
```

The most important — and impressive — part of the automatic implementation of the ThreeNumbersIterator class is the MoveNext method. Whatever looping logic, distinction of cases, or other algorithms you use in your iterator function, the compiler generates a MoveNext method that creates the same sequence as its result.

The entire pattern declared by the IEnumerable and IEnumerator interfaces is about laziness. It's about fetching data only when needed. Fetching data in this context summarizes a number of possible operations: calculating data, getting it from a remote location, or simply retrieving it from a data structure. The advantage of the pattern is that a sequence is a small flexible part in a bigger algorithm. The sequence doesn't make any assumptions about how it's going to be used. It may be that your application works with data structures that are kept in memory, but it could just as well work with data that is retrieved from a SQL database, a Web service, or some other data source. A lazy pattern like iterators in C# allows you to provide access to your data in a way that is modular and very flexible, and that doesn't impose any constraints on how the rest of your code, or code written by somebody else, works with the data.

As a final example of the laziness factor, here's code that outputs some debug information:

Available for
download on
Wrox.com

```csharp
public static IEnumerable<int> ThreeNumbersDebug( ) {
   Console.WriteLine("Returning 3");
   yield return 3;
   Console.WriteLine("Returning 11");
   yield return 11;
   Console.WriteLine("Returning 27");
   yield return 27;
}

...

Console.WriteLine("Retrieving the list object");
var list = ThreeNumbersDebug( );
Console.WriteLine("Before the foreach loop");
foreach (var item in list)
  Console.WriteLine("Got value {0}", item);
```

Code snippet Program.cs

The output is this:

```
Retrieving the list object
Before the foreach loop
Returning 3
Got value 3
Returning 11
Got value 11
Returning 27
Got value 27
```

Two important things can be seen in this result. First, no values are retrieved from the sequence at the point where the function ThreeNumbersDebug is called. It doesn't matter whether the values even exist at this point, or whether they are ever retrieved — there's no overhead involved with calling the iterator function. Second, the debug output during the loop alternates between the "Returning x" info from the iterator function itself and the "Got value x" confirmation of the code on the outer foreach loop. Every time a new value is fetched, control is passed to the body of the iterator function, which picks up where it left off (or that's what it looks like — the reality is a bit different, as the Reflector output from before showed). Once again no overhead is involved when the consumer stops retrieving values. The pattern only does as much work as required.

The following code snippet shows a practical example of an iterator that retrieves data from a web service, using a search of the Twitter stream. Data is retrieved lazily from that web service, because it employs paging automatically. The iterator retrieves new pages as needed and returns a string sequence to the caller that is of unknown length. The caller can decide to handle that sequence any way it likes — in this example by chaining into `Take`:

```
private static void TwitterSearchIterator( ) {
  foreach (var tweet in GetTweets("#msdn").Take(10))
    Console.WriteLine(tweet);
}

private static IEnumerable<string> GetTweets(string searchString) {
  var url = "http://search.twitter.com/search.atom?q=";
  int page = 1;
  var escapedSearchString = searchString.Replace("@", "%40").Replace("#", "%23");
  XNamespace ns = "http://www.w3.org/2005/Atom";

  while (true) {
    var doc = XDocument.Load(String.Format(
      "{0}{1}&page={2}", url, escapedSearchString, page));
    var entries = doc.Root.Elements(ns + "entry");
    if (entries.Count( ) == 0)
      yield break;
    foreach (var entry in entries)
      yield return
        entry.Element(ns + "author").Element(ns + "name").Value + ": " +
          WebUtility.HtmlDecode(entry.Element(ns + "title").Value);
    page++;
  }
}
```

Returning IEnumerator

Instead of the interfaces `IEnumerable` and `IEnumerable<T>` that have been used in examples so far, iterators can also return `IEnumerator` or `IEnumerator<T>`. The code created by the compiler is adjusted automatically, so that only these interfaces are implemented by the auto-created iterator class. Until now, you have seen cases where functions were used to return instances of those auto-created iterator classes. Sometimes you want to write a class that is an iterator itself. In other words, you want to be able to use `foreach` to "iterate over an instance of your class." Obviously this makes most sense if you assume that the class in question is a collection of some description. In such a scenario, it is not sufficient to include a method in the class that returns an auto-generated iterator. What you need to do is implement `IEnumerable<T>` on the class itself, which means supplying a `GetEnumerator` function.

These scenarios are what the `IEnumerator` support of the C# iterator feature is for. Here's an implementation of an alternative `EndlessList` class, based on iterator support:

```
public class EndlessListWithIterators : IEnumerable<int> {
  IEnumerator<int> IEnumerable<int>.GetEnumerator( ) {
    int val = 0;
    while (true)
      yield return val++;
  }

  IEnumerator IEnumerable.GetEnumerator( ) {
    return ((IEnumerable<int>) this).GetEnumerator( );
  }
}
```

This class only implements the "outer" `IEnumerable<T>` interface, and leaves `IEnumerator<T>` for the compiler to do. By supporting both sets of interfaces with the iterator mechanisms, the compiler makes it easy to create both convenient iterator functions and full class implementations.

CHAINING ITERATORS

Iterators in the form of functions can be used in chains very easily, creating complex processing pipelines out of them. This concept is used a lot in LINQ and also in many of the examples later in this book, and it is one key idea of functional programming. Following are a few examples of the basic idea.

You've seen the iterator `EndlessListFunction`, which returns an endless sequence of integer values. An iterator function that does something to the sequence itself can be used with it. For example, following is an implementation of `Take`. This function takes a sequence of ints as a parameter together with a count, and only returns the first few elements from the source sequence.

```
public static IEnumerable<int> Take(int count, IEnumerable<int> source) {
  int used = 0;
  foreach (var item in source)
    if (count > used++)
      yield return item;
    else
      yield break;
}
```

You can use `Take` together with `EndlessListFunction` like this:

```
var fiveElementList = Take(5, EndlessListFunction( ));
foreach (var item in fiveElementList)
  Console.WriteLine(item);
```

This is a good example of how iterators can be used as modules. The iterator created by `EndlessListFunction` can return an unlimited number of elements, but there's no problem if the algorithm requires only the first few. Only the necessary work is ever executed. You will see improved versions of the `Take` function later in the book.

The second type of function used in iterator chains is one that employs the actual content. Performing calculations is an obvious idea because all of the examples in this chapter have used integers. Here's a function that performs a calculation with an integer value:

```
public static int Square(int x) {
  return x * x;
}
```

With an iterator, you can easily apply the Square function to a sequence of values:

```
public static IEnumerable<int> Square(IEnumerable<int> values) {
  foreach (int val in values)
    yield return Square(val);
}
```

Using delegate types, you could make the pattern of applying a function to a sequence of ints a bit more general purpose:

```
public static IEnumerable<int> Apply(IEnumerable<int> values,
  Func<int, int> calculation) {
  foreach (int val in values)
    yield return calculation(val);
}
```

You can introduce your own generic parameter so the Apply function works with types other than int. For good measure, Apply<T> is also implemented as an extension method.

```
public static IEnumerable<T> Apply<T>(this IEnumerable<T> values,
  Func<T, T> calculation) {
  foreach (T val in values)
    yield return calculation(val);
}
```

The pieces all fit together. And of course a chain of such iterator functions can be as long as you like:

```
var results = Take(10,
  EndlessListFunction( ).
  Apply(Square).
  Apply(x => x / 2));
foreach (var item in results)
  Console.WriteLine(item);
```

No overhead of any significance is introduced when the elements are chained together in this way. The "endless" list still generates only the first 10 values in this last example — nothing more. That's what laziness is all about.

The iteration mechanisms described in this chapter are just one example of laziness applied to computer programming. A more general description of lazy evaluation can be found in Chapter 9, and caching techniques like those described in Chapter 10 may be useful if you want to prevent values from being recalculated under any circumstances — until now, the sequences implemented using iterators will still evaluate, fetch, or calculate from scratch every time a new iteration is started.

SUMMARY

Sequence support has been in .NET since the beginning. Its implementation in the framework is object oriented, based on interfaces. While it has always been possible to implement custom sequences, or iterators, by implementing those interfaces, the iterator support introduced in C# 2.0 made this task much easier. In spite of the heavy use Microsoft itself has made of this feature, the concept of iterators has remained vague for many developers. This chapter has demonstrated the basics of the syntax, and the rest of the book has many more iterator implementations to offer.

Encapsulating Data in Closures

➤ Constructing functions dynamically

➤ Solving scope issues with closures

The capability of a programming language to work with higher order functions means that the problem of data scope becomes apparent. When functions are passed around as parameters and return values, the compiler uses closures to extend variable scope so that data is guaranteed to be available when needed.

CONSTRUCTING FUNCTIONS DYNAMICALLY

Most of the C# functionality related to creating functions and methods has been around in programming languages for a long time. Many languages have also had the feature of variables that refer to functions. Even the C programming language had function pointers that could be used to store references to functions, pass these into other functions, and call into the functions. The C# 1.0 delegate type doesn't really add much to what was already possible in C; the idea is just more formalized through the `delegate` keyword and has been extended upon with multicast delegates and events.

The main difference between C and C# from version 2.0 onward is that C# makes it possible to create new functions anonymously. Now you may wonder why this is so important — after all, the compiler inserts these functions as methods into the class, so isn't this just syntactic sugar? To a certain extent that's true, but there is a lot of functionality gained by the capability to create functions on-the-fly and return them to the outer scope. Yes, functions can be return values, just like this:

```
private static void ReturningFunctions( ) {
  var add = GetAdd( );
```

```
      var result = add(10, 20);
   }

   static Func<int, int, int> GetAdd( ) {
      return (x, y) => x + y;
   }
```

Although appealing from a technical standpoint, this example doesn't really solve any problems. The same function is returned from every call to GetAdd, which is nothing special and could be achieved much more easily. Where it gets really interesting is when the creation of the function is dynamic, and for that purpose the support for closures is required.

THE PROBLEM WITH SCOPE

In C#, the scope of variables is defined precisely. The details aren't relevant here, but the essence of it is that all code lives in methods in classes, and all variables exist only in and below the block where they are declared. Developers can choose where they put values they want to store away for later reuse. The decision typically depends on the purpose of the variable and also how much later any reuse is going to occur. A variable may end up being local to a method or to a class instance, or it can be almost global by being stored in a static class field.

Variables are changeable — the word "variable" gives it away. On the whole, functional programming in general doesn't like the idea of changeable values in programs (more about this in Chapter 16), and the more public a variable is, the greater the issues. In general, the guideline is to have no changeable values at all, and to store everything in the smallest possible scope. A pure function is expected to work only with values that are local to its own block, and access nothing outside its own scope and certainly nothing that can be changed from elsewhere.

Many programmers have an initial reaction to this idea that is best described as incredulity. But think about it — it's probably been a long time since somebody told you how global variables of the kind that C programs had, or Pascal ones, were a bad idea. Remember what the reasoning was like? "It's a bad idea to have global variables because there's a chance of collision, and maintainability is affected because it's hard to understand what these variables contain at any given point in time, when they are changed," — or something very similar.

Having fields in classes that can be changed from any one of the methods in the class isn't much different from having global variables in your application. It's just the scope that's different. Yes, perhaps the problems of collision and maintainability resulting from having these variables aren't quite as great, especially if you keep your classes small and simple and well abstracted. But the problems of collision and maintainability remain, nevertheless. Unfortunately it often seems impossible to restrict values to the scope of functions. What if, during the initialization process, your application has a few values that are needed much later on, perhaps from more than one place in code? One possible answer is to take advantage of closures.

HOW CLOSURES WORK

To understand the nature of closures, it's best to look at some examples that utilize them. Have a look at this code:

```
static void Closures( ) {
  Console.WriteLine(GetClosureFunction( )(30));
}

static Func<int, int> GetClosureFunction( ) {
  int val = 10;
  Func<int, int> internalAdd = x => x + val;

  Console.WriteLine(internalAdd(10));

  val = 30;
  Console.WriteLine(internalAdd(10));

  return internalAdd;
}
```

Follow the path of execution: the function Closures calls into GetClosureFunction. There is an odd second pair of parentheses behind that call, with the parameter 30. This is because GetClosureFunction returns a function that is then called right away.

In GetClosureFunction, there is a local variable called val, and a local function called internalAdd, which adds val to a parameter called x. internalAdd is then called and the value 10 is passed in. What do you think the output is going to be? The answer is 20 — the value of val plus the parameter 10.

Now val is changed to 30 and internalAdd is called again. The result is 40, so you can learn something here about how the local function works with local variables that live in the same scope: obviously the change to the local variable is picked up by internalAdd, even though it happened after internalAdd had been originally created.

Finally, internalAdd is returned from GetClosureFunction, and as you saw initially, it is being called again with the parameter 30. The result is 60, the last known value of val plus the parameter 30.

So far, so good. This is just what somebody may be expecting since it's the only thing that you would really want to happen in this situation. Yet it's not really logical at first glance. val is supposed to be a local variable, living on the stack, and at least when GetClosureFunction returns, it should be gone. Right? Yes, and that shows exactly what the purpose of closures is: to prevent values from going out of scope when the compiler can clearly tell that this would result in a crash of your application.

The very high-level explanation of how closures work is now quite simple. The compiler notices that the anonymous function created within GetClosureFunction refers to an element from an outer scope (that's the variable val). Since functions can be passed around like data in C#, it is possible that the function survives longer than the value of val. If the function is called at a later point, potentially from an entirely different place in the application code, the application would crash if the value had been removed from memory by then. So the compiler goes ahead and stores that value away in a safe location (anywhere but the function stack does the job), in case it is used later.

From a technical perspective, the location where that data gets stored away is important. The compiler creates an anonymous class, and an instance of that class is created inside `GetClosureFunction`. The anonymous function is created as a function inside that anonymous class — if the closure functionality weren't required here, that anonymous function would just be created in the class where `GetClosureFunction` also lives. Finally, the local variable `val` is actually not a local variable anymore; instead it is a field in the anonymous class.

As a result, `internalAdd` now references the function that is in the anonymous class instance. That instance also contains the data, which is stored for as long as a reference to `internalAdd` is kept around.

The following code shows the schema that is implemented by the compiler in this case. You can use the Reflector tool to see this for yourself. All auto-generated names have been changed and the code cleaned up a bit for readability.

```
[CompilerGenerated]
private sealed class DisplayClass {
    public int val;

    public int AnonymousFunction(int x) {
        return x + this.val;
    }
}

private static Func<int, int> GetClosureFunction() {
    DisplayClass displayClass = new DisplayClass();
    displayClass.val = 10;
    Func<int,int> internalAdd = displayClass.AnonymousFunction;

    Console.WriteLine(internalAdd(10));

    displayClass.val = 30;
    Console.WriteLine(internalAdd(10));

    return internalAdd;
}
```

Back to the idea of dynamically generated functions for a moment: it is now possible to create new functions out of thin air that vary in behavior depending on parameters. For instance, here's a function that adds a static value to a parameter:

```
private static void DynamicAdd( ) {
    var add5 = GetAddX(5);
    var add10 = GetAddX(10);

    Console.WriteLine(add5(10));
    Console.WriteLine(add10(10));
```

```
    }

    private static Func<int, int> GetAddX(int staticVal) {
      return x => staticVal + x;
    }
```

This principle is the basis of many of the function construction techniques that will be discussed in later chapters. Even from the simple example like the last one, it becomes obvious that this is a technique in direct competition to object oriented approaches like method overloads. But in contrast to method overloads, the creation of anonymous functions can happen dynamically at runtime, triggered by a single line of code in another function. Specialized functions that are needed to make a particular algorithm easier to write and read can be created in the scope of the single method where they are going to be used, instead of cluttering the level above by being inserted on the class level. This is the core idea of functional modularization.

As a practical example for the use of closures, consider the async pattern used with the standard .NET WebRequest class. The following code shows a common implementation that uses a separate state class, as suggested by the MSDN documentation:

```
    public class StateHolder {
      public WebRequest Request { get; set; }
      public string ClientId { get; set; }
      public string Query { get; set; }
    }

    private static void QueryVersion1(string clientId, string query) {
      // Unrelated to this demo, but important: in the real world, make sure
      // 'query' has been checked to be safe!
      var request = WebRequest.Create("http://www.google.com/search?q=" + query);
      request.BeginGetResponse(QueryCallback1,
        new StateHolder {
          Request = request,
          ClientId = clientId,
          Query = query
        });
    }

    private static void FeedBackToClient(string clientId, Stream responseStream) {
      // This method does whatever it takes to get the results back
      // to the client with the given id.
    }

    private static void QueryCallback1(IAsyncResult ar) {
      var state = ar.AsyncState as StateHolder;
      if (state != null) {
        var response = state.Request.EndGetResponse(ar);
        FeedBackToClient(state.ClientId, response.GetResponseStream( ));
        response.Close( );
      }
    }
```

The async pattern decouples the place where a potentially long-running operation starts (the BeginGetResponse call in QueryVersion1) from the callback code that is triggered when the operation completes (the method `QueryCallback1`). The drawback of the pattern is that it's cumbersome to implement, because there's usually quite a lot of information that needs to be kept around for use once the callback is called. The `StateHolder` class is used in the example to store that information. `BeginGetResponse` allows for one object to pass through, which can later be retrieved from the `AsyncState` property of `IAsyncResult`. For each use case, you have to create a class that can store the relevant information, and in the callback you must downcast to the correct type to retrieve the information. Having to create a new class every time is a lot of work in the long run, and the decoupling can be confusing once you have many applications of the `async` pattern in your code.

With the help of closures, there is an alternative solution. Look at the following piece of code:

```
private static void QueryVersion2(string clientId, string query) {
    // Unrelated to this demo, but important: in the real world, make sure
    // 'query' has been checked to be safe!
    var request = WebRequest.Create("http://www.google.com/search?q=" + query);
    request.BeginGetResponse(
        (IAsyncResult ar) => {
            var response = request.EndGetResponse(ar);
            FeedBackToClient(clientId, response.GetResponseStream( ));
            response.Close( );
        }, null);
}
```

`QueryVersion2` implements the same functionality as the combination of `QueryVersion1` and `QueryCallback1` described previously. Instead of the separate callback `QueryCallback1`, a lambda expression is passed to `BeginGetResponse`. Within that lambda expression, the code accesses information from the outer scope directly: the `request` and `clientId` variables. These values are stored in a closure, so they stay available until the time when the callback code is executed. It is easy to forget that the pattern is still the same and that the lambda is executed later than the `QueryVersion2` function itself, in a different context. The implementation is simple, readable and intuitive, and closures make it possible.

Finally, to get back to the topic of scope that was explained at the beginning of this chapter: The idea that was proposed is to store data in the scope of functions, to prevent having it around in places where any changes can't be tightly controlled. Closures offer a solution for this requirement. In Chapter 8 you will find more information about the techniques of currying and partial application, which rely on the functionality provided by closures. Chapters 14 and 18 have examples of practical applications as well.

SUMMARY

Closures are an important mechanism to fully support functional approaches in a programming language. This chapter has shown how they work and when the compiler employs them in C#. For scenarios like the previously explained `async` pattern, closures are a convenient mechanism; for some functional techniques they are a vital basis.

7

Code Is Data

WHAT'S IN THIS CHAPTER?

➤ Expression trees in .NET

➤ Analyzing and generating code

➤ Special considerations for expression trees in .NET 4.0

If you ask functional programming experts about the great inventions brought along decades ago by the LISP (list processing) language, one of the common answers is "eval." These days, a lot of programming languages support functions that are similar to LISP's eval, and a term like "eval mechanism" is often used to describe a particular functionality: the capability to evaluate language expressions at runtime.

The easiest way to see this at work is simply using a string. Here's a simple mathematical expression that would be valid in many programming languages: (107.6 - 23.23) * 3.141. In a language that supports an eval mechanism, you might be able to call a function like this:

```
Eval("(107.6 - 23.23) * 3.141")
```

Pass in the string with the expression and get the result of the calculation returned from the Eval function. The expression in this example is very simple; the operators are really the only elements that have their specific implementation in the programming language itself. An eval mechanism typically goes further than this, using the syntax of the language itself and allowing access to language elements, perhaps functions, classes, or variables, that are defined in the context that eval is used in.

To illustrate this description a little more, here's an example in Python, which has strong support for eval. This is a snippet from Python interactive console:

```
>>> def square(x):
...     return x*x
```

```
...
>>> square(10) + 20
120
>>> eval("square(10) + 20")
120
```

The first three lines define a function `square`, which returns the squared value of a given parameter. The next two lines calculate `(square value of 10) + 20`. In the first case, the expression is given explicitly for evaluation by the interactive environment, while in the second case it's passed as a string to the `eval` function. The result is the same in both cases.

The use of the interactive environment in the Python example is a bit odd because it uses an eval mechanism to evaluate the expressions entered at the command line. Still, it demonstrates the use of the `eval` function and serves as an advanced example of more complex expressions (such as the instruction to define a function) being evaluated.

The obvious point of having an `eval` mechanism is simple: the capability to construct expressions dynamically at runtime and running them. In some languages this is at the core of the evaluation or execution system; in others it's just a piece of functionality offered to programmers.

A final important detail is the representation of executable/evaluable expressions. In the preceding examples, the visible representation is simply a string, which was presumably parsed into code in the case of the Python example. On the surface, it isn't always possible to tell what the actual internal representation is — this requires knowledge of the mechanisms used by the language and the associated execution environment. For instance, Python could be using a just-in-time (JIT) compilation system that translates the expression into an internal representation format in a step that takes place before the application is executed.

In compiled languages like C#, things are a bit different. Theoretically it's possible to evaluate an expression in string format at runtime, but that involves a language parser separate from the compilation infrastructure. Microsoft's C# compiler is currently written in in C/C++ and is not well enough modularized to support calling into the parser alone at runtime. There are certainly workarounds, like constructing an artificial temporary source code file to wrap a code snippet and invoking the compiler against this, but they have the character of a hack.

On the level of IL (intermediate language), .NET has supported runtime creation of executable code since version 1.0, and in recent versions this has been continuously extended to improve execution behavior. For future versions there are also improvements planned on the level of language source code. Tentative plans that have been described by Anders Hejlsberg include modularization of the C# compiler, which would make features like those just described a definite possibility.

EXPRESSION TREES IN .NET

Since version 3.5, .NET as well as Microsoft's .NET languages have had support for expression trees. These support a form of an eval mechanism for a particular restricted subset of the languages. Some additional major steps have been made in .NET 4.0, triggered by the Dynamic Language Runtime (DLR) development, but these are unfortunately not supported by the C# language in version 4.0 — apparently the C# team felt that there was work left to do on expression tree support, and that an extension of the existing language support would be incomplete and potentially confusing at this time.

Consider this simple lambda expression:

```
Func<int, int, int> add = (x, y) => x + y;
```

As you know by now, this results in a local function, which you can call in order to add two `int` values:

```
int result = add(10, 20);
// result is now 30
```

The lambda expression is compiled code. The anonymous function is translated into IL code during the C# compiler run. To create an expression tree instead, the syntax has to be modified a little:

```
Expression<Func<int, int, int>> addExpr =
  (x, y) => x + y;
```

The only difference is the type of the variable that holds the lambda expression. This difference instructs the C# compiler to create entirely different code. Instead of compiling the code to perform the addition operation into IL, the compiler generates code to create a complex hierarchy of objects, all of which are of types derived from `System.Linq.Expressions.Expression`.

Because the value stored in the variable `addExpr` is an abstract representation of the lambda expression, it can't be executed directly. But the .NET Framework can compile an expression tree at runtime:

```
Func<int, int, int> addCompiled = addExpr.Compile( );
```

`addCompiled` has the same signature as the lambda expression `add` that was used earlier, and unsurprisingly this is now a function that can be executed.

```
int result2 = addCompiled(10, 20);
// result2 is now 30
```

It's almost as if a little bit of compiler functionality is now available to you for use in your own code. But the examples are a bit pointless until you realize that the data structures created to represent the code can be analyzed and created at runtime as well. The direct support in the C# compiler is a shortcut — certainly a very important one, but still only a part of the puzzle.

ANALYZING EXPRESSIONS

One of the main driving factors behind the idea of treating code as data is that it enables you to analyze the code at runtime. This is sometimes motivated by the need to understand what the code does — for instance, for logging or debugging purposes — but it also enables you to translate code at runtime into an execution format that is best suited for the task at hand.

The sample project for this chapter contains a class called ExpressionDumper, which walks through an expression tree hierarchically and outputs information about all the elements to the console or some other stream. For the addExpr expression, a call to ExpressionDumper.Output() renders the following hierarchy:

```
LambdaExpression (
  Parameters:
    ParameterExpression (x)
    ParameterExpression (y)
  Body:
    BinaryExpression:Add (
      Left:
        ParameterExpression (x)
      Right:
        ParameterExpression (y)
    )
)
```

This is one of the easiest ways to familiarize yourself with the structures used by expression trees: make use of the C# compiler's capability to generate the trees from code, output them using ExpressionDumper and see how certain constructs are represented.

The following code shows one of the core methods (just the first 20 lines for brevity) in the ExpressionDumper class:

Available for download on Wrox.com

```
private static void Output(Expression expression, TextWriter textWriter,
  int indent) {
  switch (expression.NodeType) {
    case ExpressionType.Add:
      Output((BinaryExpression) expression, textWriter, indent);
      break;
    case ExpressionType.AddChecked:
      Output((BinaryExpression) expression, textWriter, indent);
      break;
    case ExpressionType.And:
      Output((BinaryExpression) expression, textWriter, indent);
      break;
    case ExpressionType.AndAlso:
```

```
      Output((BinaryExpression) expression, textWriter, indent);
      break;
    case ExpressionType.ArrayLength:
      Output((UnaryExpression) expression, textWriter, indent);
      break;
    case ExpressionType.ArrayIndex:
      Output((BinaryExpression) expression, textWriter, indent);
      break;
  ...
```

Code snippet ExpressionDumper.cs

Expression trees use a structure that's quite common for syntax trees. Each of the elements that can be contained in the hierarchy derives from a common base class, and there's one derived class for each of the possible types. But at the same time, the common base class has a field of an enum type that you can use to check for the type before performing any casts. Looking at the enum field first is a much more efficient way to discover the type of a particular element than it would be to use runtime type information. ExpressionDumper simply checks for all possible elements of the enum ExpressionType and calls into other overloads of the Output function, which handle the type specific outputs.

There are certain restrictions to the language elements that can be represented by expression trees. In .NET 3.5, this is easy to summarize: expressions are only supported as long as they have expression bodies. The language support in C# 3.5 covers exactly the same features. In .NET 4.0, things are a bit more confusing because the feature set of expression trees in the .NET Framework has been extended, but the C# feature set of language version 4.0 has stayed the same.

.NET 4.0 covers statements in addition to expressions. Declarations of new types aren't supported yet; this is left as a target for future versions. The next section about the dynamic generation of expressions has an example of .NET 4.0–specific functionality.

In real-world applications, the purpose of analyzing expression trees is usually a translation into a different format that represents the same or an analogous expression. The functionality was initially introduced in conjunction with LINQ in .NET and C# 3.5, and the database-independent querying support provided by the LINQ infrastructure is the most common place where expression tree analysis is required.

A full example of a custom LINQ provider is beyond the scope of this book because there are complex aspects to the infrastructure of LINQ extensibility, which are not relevant to functional programming. Nevertheless, the idea of transforming an expression tree into a format that can be interpreted by some other engine is a useful and common one. Consider this LINQ expression:

```
var peopleWithIInTheirName =
  from p in people
  where p.Name.Contains("i")
  select p;
```

This valid little query finds all those elements in the collection people that have an "i" in the string returned by the property Name. Of course this piece of code is supported by a type (called Person) that declares the property Name of type string, and there is also a data source called `people`. In the sample code for this chapter, people is simply a `List<Person>`, but the LINQ system can also work with data sources that aren't really lists of things. There are interfaces that can be implemented by data source classes, and through those interfaces, LINQ interacts with the data sources in order to have the actual query code translated into whatever format is preferred by the data source in question.

For instance, imagine that the thing called people represents a table in a database. That database might understand SQL, and in that case it would be much better to make use of the SQL language to execute the query for elements with an "i" in the name. With SQL, the query would run on the database server, and only the elements that satisfy the condition would ever be returned to the client application. This is what LINQ supports: writing a query in your C# code that can be translated into a query that runs on a database server, or any other format of query that you can come up with.

The important bit of the query in the example is the `where` clause. The other parts aren't irrelevant, but for the sake of this simplified example the `where` clause shall suffice. For LINQ, the C# compiler translates a query expression like the example into a chained sequence of method calls, and elements like the `where` clause are translated into lambda expressions. The `where` clause of the preceding example results in this lambda expression:

```
p => p.Name.Contains("i")
```

The expression takes an object p and returns whether a particular conditions is true for this object. This type of expression is called a *predicate*, and there is a pre-defined delegate type in the .NET Framework for these, called `Predicate<T>`:

```
Predicate<Person> nameContainsI = p => p.Name.Contains("i");
```

`Predicate<T>` is functionally equivalent to `Func<T, bool>`: it takes an item of type T as a parameter and returns a `bool` value that indicates whether the given T parameter fulfills a certain criterion. This predicate delegate can now be called for each of the `Person` objects in a list, and it will return true or false to indicate whether each element should be included in a result list or not. If further analysis of the predicate is necessary, it should be created in the form of an expression:

```
Expression<Predicate<Person>> nameContainsI =
    p => p.Name.Contains("i");
```

To perform a similar operation in a SQL query on a database server, this predicate would have to be translated into a SQL compatible query string. Advanced string operations like `Contains` aren't standardized in SQL, so the translation would have to be specific to the database system that is targeted. For T-SQL, the SQL dialect used by Microsoft SQL Server, the expression could be this:

```
CHARINDEX("i", Name) > 0
```

This is simplified a bit, leaving out the part where a particular table name might have to be included to supplement the column name. The task is clear nevertheless: take an expression representing a predicate, and convert it into a T-SQL-compatible expression (within the boundaries of this example). The task is accomplished by the following code. Note that the implementation is rather agile (with a few minor add-ons for error handling) — only those exact features required by the task at hand have been implemented, which reduces the complexity of the example, but leaves countless other execution branches unconsidered.

Available for download on Wrox.com

```
static string ConvertExpressionToTSQL(Expression expression) {
  switch (expression.NodeType) {
    case ExpressionType.Lambda:
      return ConvertLambdaExpressionToTSQL(
        (LambdaExpression) expression);
    case ExpressionType.Call:
      return ConvertMethodCallExpressionToTSQL(
        (MethodCallExpression) expression);
    case ExpressionType.Constant:
      return ConvertConstantExpressionToTSQL(
        (ConstantExpression) expression);
    case ExpressionType.MemberAccess:
      return ConvertMemberExpressionToTSQL(
        (MemberExpression) expression);
    default:
      return "Unsupported expression type";
  }
}

static string ConvertLambdaExpressionToTSQL(
  LambdaExpression lambdaExpression) {
  // skipping things here, only interested in the body
  return ConvertExpressionToTSQL(lambdaExpression.Body);
}

static string ConvertMethodCallExpressionToTSQL(
  MethodCallExpression methodCallExpression) {
  // the only method that's currently supported for an actual
  // conversion is String.Contains

  var stringContainsMethodInfo = typeof(String).GetMethod("Contains");
  if (methodCallExpression.Method == stringContainsMethodInfo) {
    return String.Format("CHARINDEX(\"{0}\", {1}) > 0",
      ConvertExpressionToTSQL(methodCallExpression.Arguments[0]),
      ConvertExpressionToTSQL(methodCallExpression.Object));
  }
  else
    return ConvertUnknownMethodCallExpressionToTSQL(
      methodCallExpression.Method.Name, methodCallExpression.Arguments);
}

static string ConvertMemberExpressionToTSQL(
  MemberExpression memberExpression) {
  return memberExpression.Member.Name;
}

static string ConvertConstantExpressionToTSQL(
```

```
      ConstantExpression constantExpression) {
      return constantExpression.Value.ToString( );
    }

    static string ConvertUnknownMethodCallExpressionToTSQL(
      string methodName,
      ReadOnlyCollection<Expression> methodArguments) {
      // try to build a somewhat helpful string for
      // method calls that aren't supported
      StringBuilder builder = new StringBuilder( );
      builder.AppendFormat("UnsupportedMethod{0}(", methodName);
      bool firstArg = true;
      foreach (var argument in methodArguments) {
        if (!firstArg)
          builder.Append(", ");
        else
          firstArg = false;
        builder.Append(ConvertExpressionToTSQL(argument));
      }
      builder.Append(")");
      return builder.ToString( );
    }
```

Code snippet chapter7/Program.cs

Looking at this code, you might notice the similarities to the implementation of the
ExpressionDumper. Both are, in fact, algorithms that translate a given expression into
some other format — a readable output format in the case of the ExpressionDumper,
a SQL format in the case of this example.

GENERATING EXPRESSIONS

Making the step from analyzing expressions to constructing them isn't difficult. With the help
of the ExpressionDumper and the support of the C# compiler (as far as it currently goes), it's
easy to find out how common expressions are represented in the trees. The Expression class
has a lot of helper functions that make it easy to construct new expression trees at runtime.
These can then be used in any APIs that use function passing (by compiling the expression trees)
or in those that use the expression trees directly (like LINQ). This can be a modern form of
dynamic querying, using expression trees as an intermediate step and thereby increasing
flexibility, security, and type safety.

Here's the expression tree again for the add function:

```
LambdaExpression (
  Parameters:
    ParameterExpression (x)
    ParameterExpression (y)
  Body:
    BinaryExpression:Add (
      Left:
```

```
      ParameterExpression (x)
   Right:
      ParameterExpression (y)
   )
)
```

Such a tree makes it easy to see the elements that are being used, and with the helper functions in the `Expression` class it's just as easy to construct the same tree. Here's the code for this function:

```
ParameterExpression xParam = Expression.Parameter(typeof(int), "x");
ParameterExpression yParam = Expression.Parameter(typeof(int), "y");

var addExpr = Expression.Lambda<Func<int, int, int>>(
  Expression.Add(xParam, yParam), xParam, yParam);
```

Starting from the innermost element, `Expression.Add` is used to create the `BinaryExpression` with the subtype `Add`. It gets passed the two parameters to work with. The result is passed on to the helper function `Lambda<T>`, which returns a fully typed expression tree. The slightly odd-looking duplication of the `xParam, yParam` parameters in the second line is just accidental — the helper function `Lambda` has the list of all parameters taken by the lambda expression as its final arguments.

The sample source code for this chapter contains a slightly more complex example, to construct an expression tree for this expression:

```
(x, y) => (x + 11) > 30 && x < y
```

The algorithm for the SQL conversion has also been extended in the download example, so it can deal with a variety of `BinaryExpression` types as well as the `ParameterExpression`. Following is the replacement `ConvertExpressionToTSQL` method, as well as a few new helper methods.

Available for download on Wrox.com

```
static string ConvertExpressionToTSQL(Expression expression) {
  switch (expression.NodeType) {
    case ExpressionType.Lambda:
      return ConvertLambdaExpressionToTSQL(
        (LambdaExpression) expression);
    case ExpressionType.Call:
      return ConvertMethodCallExpressionToTSQL(
        (MethodCallExpression) expression);
    case ExpressionType.Constant:
      return ConvertConstantExpressionToTSQL(
        (ConstantExpression) expression);
    case ExpressionType.MemberAccess:
      return ConvertMemberExpressionToTSQL(
        (MemberExpression) expression);
    case ExpressionType.Parameter:
      return ConvertParameterExpressionToTSQL(
        (ParameterExpression) expression);
    case ExpressionType.GreaterThan:
      return ConvertBinaryExpressionToTSQL(
        (BinaryExpression) expression);
    case ExpressionType.GreaterThanOrEqual:
```

```
        return ConvertBinaryExpressionToTSQL(
          (BinaryExpression) expression);
      case ExpressionType.LessThan:
        return ConvertBinaryExpressionToTSQL(
          (BinaryExpression) expression);
      case ExpressionType.LessThanOrEqual:
        return ConvertBinaryExpressionToTSQL(
          (BinaryExpression) expression);
      case ExpressionType.Equal:
        return ConvertBinaryExpressionToTSQL(
          (BinaryExpression) expression);
      case ExpressionType.AndAlso:
        return ConvertBinaryExpressionToTSQL(
          (BinaryExpression) expression);
      case ExpressionType.OrElse:
        return ConvertBinaryExpressionToTSQL(
          (BinaryExpression) expression);
      case ExpressionType.Add:
        return ConvertBinaryExpressionToTSQL(
          (BinaryExpression) expression);
      case ExpressionType.Subtract:
        return ConvertBinaryExpressionToTSQL(
          (BinaryExpression) expression);
      case ExpressionType.Multiply:
        return ConvertBinaryExpressionToTSQL(
          (BinaryExpression) expression);
      case ExpressionType.Divide:
        return ConvertBinaryExpressionToTSQL(
          (BinaryExpression) expression);
      default:
        return "Unsupported expression type";
    }
  }

  static string ConvertParameterExpressionToTSQL(
    ParameterExpression expression) {
    return expression.Name;
  }

  static string ConvertBinaryExpressionToTSQL(
    BinaryExpression expression){
    string op = "UNKNOWN_BINOP";
    switch (expression.NodeType) {
      case ExpressionType.GreaterThan:
        op = ">";
        break;
      case ExpressionType.GreaterThanOrEqual:
        op = ">=";
        break;
      case ExpressionType.LessThan:
        op = "<";
        break;
      case ExpressionType.LessThanOrEqual:
        op = "<=";
```

```
        break;
      case ExpressionType.Equal:
        op = "==";
        break;
      case ExpressionType.AndAlso:
        op = "&&";
        break;
      case ExpressionType.OrElse:
        op = "||";
        break;
      case ExpressionType.Add:
        op = "+";
        break;
      case ExpressionType.Subtract:
        op = "-";
        break;
      case ExpressionType.Multiply:
        op = "*";
        break;
      case ExpressionType.Divide:
        op = "/";
        break;
    }
    return String.Format("(({0}) {1} ({2}))",
      ConvertExpressionToTSQL(expression.Left),
      op, ConvertExpressionToTSQL(expression.Right));
  }

  static string ConstructWhereClause(Expression expression) {
    return String.Format("WHERE {0}",
      ConvertExpressionToTSQL(expression));
  }
```

Code snippet chapter7/Program.cs

Building the expression requires the following code:

```
var complexPredicate = Expression.Lambda<Func<int, int, bool>>(
  Expression.AndAlso(
    Expression.GreaterThan(
      Expression.Add(xParam, Expression.Constant(11)),
      Expression.Constant(30)),
    Expression.LessThan(xParam, yParam)),
  xParam, yParam);
```

With the help of the newly extended conversion functionality, the tree can be transformed into something that could almost be used in a SQL query:

```
var predicateSql = ConstructWhereClause(complexPredicate);
...
"WHERE (((((x) + (11))) > (30))) && (((x) < (y))))"
```

The conversion algorithm is rather careful about putting parentheses everywhere and there's no logic implemented to reduce those afterward, but it is nevertheless easy to recognize that the expression is the same one that was previously shown as a lambda expression.

.NET 4.0 SPECIFICS

As mentioned earlier, .NET 4.0 has extended the supported language elements for expression trees, but the C# language hasn't seen any corresponding extensions yet. As a result, expression trees can currently be constructed through helper functions of the `Expression` class in .NET 4.0, which don't have a syntactic representation in the language itself. It's possible to implement a function or a lambda expression with the same functionality as any given expression tree, but the automatic conversion into an expression tree doesn't work.

For instance, here is a simple function to calculate a factorial using an iterative algorithm:

```
static int Fact(int x) {
  int result = 1;
  for (int m = 2; m <= x; m++)
    result *= m;
  return result;
}
```

As a lambda expression, this is what the function looks like:

```
Func<int, int> fact = x => {
  int result = 1;
  for (int m = 2; m <= x; m++)
    result *= m;
  return result;
};
```

But that is not possible and results in the compilation error "A lambda expression with a statement body cannot be converted to an expression tree."

```
Expression<Func<int, int>> factExpression = x => {
  int result = 1;
  for (int m = 2; m <= x; m++)
    result *= m;
  return result;
};
```

Constructing the expression tree for this simple algorithm is quite complicated. Here's the function that does it:

```
static Func<int, int> ConstructRuntimeFact( ) {
  var param = Expression.Parameter(typeof(int), "x");
  var resultVar = Expression.Variable(typeof(int), "result");
  var mVar = Expression.Variable(typeof(int), "m");
  var loopEnd = Expression.Label();
```

```
      return Expression.Lambda<Func<int, int>>(
        Expression.Block(
          new[] { resultVar },
          Expression.Assign(resultVar, Expression.Constant(1)),
          Expression.Block(
            new[] { mVar },
            Expression.Assign(mVar, Expression.Constant(2)),
            Expression.Loop(
              Expression.Block(
                Expression.IfThen(
                  Expression.Not(
                    Expression.LessThanOrEqual(mVar, param)),
                  Expression.Break(loopEnd)),
                Expression.MultiplyAssign(resultVar, mVar),
                Expression.PostIncrementAssign(mVar)),
              loopEnd)),
          resultVar),
        param).Compile();
    }
```

To start, all the elements that you need to refer to more than once in the tree need to be created up front. There's the parameter that the lambda expression takes, but there are also two new variable elements (these are actually also of type ParameterExpression) and one of type LabelTarget.

The process of constructing the tree is a bit like programming assembly language. Many high-level constructs that you are familiar with in C# are not available. The example was chosen to include a for loop, which is one element that doesn't have a direct representation in the expression tree system.

An important new element is the BlockExpression, which is returned by the helper function Expression.Block. This is used to encapsulate more than one expression in cases where statements are being executed linearly — one of the foundations of imperative programming. Any variables that are going to be declared for the block need to be passed in as the first argument to the helper function, and since the parameter is an IEnumerable<ParameterExpression>, you need to construct a temporary list even when there's just one variable. The assignment of a value to a variable is a second explicit operation, implemented by the BinaryExpression returned by Expression.Assign.

Finally, the semantics of the C# for loop need to be decomposed. A for loop is rather complex because it can contain variable declarations and assignments, checks for break criteria as well as iteration instructions. The helper function Expression.IfThen is used to create a ConditionalExpression, which potentially executes a Break. This, in turn, is of type GotoExpression and results in a jump to the label called loopEnd, which is added into the tree right after the body of the LoopExpression.

The return value of a BlockExpression is the result of the final expression passed to the Expression.Block helper function — in this case, resultVar.

This example makes for an interesting study, and the advantages of being able to create code at runtime in such an orderly fashion are potentially great. The lack of support in the language is an issue, and learning to work with expression trees by looking at automatically generated examples with the ExpressionDumper is therefore only an option for those elements that were already supported in .NET 3.5.

SUMMARY

You have seen in this chapter that expression trees cover many different scenarios around the idea of handling code at runtime — whether it is the need to understand and analyze code or create it dynamically. Creating code dynamically is more likely to be relevant to a majority of programmers, and in that area expression trees are today the mechanism of choice, instead of the older approaches using reflection or IL emission — at least as long as the slightly restricted expression tree language coverage is sufficient. For a further example, look at Chapter 16, which demonstrates a technique for object cloning that takes advantage of expression trees for dynamic property access.

PART III
Implementing Well-known Functional Techniques in C#

Currying and Partial Application

At its core, functional programming is all about the application of functions and their use as building blocks of algorithms. Haskell Curry is the mathematician whose name is the origin of the term *currying* (as well as the functional language Haskell). He invented the concept of currying at roughly the same time as Moses Schönfinkel and Gottlob Frege. Currying makes it possible to view all functions as members of the class of functions that take only one parameter, regardless of the number of arguments needed to perform the actual calculation. It enables partial application, which is one of two techniques (the other being composition) that make functional modularization possible.

In some publications, the term currying is used to cover the technique of partial application as well as currying itself. Because C# is a language in which the curried form of a function is not the native approach, it makes sense to keep these two separate and define them distinctly.

DECOUPLING PARAMETERS

Function or method calls can accept parameters — that is true in almost all programming languages. The underlying mechanisms to transfer the parameters and to make them available to the code executed in the function or method vary, and so does the terminology used to describe this process.

In most .NET languages the parameter list that is declared for a particular function is static. That means that the function in question can only be called with all the parameters at once. In fact, the notion of calling a function with an incomplete list of parameters probably strikes many C# programmers as rather odd. Nevertheless, this is exactly what currying is all about: splitting up the parameter list, so it becomes possible to call functions with an incomplete set of parameters.

You might think at this point that object oriented languages, or even imperative languages in general, have their own mechanisms for the purpose of providing convenient variants of functions or methods, for those cases where the standard implementations are found to be too complex to use. This is an absolutely correct association. Mechanisms like method overloading or extension methods have a similar purpose. However, the functional alternatives have advantages when it comes to function level reuse and modularization, which makes them an interesting option.

Manual Currying

Currying is a transformation technique that starts with a function with multiple parameters and converts it into a sequence of functions that each accept only one parameter at a time and return the next function in the sequence. At the end of this chain of functions, all parameters are available at once, allowing the original algorithm to do its work.

To illustrate this process, consider the following simple function in C# 2.0-compatible anonymous method syntax:

```
Func<int, int, int> add =
  delegate(int x, int y) {
    return x + y;
  };
```

This is a function add that takes two parameters and returns the result of adding the two values. When this function is called, the caller must supply both arguments x and y at once; the syntactic constraints of C# don't allow any other approach.

Applying currying to this function means creating a function that accepts only one parameter, returns another function that takes the second parameter, and then returns the result of the addition. Typically the order of parameters after the application of currying will be the same as before, although it doesn't have to be. You can find more information on the topic of parameter order in the section "Why Parameter Order Matters" later in this chapter.

This is what the function looks like after currying has been applied:

```
Func<int, Func<int, int>> curriedAdd =
  delegate(int x) {
    return delegate(int y) {
      return x + y;
    }
  };
```

As you can see, this implementation is exactly what was just described: a function that takes the first parameter and returns another function, which takes the second parameter and returns the result of the computation.

The type of the function has changed, from `Func<int, int, int>` to `Func<int, Func<int, int>>`. This reflects the new structure of the function, but is also one of those unfortunate situations where syntactic requirements of the C# language are quite inconvenient. The C# compiler refuses to use type inference for variables that store anonymous methods (whether using delegate syntax or lambda syntax), even though at least in the delegate case the types are readily available. Fortunately, the explicit type is only required with the declaration of a new function. In cases where functions are returned by other functions, the calling code can remain free of verbose type declarations and the `var` keyword can be used instead.

The representation of the functions using the anonymous methods syntax from C# 2.0 was chosen in these examples because it is much easier to see why the two parameters that have been passed in one by one are in fact available at the same time on the deepest nesting level of the curried format function. The technical answer to that question is, of course, closures. Because the inner function uses the parameter x that is a local variable in the outer function, the compiler creates a closure for that variable.

The principles of currying also apply to functions in lambda syntax. The `add` function could be written as a lambda expression like this:

```
Func<int, int, int> add = (x, y) => x + y;
```

The curried add function looks like this:

```
Func<int, Func<int, int>> curriedAdd = x => y => x + y;
```

As you can see, the syntax is so much more concise that it seems quite hard to believe these examples implement the exact same code as the earlier anonymous methods. This can be visualized a little better by inserting parentheses to make the nesting of functions more obvious in the lambda case:

```
Func<int, Func<int, int>> curriedAdd = x => (y => x + y);
```

The technique of currying applies to functions with any number of parameters. Assuming a function with a list of parameters:

```
Func<...> f = (par1, par2, ..., parX) => ...;
```

The curried format function always has this signature:

```
Func<...> cf = par1 => par2 => ... => parX => ...;
```

The code in the "body" of the lambda expression — that is, the expression to the right of the last goes-to operator — remains the same during the transformation.

The shape of the type changes according to very similar rules. Consider this original generic delegate type:

```
Func<int, bool, string, decimal, double>
```

The resulting type after the application of currying is this:

```
Func<int, Func<bool, Func<string, Func<decimal, double>>>>
```

Automatic Currying

It is quickly becoming clear that the process of currying follows hard rules, and it is possible to automate it entirely. There are cases where the manual application of currying has advantages — some will be described in later chapters on parameter order and pre-computation — but most of the time it is a relief to have a helper function that performs the process automatically.

Here is the function `Curry`, which takes another function as a parameter and returns a curried format function:

```
public static Func<T1, Func<T2, TR>> Curry<T1, T2, TR>(
  this Func<T1, T2, TR> func) {
  return par1 => par2 => func(par1, par2);
}
```

You will recognize the important details that have been discussed previously:

> ➤ The input parameter `func` is of type `Func<T1, T2, TR>` and the return type of the `Curry` function is `Func<T1, Func<T2, TR>>`

> ➤ The shape of the function that is returned follows the same schema as the lambda expressions that have been curried manually.

Using the helper function `Curry`, a curried format of a function can be retrieved with a simple call. This helper function is part of FCSlib and lives in the class `Functional`, so all further examples will call it as `Functional.Curry(...)`.

The main detail to pay attention to is the requirements of C# type inference. Basically, the compiler needs to be able to infer the parameter and return types of the function from at least one location. Of course, it is possible to declare the type of the source function explicitly and then use `var` with the `Curry` function:

```
Func<int, int, int> add = (x, y) => x + y;
var curriedAdd = Functional.Curry(add);
```

In this case, even though `Curry` is a generic function, it is not necessary to pass in the generic parameters explicitly. The compiler infers the generic parameters because the parameter passed into `Curry` is already typed. For inline use of lambda expressions it can also make sense to pass the generic parameters explicitly:

```
var curriedAdd = Functional.Curry<int, int, int>((x, y) => x + y);
```

Interestingly, type inference can also infer the generic parameters if the types of the lambda expression, or those of a C# 2.0 anonymous method, are given explicitly. This is curious because in the same situation the use of the var keyword to store the function in a variable is not valid.

```
// this is invalid
var mult = (int x, int y) => x * y;

// this is valid
var curriedMult = Functional.Curry((int x, int y) => x * y);
```

Since the function Curry has been declared as a C# 3.0 extension method, it is also possible to call it directly on a variable that stores a compatible function:

```
Func<int, int, int> mult = (x, y) => x * y;
var curriedMult = mult.Curry();
```

Calling extension methods is not possible on inline lambda expressions, so the following syntax is not valid:

```
// invalid
((int x, int y) => x * y).Curry();
```

In addition to the Curry function shown previously, there are many other overloads declared in FCSlib. You can curry functions with much larger numbers of arguments with overloads like this:

```
public static Func<T1, Func<T2, Func<T3, Func<T4, Func<T5, Func<T6, Func<T7,
TR>>>>>>>
 Curry<T1, T2, T3, T4, T5, T6, T7, TR>(this Func<T1, T2, T3, T4, T5, T6, T7, TR>
func) {
 return p1 => p2 => p3 => p4 => p5 => p6 => p7 => func(p1, p2, p3, p4, p5, p6, p7);
}
```

Overloads to curry Action delegates are also included:

```
public static Func<T1, Action<T2>> Curry<T1, T2>(this Action<T1, T2> action) {
  return p1 => p2 => action(p1, p2);
}
```

These are useful for cases where the function you need to curry doesn't have a return value, like this assertion for easy use in a unit test:

```
public class Assert {
  public static void Equals(int x, int y) {
    Debug.Assert(x == y);
  }
}

...

var curriedAssertEquals = Functional.Curry<int, int>(Assert.Equals);
var assertEquals5 = curriedAssertEquals(5);
```

Calling Curried Functions

Whether a function has been curried manually or automatically, or even created from scratch in this format, there are some common consequences regarding the way the function can and has to be used. A basic call to the function `curriedAdd` looks like this, passing in both parameters:

```
int result = curriedAdd(5)(3);
```

or:

```
var curriedAdd5 = curriedAdd(5);
var result = curriedAdd(3);
```

At first glance, the way there are several pairs of parentheses on the line is confusing, but of course this is the result of the function chaining that currying creates. The call to the first function just takes one parameter, and it returns a second function which is being called with the second parameter list. Agreed, it does look unfamiliar, but it's easy enough to get used to.

The Class Context

Although examples so far have dealt with functions that are declared as lambda expressions or anonymous methods, currying works just as well with more conventional methods declared in C# classes. Both static class methods and instance methods can be curried. Classes also offer an easy way of making curried functions available for external calls. The following listing shows the class `Calculator`, which publishes curried versions of the `Add` and `Mult` functions for public consumption. This example uses static methods and fields, which is quite common with fully functional approaches, but the same techniques can be used equally well with instance methods and fields.

```
class Program {
  static void Main(string[] args) {
    // The results of these two calls are the same
    Console.WriteLine(Calculator.AddC(20)(30));
    Console.WriteLine(Calculator.Add(20, 30));
  }
}

public static class Calculator {
  public static int Add(int x, int y) {
    return x + y;
  }

  public static readonly Func<int, Func<int, int>> AddC =
    Functional.Curry<int, int, int>(Add);

  public static int Mult(int x, int y) {
    return x * y;
  }

  public static readonly Func<int,Func<int,int>> MultC =
    Functional.Curry<int, int, int>(Mult);
}
```

Currying class methods is another situation where C# type inference lets you down, so you need to specify the generic type parameters on the `Curry` call explicitly. Unfortunately the compiler is also unable to distinguish between the field Add and the method `Add` in that same call to `Curry`. If that worked better, it would be possible to have both a curried and a normal method called Add because these two have different parameter lists. But the compiler complains about a line like this:

```
// invalid
public static readonly Func<int, Func<int,int>> Add =
  Functional.Curry<int, int, int>(Add);
```

It seems clear that the Add that's passed to the `Curry` function can only be the static method declared before, and not a reference to the static field Add because only the method is compatible with the type `Func<int, int, int>` that is expected by the `Curry` function. But C# is unable to infer this, so it becomes necessary to establish a naming convention that distinguishes between the original and the curried versions of the same functions. In these examples the curried functions all end in a capital C for "curried."

The suggested syntax declares two curried functions that are independent from each other. In cases where there are dependencies between functions, it is unwise to rely on the compiler to initialize the static fields in a particular order. The safe approach is to have a static constructor and to use that to initialize the static fields instead of in-place initialization. The following listing shows a version of the `Calculator` class that uses this alternative initialization approach:

```
public static class Calculator {
  static Calculator2( ) {
    AddC = Functional.Curry<int, int, int>(Add);
    MultC = Functional.Curry<int, int, int>(Mult);
  }

  public static int Add(int x, int y) {
    return x + y;
  }

  public static int Mult(int x, int y) {
    return x * y;
  }

  public static readonly Func<int, Func<int, int>> AddC;
  public static readonly Func<int, Func<int, int>> MultC;
}
```

In some situations it can be useful to use properties instead of fields to publish curried versions of functions. There are at least three potential advantages to this approach that go hand in hand, and one that's more general:

1. The precise mechanism used to "prepare" the function before it's published can be much more complex than simple currying. Examples include memoization and precomputation, explained in Chapter 10.

2. When the cost of preparing functions and the number of functions prepared in some way rise, it becomes desirable to do this only when it is really needed. A property

implementation allows the use of a create-on-demand approach, which can result in considerable efficiency improvements.

3. When a create-on-demand technique is used, the static constructor is not needed any more. This has the advantage of keeping related operations in one block instead of spreading things around.

4. Properties provide encapsulation of implementation logic, which is the typical reason to use properties for anything at all. If a class uses public fields and you see a need later to replace them with properties, your own code might not break because the calling syntax is identical. But you will still have to rebuild all consuming code because the IL generated for a field access is different from that used for a property access.

One downside is that the syntax for this technique isn't quite as concise anymore as the public field approach above. There is really no silver bullet for this; it all depends on the priorities of a particular use case.

The following example shows yet another implementation of the `Calculator` class. It uses static properties with a create-on-demand approach to currying. It also works without any "normal" functions in place, making the implementation of the curried functions almost entirely self-contained (with the exception of the private field — you will see later how it is possible to get rid of that field as well).

```
public static class Calculator {
  private static Func<int, Func<int, int>> add;
  public static Func<int, Func<int, int>> Add {
    get {
      if (add == null)
        add = Functional.Curry<int, int, int>((x, y) => x + y);
      return add;
    }
  }
  private static Func<int, Func<int, int>> mult;
  public static Func<int, Func<int, int>> Mult {
    get {
      if (mult == null)
        mult = Functional.Curry<int, int, int>((x, y) => x * y);
      return mult;
    }
  }
}
```

This last example is one that has purely academic value. It hasn't been pointed out so far, but if there isn't actually an existing function with multiple parameters, it is much easier and more concise to create the functions in curried format from the start. Using curried format functions directly, the shortest version of the `Calculator` could look like this (neglecting the earlier arguments against using fields):

```
public static class Calculator4 {
  public static readonly Func<int, Func<int, int>> Add =
    x => y => x + y;
```

```
      public static readonly Func<int, Func<int, int>> Mult =
        x => y => x * y;
}
```

This implementation hardly needs any further explanation. It uses the syntax of a curried lambda expression and implements the calculation directly in the body of the final part of the expression instead of calling some other function for the result.

What FCSlib Contains

The function `Curry` is provided by FCSlib in the class `Functional`. There are two sets of overloads, one that curries functions compatible with `Func<...>`, the other for `Action<...>`. The delegates `Func<...>` and `Action<...>` are part of .NET 3.5, and both have a number of overloads themselves, for functions taking up to four parameters. FCSlib takes this a few steps farther by providing additional `Func<...>` and `Action<...>` delegates for functions with up to nine parameters.

There are nine variations of `Curry` that work with `Func<...>`, where the difference is the number of parameters the original function accepts. These overloads all follow the same pattern:

```
    public static Func<T1, Func<T2, TR>> Curry<T1, T2, TR>(
      this Func<T1, T2, TR> func) {
      return par1 => par2 => func(par1, par2);
    }

    public static Func<T1, Func<T2, Func<T3, TR>>> Curry<T1, T2, T3, TR>(
      this Func<T1, T2, T3, TR> func) {
      return par1 => par2 => par3 => func(par1, par2, par3);
    }

    public static Func<T1, Func<T2, Func<T3, Func<T4, TR>>>>
      Curry<T1, T2, T3, T4, TR>(this Func<T1, T2, T3, T4, TR> func) {
      return par1 => par2 => par3 => par4 => func(par1, par2, par3, par4);
    }

    ...
```

The schema for the overloads that accept `Action<...>` delegates is slightly different because the last element in the chain of functions is always an `Action<T>` instead of a `Func<T, R>`. Here are the first three overloads from that group for comparison:

```
    public static Func<T1, Action<T2>> Curry<T1, T2>(this Action<T1, T2> action) {
      return par1 => par2 => action(par1, par2);
    }

    public static Func<T1, Func<T2, Action<TR>>> Curry<T1, T2, TR>(
      this Action<T1, T2, TR> action) {
      return par1 => par2 => par3 => action(par1, par2, par3);
    }

    public static Func<T1, Func<T2, Func<T3, Action<TR>>>> Curry<T1, T2, T3, TR>(
```

```
      this Action<T1, T2, T3, TR> action) {
      return par1 => par2 => par3 => par4 => action(par1, par2, par3, par4);
   }
```

The purpose of FCSlib is to provide all the overloads that would reasonably be needed, so you don't have to create any such functions in your own code.

A second set of functions provided by FCSlib in relation to currying is a set of overloads of Uncurry. To be clear: this converts functions from curried format into non-curried format. Here is the overload for a function with two arguments:

```
public static Func<T1, T2, TR> Uncurry<T1, T2, TR>(this Func<T1, Func<T2, TR>> func)
{
   return (p1, p2) => func(p1)(p2);
}
```

The overloads provided by FCSlib allow to reverse all the operations that can be performed by the Curry overloads, both for Func and Action delegate types.

There's a final set of functions in FCSlib that helps deal with lambdas in curried and uncurried format. These overloads are called Lambda, and they construct a typed lambda expression. Many overloads are included for consistency, although in simple cases they don't provide any benefits:

```
var addL = Functional.Lambda<int, int, int>((x, y) => x + y);
Func<int, int, int> add = (x, y) => x + y;
```

Both these lines have the same effect, one using a helper function to retrieve the typed delegate, the other using declaration syntax for the same purpose. However, there are also overloads of Lambda that take curried format functions as their argument:

```
var mult4L = Functional.Lambda<int, int, int, int, int>(
   a => b => c => d => a * b * c * d);
Func<int, Func<int, Func<int, Func<int, int>>>> mult4 =
   a => b => c => d => a * b * c * d;
```

As you can see, the amount of code you need to write is still roughly the same. The advantage of using Lambda in a case like this is that the type signature of the curried function grows in complexity with the number of arguments it has, due to the nesting of the Func delegate types. The call to the Lambda helper function has a flat list of type arguments instead. This makes the line easier to read. On the other hand, you may want the additional information provided by the explicit type signature — this is a matter of your own priorities.

CALLING PARTS OF FUNCTIONS

The most important reason to use a curried format function is that it becomes possible to call this function with only some, but not all, the parameters that are needed for the computation it performs. This process is called *partial application*, for obvious reasons: the function is applied, but only in part. Partial application is one technique used for function construction.

Consider the following piece of code, which uses a function created from scratch in curried format:

```
Func<int, Func<int, int>> add = x => y => x + y;
var add5 = add(5);
```

The curried function `add` is called, but only one parameter is passed to it. Obviously the calculation can't be performed at this point because it requires two parameters. The call with one parameter returns a new function, and instead of calling this immediately, it is stored away in the variable `add5` for later use.

This new function that has been created can now be called like any other function:

```
// the result will be 42
int result = add5(37);
```

The technique of partial application has created a new function out of an existing one. In general, partial application takes a function that is rather generic in nature and creates a new function with a more specific purpose. In the example, the function `add` is generic in the sense that it can take any two arbitrary integer values and add them. Every time the function is called, a new combination of integer values is passed in and a new result returned. While this is flexible, it also has the requirement that both parameters need to be passed in every time. Sometimes this is not desirable if a given algorithm needs the functionality in question (adding two values in this case) but not all the flexibility offered by the function.

There is a different approach with a very similar purpose available in many programming languages, including C#: overloading. A programmer could have the following two methods in a class:

```
int Add(int x, int y) {
  return x + y;
}

int Add5(int y) {
  return Add(5, y);
}
```

It is important to understand that partial application is used for the same reasons that overloads are created. These reasons evolve largely around the usability of APIs. An existing class will provide certain functions or methods that have been created with particular use cases in mind. In some cases the programmers of frameworks and similar large collections of APIs will have had an eye on usability, and they might have provided convenient overloads for functions where it made sense to them. In other cases they might not have done so, and it is almost a philosophical question whether this should even be done.

Without functional approaches like partial application, there is no really good way of creating convenience functions that haven't been prepared by the creators of an API. Imagine you are using a class that has been created by somebody else. The class has a function that does something you need, and it's extremely flexible and has lots of parameters. In your algorithm, however, you only need part of that flexibility and all your calls use the same values for some of the parameters. Your code will be much less readable than it could be, if only you had a function that was stripped down to those few of the parameters that you actually need.

An overload would be a solution, but you can't create that overload in the class in question because you don't have the source code. Even if you did have the source code, perhaps creating a convenience function for your particular use case right there in the class wouldn't be the right approach. Alternatively you could create a helper function in a class of your own, and this is probably the approach chosen by most programmers. But is that the right one? A new method in your class just for the use of the one algorithm you are writing right now? This is the approach suggested by the extension method feature in C# 3.0, but it isn't always the right one.

With the help of partial application, you have one new choice: you can create that helper function in the exact place where it is needed. The context is correct because the function lives right next to the algorithm that utilizes it. It doesn't "pollute" the class context with functionality that is really specific to a particular algorithm. And the approach can be used in all situations, whether you are working with functions you have under your own control or ones that have been created by somebody else.

Partial application (and other function construction techniques; see Chapter 14) enables modularization on a functional level. Building blocks in your application don't have to be high-level entities like classes. Instead it's possible to modularize and reuse on a low level, on the functional level. Reusability and modularization is thereby shifted from being an architecture concern into the realm of responsibility and capability of every programmer.

WHY PARAMETER ORDER MATTERS

There is a simple reason why parameter order matters when the techniques of currying and partial application are used: it is only possible to partially apply from the start of the parameter list. When a function has three parameters — x, y, and z, in that order — it can be partially applied by passing x, or x and y, but not just y, or z, or y and z.

As a result, when writing functions for use in functional scenarios, where it is likely that partial application will be used on them, it is a good idea to consider parameter order from that point of view. This applies to "normal," multi-parameter functions as well as those that are written in curried format from the start.

The important thing to decide about parameter order is which parameter in your function is most likely to be partially applied. In simple cases like those add and mult functions demonstrated earlier, it might not matter at all. But in the case of that ADO.NET helper function from the practical use case, it matters a lot — if the helper function ExecuteModification had the command as the first parameter, partial application couldn't be readily used. It is much more likely that a caller to this function would want to fix the first parameter, the connection object, than the second one, the SQL command. As it is in most such cases, it is certainly possible that somebody would have a different point of view — a replication scenario where the same statements need to be executed through different connections, for instance. It is a choice you have to make about the priorities of different use cases you try to cover.

For the most part, personal preference is the only criterion to consider when it comes to parameter order. However, there is one feature in C# 3.0 that requires a specific parameter order: extension methods. The first parameter in an extension method signature defines the type that is being extended, and so there are cases when a "good" parameter order from a functional point of view can't be used because of the extension requirements.

Fortunately, it is possible to swap the order of parameters using an approach similar to currying. For example, using the function ExecuteModification from the previous code sample:

```
private static void ExecuteModification(SqlConnection connection,
  string sqlCommand) {
...
}
...
Func<string, Action<SqlConnection>> modify =
  command => connection => ExecuteModification(connection, command);
```

The order of the parameters in the sequence of the curried function has been swapped, compared to the original order in the ExecuteModification function. It is necessary to make this step manually because there's not much you can do to automate it. And of course it's an additional step in cases where the function is already available in curried format. Nevertheless, the approach applies to curried functions in the same way:

```
Func<int, Func<int, int>> add = x => y => x + y;
Func<int, Func<int, int>> reorderedAdd = y => x => add(x)(y);
```

SUMMARY

In this chapter you have seen how parameters can be decoupled from one another using the currying technique, so they don't have to be passed all at once. This promotes modularization on a functional level with the help of partial application.

Lazy Evaluation

WHAT'S IN THIS CHAPTER?

➤ Strict and non-strict evaluation

➤ Laziness through function passing

➤ Lazy<T>

➤ How lazy can you be?

C# is a language that uses a strict evaluation strategy most of the time. The topic of evaluation strategies is a complex one that applies to the techniques of passing parameters to functions, applying operators, the order in which expressions are evaluated, and several other related subjects.

As far as function calls go, strict evaluation means that parameters are evaluated before they are passed to functions. For instance, this function call uses an expression as a parameter:

```
MyFunction(23 * 4);
```

In C#, the fact that an expression was used on the calling side is no longer visible from the inside of MyFunction. The code inside the function can only see the value that is the result of an evaluation of that expression: 92.

Strict evaluation is very common, even more so in what can be considered mainstream programming languages these days. But there is competition in the form of non-strict evaluation strategies, which many programming languages use as well. Non-strict evaluation is often called lazy evaluation because the essence of it is that expressions, or parts of expressions, are only evaluated when their results are actually needed.

To see a case where C# uses non-strict evaluation, take a look at this Boolean expression:

```
bool isTrue = (10 < 5) && (MyCheck());
```

C# has a feature called short-circuiting, which is used during the evaluation of expressions like this. Its result is that the `MyCheck` function call is actually never executed in the previous expression because the first part of the expression already evaluates to `false` and so the whole expression can't be true anymore. The same works in the opposite case for the Boolean `or` operator:

```
bool isTrue = (10 > 5) || (MyCheck());
```

This time the first part of the expression evaluates to `true`, and so the second part doesn't have to be checked because it's already clear that the whole expression is going to be true as well.

Many programming languages use a mix of evaluation strategies, like C# does, but only few apply non-strict evaluation as the default. The most prominent example of a non-strict language is the pure functional programming language Haskell. In Haskell, you can define a simple function like this:

```
myfunc a b = if a then b else 0
```

This is a call to the function:

```
myfunc True (37+5)
```

Even if you don't know Haskell, I'm sure you can easily see that the result is 42 in this case. The parameter `a` is a Boolean value and since it is `True` in this call, the expression is evaluated and returned from the function. But here's a second call:

```
myfunc False (37+5)
```

This returns 0 (zero), of course, because now the Boolean value that's passed in is `False`. What is not obvious (and actually extremely hard to demonstrate visibly in Haskell) is that in this second case Haskell never evaluates the expression `37+5`! Due to the non-strict nature of its evaluation strategy, Haskell passes the entire expression into `myfunc`, without evaluating it first. Technically, it uses a so-called thunk to store and transfer the expression. This is not related to Haskell directly. A *thunk* is a general term to describe a piece of code stored away for later evaluation.

In C#, it is not possible to introduce the same concepts that Haskell uses for two reasons: it is naturally an imperative language, where evaluation order is often important, and unless you work for Microsoft, you can't change the C# compiler. Nevertheless, some techniques of lazy evaluation can be used in C# as well. The structure of `IEnumerable` and `IEnumerator` since .NET 1, the introduction of iterators in C# 2.0, and the architecture of LINQ have demonstrated that Microsoft also cares about these topics. The following sections explain two more general approaches that can be used in everyday C# programming, using function passing as well as explicit laziness with the help of an encapsulation unit.

WHAT'S GOOD ABOUT BEING LAZY?

There are two main intentions in lazy evaluation. First, it can make program execution more efficient. In imperative programming, execution order is always important. In complex algorithms it is often difficult to decide under which circumstances something should or shouldn't be done, and the techniques used to "get it right" typically rely on a very specific execution order. Lazy evaluation offers an alternative approach, which comes with its own practical considerations and the need for a different style, but also the promise of optimal efficiency gains and vastly simplified algorithms in many situations. In languages that default to non-strict, lazy evaluation, programmers need ways to trigger strict evaluation occasionally. The important thing is having a choice.

Second, in traditional functional languages execution order typically doesn't play a big role at all. Functions have dependencies, which result in requirements for the order of evaluation. But should it be the programmer's task to figure this out? It shouldn't, and as this book continuously describes, the science of pure functions makes it possible to describe algorithms as a network of functions, with the "connections" defined by the dependencies. In this world, being lazy is an important part of being efficient, to avoid the side effect of executing expensive computations in places where the need isn't really clear yet.

Finally, of course, being lazy is always a virtue for a programmer — it makes you write better code if you continuously question whether there isn't a more efficient way you could go, or whether you could get by somehow with writing even fewer lines of code.

PASSING FUNCTIONS

A very simple approach to lazy evaluation is preferring higher order functions where possible. Consider this piece of imperative code:

```
private static int BigCalculation( ) {
  Console.WriteLine("BigCalculation called");

  return 42;
}

private static void DoSomething(int a, int b) {
  Console.WriteLine("DoSomething called");

  if (a != 0)
    Console.WriteLine(b);
}
```

The function BigCalculation is meant to model a function that takes a very long time to return its result. It may actually be a calculation, or it may be a process that takes long to complete for other reasons.

The function DoSomething is entirely unconnected, it takes two parameters, a and b, and does something with b depending on a. In fact, it is not really relevant that the action depends on a; in reality it could depend on a whole number of circumstances outside the scope of the function. Imperative programming is all about the management of state, so there are typically many external details that influence the precise code path through any given function. In this example, the line of code that "does something with" b simply outputs the value on the console, which is again a placeholder for any other kind of action that requires the value of b.

Now, in an imperative application a call into this function might well look like this:

```
DoSomething(0, BigCalculation());
```

It doesn't have to be a literal zero that is passed as the first parameter; it could be a variable instead. The important thing is that the thought process of the imperative programmer dictates: "Before I can call `DoSomething()`, I need to calculate the values I must pass in as parameters." As a result, an execution of this sequence will output the following debug lines on the console:

```
BigCalculation called
DoSomething called
```

Note that the value 42 is not shown. In fact, in the given scenario that value was never needed, because for reasons known only to the function `DoSomething`, it turned out that the code path passed by any lines where b would have been required. A call into `BigCalculation` — and thereby a rather large amount of time — has been wasted. Outside `DoSomething` there is no elegant way to anticipate whether the value for b is going to be required or not because that would involve a much more complex algorithm, or even a duplication of the code that checks the relevant state information. In any case, some value for b would need to be passed because `DoSomething` expects such a value even if it doesn't end up using it.

So what does "preferring higher order functions" mean in this context? Look at this variation of the function `DoSomething`:

```
private static void HigherOrderDoSomething(Func<int> a, Func<int> b) {
  Console.WriteLine("HigherOrderDoSomething called");

  if (a() != 0)
    Console.WriteLine(b());
}
```

The difference is that instead of taking two integer parameters, a and b, the parameters are now functions that return those integers. The lines where the values of a and b are being used have been changed as well to reflect the fact that these functions have to be called to return the values. It is a minor change really, and quite easy to make in any existing function.

The call into this function also changes:

```
DoSomething(() => 0, BigCalculation);
```

The zero value for the first parameter has been wrapped in a lambda expression (the empty pair of parentheses means that the expression doesn't take any parameters), and for the second parameter the function `BigCalculation` is passed instead of the value returned by `BigCalculation`. Executing this code now renders the following console output:

```
DoSomething called
```

There is no output from a call to BigCalculation, because such a call never happens. The algorithm now retrieves the result of the BigCalculation only if and when it is actually needed.

EXPLICIT LAZY EVALUATION

The technique of explicit lazy evaluation uses an encapsulation of a function call, which can be passed around and evaluated at any point. This encapsulation also provides caching, so that the actual method call only happens (at most) once.

This technique is quite close to the approach used by Haskell that was mentioned in the introduction to this chapter. Unfortunately, it can't be fully automatic in C#; instead, the encapsulating type must be specified explicitly in place of the "real" return type.

FCSlib provides a class Lazy<T>, which can be used as an encapsulation container for a function call:

Available for download on Wrox.com

```
public sealed class Lazy<T> {
  public Lazy(Func<T> function) {
    this.function = function;
  }

  public Lazy(T value) {
    this.value = value;
  }

  readonly Func<T> function;
  T value;
  bool forced;
  object forceLock = new object( );
  Exception exception;

  public T Force( ) {
    lock (forceLock) {
      return UnsynchronizedForce( );
    }
  }

  public T UnsynchronizedForce( ) {
    if (exception != null)
      throw exception;
    if (function != null && !forced) {
      try {
        value = function( );
        forced = true;
      }
      catch (Exception ex) {
        this.exception = ex;
        throw;
      }
    }
    return value;
```

```
    }

    public T Value { get { return Force( ); } }

    public bool IsForced { get { return forced; } }

    public bool IsException { get { return exception != null; } }

    public Exception Exception { get { return exception; } }

  }
```

code snippet Lazy.cs

The implementation and public interface of the class resemble a similar class that is used in the F# libraries. The class is quite straightforward — the code has not been copied from F#, but simply re-implemented in C# by looking at the public API of the class. It is initialized through its constructor with either a function or a value that is stored internally. The Force() and UnsynchronizedForce() methods as well as the Value property can be used to retrieve the value, which will be either returned directly or retrieved from the function first. The value will only be retrieved (at most) once.

Exceptions are handled by Lazy<T> as well. Any exception thrown by the encapsulated function is stored away and rethrown every time the value of the Lazy<T> instance is accessed. This behavior is especially desirable in use cases that involve multiple threads, because you can rely on the Lazy<T> instance to "keep each thread informed" correctly when an exception is thrown by the function.

The final feature of Lazy<T> is its thread safety. To avoid restrictions on T, the class is coded with a lock that encompasses the entire section with access to the value, not just the write operation. It would be possible to make this more efficient by locking only the write access, or even using a lock-less approach, but then T would have to be restricted to reference types.

Using Lazy<T> is simple, as it can be used in place of the value that it represents, whether that is a value known at the time of instantiation or one that still needs to be retrieved by calling another function. There are several ways to instantiate a Lazy<T> instance. First, it can be instantiated to represent a value that is already known:

```
    var lazy42 = new Lazy<int>(42);
```

This format is convenient if functions have been written to accept lazy parameters. In this case, Lazy<T> can represent the value directly, eliminating the need to wrap it into a function (as shown in the section "Passing Functions"). If another function needs to be called to retrieve the value, Lazy<T> can be instantiated like this:

```
    var lazyCalc = new Lazy<int>(BigCalculation);
```

In this line, BigCalculation represents a function that returns an integer, like the one in the "Passing Functions" example. The Lazy<T> instance represents this function and calls it as necessary when the value is requested through a call to the Force() or UnsynchronizedForce method or the Value property.

There is also a pair of helper functions in the `Functional` class that instantiate `Lazy<T>` for either a value or a function. The previous examples could also be written like this:

```
var lazy42 = Functional.Lazy(42);
var lazyCalc = Functional.Lazy<int>(BigCalculation);
```

Generally speaking, the advantage of the helper functions is that they can sometimes be called without explicit generic type parameters. Unfortunately, C# type inference doesn't always support this, as you can see in the `BigCalculation` line. Often it's just a matter of personal preference — some people find it easier to read a function call than an object instantiation when generics are being used.

A more interesting example of using `Lazy<T>` involves situations where it is used as the return type of a function that performs some calculation. Here are two variations of a lazy add function:

```
private static Lazy<int> LazyAdd(int x, int y) {
  return Functional.Lazy(( ) => x + y);
}

Func<int, Func<int, Lazy<int>>> lazyAdd =
  x => y => Functional.Lazy(() => x + y);
```

Both these cases have the same result: a function that takes two parameters and returns a `Lazy<int>` as its result. The `Functional.Lazy` helper function takes a function as a parameter, and the C# compiler makes the actual values of x and y available in a closure. So it is possible to call any of these functions for the result of an addition, but the actual calculation is delayed to the point where the `Value` is accessed from the `Lazy<int>` instance. Have a look at this more complete example:

```
private static Lazy<int> LazyAdd(int x, int y) {
  Console.WriteLine("Calling LazyAdd");
  return Functional.Lazy(( ) => {
    Console.WriteLine("Performing calculation");
    return x + y;
  });
}

...

Console.WriteLine("      Getting result");
var result = LazyAdd(37, 5);
Console.WriteLine("     Accessing the result");
Console.WriteLine(result.Value);
Console.WriteLine("     Accessing the result a second time");
Console.WriteLine(result.Value);
```

Here, the `LazyAdd` method has been instrumented with a few debug statements, so you can follow the sequence of events. In the calling code, there's one step to retrieve the result from `LazyAdd` and a second one to evaluate the result. The output on the console is this:

```
      Getting result
Calling LazyAdd
      Accessing the result
```

```
Performing calculation
42
    Accessing the result a second time
42
```

The actual calculation of the result happens only when the value is retrieved the first time. After that first evaluation, the value is cached, so it can be retrieved directly the second time.

As promised, the class `Lazy<T>` provides an encapsulation of an operation in a similar way to laziness in Haskell. This is about as far as lazy evaluation can be taken in C# — the syntax tends to grow more complex while the functionality improves, so to an extent this is a tradeoff between functionality and readability.

The class `Lazy<T>` used in this chapter is part of FCSlib, together with the utility functions in the Functional class. In .NET version 4.0, Microsoft has included `Lazy<T>` in the framework as `System.Lazy<T>`, so this mechanism is available to a wider audience now.

COMPARING THE LAZY EVALUATION TECHNIQUES

Both techniques demonstrated in the preceding sections have their various good and bad sides. The next few paragraphs describe some of the considerations you should make when applying one or both of these techniques to a problem.

Usability

If you have existing functions that take values as parameters, it is an easy change to replace these either with function types or with a `Lazy<T>` encapsulation. In both cases you must also change the call sites — that is, the places where the parameters are being evaluated — but those are simple changes and the compiler will help you because your code breaks once you have changed the types of the parameters.

For new code, you may find that depending on your style of programming as well as the extent to which you have adopted pure functions, it might come very naturally to pass functions in a lot more places than you used to do. If your code is already a network of functions, as suggested in the introduction, it is often an easy afterthought to add laziness through function passing into the mix — or you might even find yourself using it without noticing. However similar the `Lazy<T>` approach may be to Haskell, in C# it means using different types, so this will never happen by chance.

Another reason why `Lazy<T>` requires some additional consideration is that it can only represent operations without parameters. As the samples have shown, it is not hard to incorporate this necessity into your code, but again, it has to be done consciously.

Efficiency

One of the purposes of the whole laziness idea is to promote efficiency by making sure that computations aren't executed when they are not needed. Function passing, on the other hand, has the disadvantage that there's no automatic caching of result values. When the scope is left where the value has been evaluated, the result is forgotten, and recalculated on any further calls. It is easy to come up with an algorithm similar to the previous function passing example, in which performance will deteriorate vastly due to function passing:

```
private static void PassingFunctionsWithReallyBadPerformance( ) {
  DoSomethingBad(( ) => true, BigCalculation);
}

private static void DoSomethingBad(Func<bool> squareFirst,
  Func<int> bigCalculation) {
  Console.WriteLine("Result: {0}",
    squareFirst() ? bigCalculation( ) * bigCalculation( ) : bigCalculation( ));
}
```

In the example call, the `bigCalculation` function is evaluated twice. It would be easy to introduce a local variable to store the result, but then you'd be back at square one, having to find the correct place in your algorithm where that computation must be executed.

In contrast to function passing, `Lazy<T>` implements a simple cache because it doesn't reevaluate the function when the value is retrieved multiple times. It is also possible to do something similar for the case of function passing, but that's a separate topic and doesn't happen automatically — the key is a technique called memoization, which is discussed more in Chapter 10.

HOW LAZY CAN YOU BE?

Lazy evaluation is simple, or at least that's one possible impression you might get from reading this chapter. It is quite easy to make a few changes to existing code and make it lazy, using either of the approaches that were discussed. The trouble is that this can quickly lead to problems, and the reason is that evaluation order is often important in imperative code.

Your code, which you wrote in the past in C#, is likely to be imperative and object oriented. Most probably it uses classes a lot, and these classes have state; that is, fields that store information. That state is mutable, as state tends to be. Some people say the central focus of imperative programming is the handling and changing of state. Typically, the order in which state changes is important. In the narrowest sense, you can think of a state machine with certain transitions — obviously these transitions must not suddenly change. In a more general sense, algorithms in your classes assume information to be in a particular state when they run. If you write unit and/or functional tests, you can attest to the amount of work that goes into preparing the environment in which your code runs, into emulating the real working scenario of a piece of code as exactly as possible. State, and the precise way it is handled, is important.

Lazy evaluation changes the order in which your code is executed. It doesn't just change it once; it changes it, potentially, on every single run of your application, or even any particular algorithm. You could argue that this is the point of lazy evaluation, but at the same time it is obvious that this is absolutely incompatible with the requirements of state handling in imperative code.

The only situation where lazy evaluation makes no difference (well, almost no difference) to the functionality of your application is when your code consists entirely of pure functions. Remember, those are the ones that don't have any side effects, the ones that don't access information outside their own scope in any way. The language Haskell, which has been mentioned several times in this chapter, is a pure functional language, where functions are not usually allowed to have side effects, and special handling through the type system provides for safety in the cases where side effects need to be managed.

If you can't claim that your functions are pure, at least all those that you want to use lazy evaluation with, you will be in trouble.

The previous arguments dealt mainly with considerations about existing code that is to be converted. If you are writing new code, these same considerations are just as valid. But it becomes a matter of strategy and discipline to decide for or against lazy evaluation. It is much easier to write pure functions from scratch than to check large amounts of existing code for purity.

SUMMARY

C# is mostly a strict evaluation language, but there are some approaches you can take to evaluate lazily when needed. This chapter has shown examples of function passing as well as the use of the `Lazy<T>` type for this purpose.

10

Caching Techniques

WHAT'S IN THIS CHAPTER?

➤ Why remembering previous results is important in functional programming

➤ Computing information before you need it

➤ Caching data as you go

➤ Considerations on memoization

THE NEED TO REMEMBER

Computers are great at remembering things. In fact, if you look at typical business applications, you could easily get the impression that remembering things, not computing things, is the main purpose of computers these days. The data that computer programs work with is more often stored in a database than it is actually created or computed during the run of those programs. The ubiquity of database systems is testament to this fact.

In functional programming, as has been said before, the focus is on applying functions as opposed to handling state, and arguably all persisted data is a kind of state. Of course, handling persisted data is a reality of computer applications today, so functional programming has to find a way to deal with that. The details of accessing data from databases are not the subject of this chapter, but there is a more general need to remember data in functional programming: that which has been returned from calculations before, and therefore shouldn't be calculated again.

There are two main cases where you want to remember results of computations performed previously, and both of those are covered in this chapter. The first is *precomputation*, which is when you purposefully compute values before the actual algorithm runs that uses those values. The second is the situation in which you have function calls that are performed repeatedly, with the same set of arguments, and you want to optimize by storing and reusing the values that have been calculated.

There's a piece of objective wisdom about optimization that says it's almost always a bad idea when it happens prematurely. "Prematurely," on the other hand, is not a clearly defined point in time. In any case, this doesn't invalidate the techniques introduced in this chapter; it merely poses the question when, not if, they should be applied.

In Chapter 9, the type `Lazy<T>` used a type of caching to prevent multiple evaluation of the same computation. It was also said that the pure functional programming language Haskell uses a similar technique for its non-strict evaluation approach. So, is it correct to regard this type of caching as an optimization strategy, which should be applied only after thorough testing and profiling has proved a non-optimized algorithm to perform poorly? It seems that in some cases, caching techniques can also be regarded as an algorithmic choice rather than an optimization. Functional approaches like those discussed in this chapter can be used "in-line," so that they don't pervade the algorithms. On the other hand, C# doesn't provide for a highly efficient and automatic implementation like Haskell does. In the end there's no final answer to this dilemma. In C#, caching is an option, while in Haskell it's not, and the implementations differ in a variety of ways. For C# programmers, it should be a technique used with consideration, whether as an optimization applied after the original implementation or as an algorithmic choice.

PRECOMPUTATION

Precomputation is a technique with which most programmers are familiar in one or another manifestation. For example, trigonometric calculations are very important for 3D animation. At the same time, they are comparatively expensive. As a result, a technique similar to this is often used:

```
tatic void ImperativePrecomputation( ) {
  double[] sines = new double[360];
  for (int i = 0; i < 360; i++) {
    sines[i] = Math.Sin(i);
  }

  // Now your algorithm is just going to look up the sine
  // values in 'sines' instead of having to calculate them.
}
```

There's a clear separation here between the calculations that are performed first, and the actual algorithm that uses the results. In practice, a class is usually used to encapsulate the pre-computation and the algorithms that use the results in object oriented programming. Here is such a class that pre-computes trigonometric functions and uses the results to rotate (2-dimensional) points:

Available for download on Wrox.com

```
public class PointRotator {
  public PointRotator( ) {
    InitLookups( );
  }

  float[] sines, cosines;

  private void InitLookups( ) {
    sines = new float[360];
    cosines = new float[360];
```

```
      for (int i = 0; i < 360; i++) {
        sines[i] = (float) Math.Sin(ToRad(i));
        cosines[i] = (float) Math.Cos(ToRad(i));
      }
    }

    public PointF RotatePointWithLookups(PointF sourcePoint,
      double angle) {
      double polarLength = Math.Sqrt(Square(sourcePoint.X) +
        Square(sourcePoint.Y));
      double polarAngle = ToDeg(Math.Atan(sourcePoint.Y / sourcePoint.X));
      int newAngleInt = (int) Math.Round(polarAngle + angle);
      float cartesianX = (float) polarLength * Cos(newAngleInt);
      float cartesianY = (float) polarLength * Sin(newAngleInt);
      return new PointF(cartesianX, cartesianY);
    }

    private int NormalizeAngle(int angle) {
      return ((angle % 360) + 360) % 360;
    }

    private float Cos(int angle) {
      return cosines[NormalizeAngle(angle)];
    }

    private float Sin(int angle) {
      return sines[NormalizeAngle(angle)];
    }


    static double Square(double x) { return x * x; }

    static double ToRad(double deg) { return deg * Math.PI / 180.0; }

    static double ToDeg(double rad) { return rad / (Math.PI / 180.0); }
  }
```

code snippet PointRotator.cs

The important part of this is not the point rotation computation itself, and if you're a graphics programmer, you'll probably find that there are more efficient ways of doing the same thing. The interesting detail is how the class uses pre-calculated tables for sine and cosine values. In this case it's a trade-off of precision for performance, and the implementation actually saves a third in processing time compared to one that calculates these values as needed.

This example is quite complex regarding the functionality it provides. It uses two different lookup tables and two functions to access those. You will see how this can be done in a functional style later, but first consider the following example, which is a simpler case of pre-computation:

```
static bool IsInListDumb<T>(IEnumerable<T> list, T item) {
  var hashSet = new HashSet<T>(list);
  return hashSet.Contains(item);
}
```

This case is about performing lookups. There is a list of things, called `list`, and the function `IsInListDumb` is supposed to return a `bool` value indicating whether a particular given thing is part of the list or not. Since the type `IEnumerable<T>` doesn't lend itself well to such lookups, the function first creates a data structure that is more efficient for the purpose, and then uses that for the actual lookup. Some calls to `IsInListDumb` could look like this:

```
static void DumbDemo1( ) {
  string[] strings = {
    "One", "Two", "Three", "Four", "Five",
    "Six", "Seven", "Eight", "Nine", "Ten"
  };

  Console.WriteLine(IsInListDumb(strings, "Three"));
  Console.WriteLine(IsInListDumb(strings, "NotInList"));
}
```

The problem with this approach is quite obvious: the function `IsInListDumb` tries to be efficient by using a dedicated lookup data structure, but it computes this structure on every lookup, eliminating any positive effect. So how about using partial application to solve that problem? Look at this:

```
var curriedLookup =
  Functional.Curry<IEnumerable<string>, string, bool>(IsInListDumb<string>);

var precomputedLookup = curriedLookup(strings);
Console.WriteLine(precomputedLookup("Three"));
Console.WriteLine(precomputedLookup("NotInList"));
```

First, a curried version of the function `IsInListDumb` is retrieved, typed to work with strings. Then partial application is used to pass in the strings list on its own. The idea is that the strings list is all that's needed to pre-compute the efficient `HashSet`. Finally, several lookups are performed using the new function `precomputedLookup`. Does this work? No. Well, yes, but it doesn't perform any better than the first attempt. Why?

Even though partial application is used, the function isn't prepared to do anything with the `list` parameter that's passed in — not before the second parameter is supplied as well. Remember, the curried format of the function looks like this:

```
list => item => IsInListDumb(list, item)
```

If you put in some nesting, it becomes even clearer:

```
list => (
  item => IsInListDumb(list, item)
)
```

After `list` has been passed in, the only thing that is returned is the new function that takes the `item` parameter. Nothing else goes on, in particular the functionality of the `IsInListDumb` function itself is not triggered at this point. And how could it? Look at the code again:

```
static bool IsInListDumb<T>(IEnumerable<T> list, T item) {
  var hashSet = new HashSet<T>(list);
```

```
   return hashSet.Contains(item);
}
```

The function body has two statements, one to construct the `HashSet`, the other to perform the lookup and return the result. Partial application can't divide this function in half by magic, executing the first line when the first parameter has been passed in and leaving the second line for later. Nevertheless, this mistake has been made before. In fact, it's probably one of the most common misunderstandings about partial application.

To find a solution, have another look at this structure:

```
list => (
  item => IsInListDumb(list, item)
)
```

As was pointed out earlier, there's nothing happening after the first parameter has been passed in. So how about making something happen as soon as that parameter is available? Here's the solution to the puzzle:

```
static Func<T, bool> CleverListLookup<T>(IEnumerable<T> list) {
  var hashSet = new HashSet<T>(list);
  return item => hashSet.Contains(item);
}
```

This function takes just one parameter, or at least first it does. It uses the parameter immediately to compute the `HashSet` for the lookup. Then it returns a new function, which takes the item parameter and performs the lookup using the `HashSet`. Interestingly, the overall signature of this function is this:

```
list => item => bool
```

That is exactly the same signature as before, only this time there is something happening as soon as the first parameter becomes available. To compare with the nested and parenthesized curried construct shown earlier, here's the same abstract syntax:

```
list => (
  var hashSet = new HashSet<T>(list);
  item => hashSet.Contains(s);
)
```

Here's how to use this function:

```
var lookup = CleverListLookup(strings);
Console.WriteLine(lookup("Three"));
Console.WriteLine(lookup("NotInList"));
```

This is very much like partial application, but the curried format function has been "split in the middle," in a manner of speaking, and code has been inserted in the sequence. This is pre-computation in a functional style.

The HashSet *is kept in a closure once it's been created because the newly created lambda expression makes use of it. If you need a review of closures, see Chapter 6.*

Here is a functional solution for the point rotation example, based on the same approach as the list lookup:

```
static Func<PointF, Func<double, PointF>> CreateFunctionalRotator( ) {
  Func<double, double> toRad = x => x * Math.PI / 180.0;
  Func<double, double> toDeg = x => x / (Math.PI / 180.0);

  float[] sines = Functional.InitArray<float>(360,
    i => (float) Math.Sin(toRad(i)));
  float[] cosines = Functional.InitArray<float>(360,
    i => (float) Math.Cos(toRad(i)));

  Func<int, int> normalize = v => ((v % 360) + 360) % 360;
  Func<int, float> sin = v => sines[normalize(v)];
  Func<int, float> cos = v => cosines[normalize(v)];
  Func<float, float> square = x => x * x;

  return p => a => {
    double polarLength = Math.Sqrt(square(p.X) + square(p.Y));
    double polarAngle = toDeg(Math.Atan(p.Y / p.X));
    int newAngleInt = (int) Math.Round(polarAngle + a);
    float cartesianX = (float) polarLength * cos(newAngleInt);
    float cartesianY = (float) polarLength * sin(newAngleInt);
    return new PointF(cartesianX, cartesianY);
  };
}
```

This example uses functional approaches extensively, just as the object oriented code goes in that direction all the way. Of course you can combine strategies, but these examples present the greatest possible differences.

First, the function creates several local elements: the helper functions and the lookup arrays. The helper function InitArray<T> from the Functional class is used to initialize the lookup arrays. This is a higher order function, which creates an array of a particular type (determined by the generic parameter) and of a certain length, and initializes all the array values by passing the indices into the function that is passed for element initialization.

After all the helper elements have been constructed, the function creates a new function that takes a point and an angle as parameters. The function performs the same calculation as the class PointRotator, but it uses the locally defined helpers for its work. These are stored in a closure by the compiler, so they stay available when the newly constructed function is returned to the caller. Here's how to use CreateFunctionalRotator:

```
var rotate = CreateFunctionalRotator( );

Console.WriteLine(rotate(new PointF(4, 3))(3));
Console.WriteLine(rotate(new PointF(10, 25))(74));
```

MEMOIZATION

Memoization is a technique to cache values that have been returned previously by function calls. This depends on the parameters and assumes that the function is referentially transparent. There is a distinction between internal and external memoization; both are explained in this chapter.

 Referential transparency, or function purity, means that the function returns the same value for every call that uses the same set of parameters, and that the function doesn't have side effects. If you want to review this topic, see Chapter 3.

You have probably implemented internal memoization or some variation of it in the past. Here's a simple function:

```
static int SquareSimple(int x) {
  return x * x;
}
```

This function is pure, so it's a candidate for memoization. Before doing so, you should consider these points:

➤ The algorithm that uses the function should make extensive use of it. There is overhead involved with memoization, and unless the function is going to be called many times, it is more efficient to leave it as it is.

➤ The parameters that the function is called with are also important, for the same reason. If it is unlikely that the function will be called many times with the same parameter, there will be overhead but no benefit in memoization.

➤ The function should be sufficiently complex in nature. In reality, simple operations like squaring an integer value are so fast that memoization can't provide any benefit.

Here's a version of this function that applies internal memoization:

```
static Dictionary<int, int> squareInternalMemory;

...

private static int SquareInternalMemoized(int x) {
  if (squareInternalMemory == null)
    squareInternalMemory = new Dictionary<int, int>( );
  if (!squareInternalMemory.ContainsKey(x)) {
    int result = x * x;
    squareInternalMemory[x] = result;
```

```
        return result;
    }
    return squareInternalMemory[x];
}
```

The function now uses a dictionary that maps parameters to results. A check is performed to see if the result value for the given input parameter is already in the dictionary, and if it can't be found, it's calculated. If the value is already in the dictionary, it is returned right away.

> *It is often recommended to use the method* `Dictionary<K,V>.TryGetValue` *instead of the separate* `ContainsKey` *call and the indexer access in the previous code snippet. This is a valid recommendation given the performance characteristics of the* `Dictionary` *implementation, which uses array storage internally. On the other hand, the* `Dictionary` *class follows design guidelines that promote naming independent from implementation details — in other words, when interfacing with a class called* `Dictionary`, *you shouldn't think about how it works internally.*
>
> *In examples in this book as well as in FCSlib, the approach of calling* `ContainsKey`, *followed by a separate indexer access, has been used occasionally for clarity. The code structure it enables is so much better than the combination of out parameter and* `TryGetValue` *call that the potential performance implications were disregarded. It goes without saying that you may have different priorities, or that your real-world implementation may require the use of* `TryGetValue` *or even an alternative to* `Dictionary` *as a whole.*

This pattern is quite simple, but applying it internally is very repetitive. A field outside the function is needed for the dictionary, and if a class has a number of methods that use internal memoization, the resulting amount of code degrades readability and maintainability of the class. To improve that situation, FCSlib offers several classes that provide the common functionality around memoization. Because the pattern is still the same, the following example goes a long way in explaining the API:

```
static int SquareInternalAutoMemoized(int x) {
    var memory = Memoizer<int, int>.GetMemory("SquareInternalAutoMemoized");
    if (!memory.HasResultFor(x)) {
        int result = x * x;
        memory.Remember(x, result);
        return result;
    }
    return memory.ResultFor(x);
}
```

The class `Memoizer<P,R>` is the main entry point, which takes two generic parameters for the parameter and return type of the function. The `GetMemory` function requires a key, which must be unique in its scope — the function name is used in the sample code, although in circumstances where the class is used a lot, the full namespace, class, and function name might be smarter.

`GetMemory` returns an `IMemory<P,R>`, which encapsulates a `Dictionary<P,R>` in its default implementation.

It is possible to create a key for the current function automatically, for instance using the following lines of code:

```
var mInfo = MethodInfo.GetCurrentMethod;
var key = mInfo.DeclaringType.FullName + mInfo.Name;
```

Unfortunately, this approach analyzes the stack frame so it can be a serious performance hog — not the most important issue here because memoization rarely occurs in situations where performance is of importance. More significantly, a helper function only makes the process of analyzing the stack even more complex. If you want to go this way and save yourself coming up with a key for each method, feel free, but for these reasons this approach is not used in FCSlib.

A function that has been memoized internally can never be used without that memoization in place. As you have seen, there are arguments for and against memoization that have to do with the algorithm that is using the function — in other words, they depend on circumstances outside the function's control. Using internal memoization is a rather static approach.

The solution to this problem is external memoization. This means that instead of changing the function implementation itself, the pattern of memoizing parameters and return values is wrapped around a function that has been implemented without any such approaches. A helper function can be constructed to perform this wrapping:

```
static Func<P, R> Memoize<P, R>(this Func<P, R> f) {
  var memory = new Dictionary<P, R>( );

  return arg => {
    if (!memory.ContainsKey(arg))
      memory[arg] = f(arg);
    return memory[arg];
  };
}
```

`Memoize` takes a function parameter and returns a new function of exactly the same type. This new function consults a memory first and generally implements the exact same pattern you've seen for internal memoization. The memory lives in a closure in this case, so that an external memory is no longer needed.

It is also possible to use the `Memoizer` helper class in the definition of `Memoize`, and that's how the implementation in FCSlib works. There are, in fact, two overloads, one of which automatically constructs a key for the (potentially anonymous) function that gets passed in:

```
static Func<P, R> Memoize<P, R>(this Func<P, R> f, string memoryKey) {
  return arg => {
    var memory = Memoizer<P, R>.GetMemory(memoryKey);
    if (!memory.HasResultFor(arg))
      memory.Remember(arg, f(arg));
    return memory.ResultFor(arg);
  };
```

```
}

static Func<P, R> Memoize<P, R>(this Func<P, R> f) {
  MethodInfo fInfo = f.Method;
  return Memoize<P, R>(f, GetDefaultMemoryKey(fInfo));
}

static string GetDefaultMemoryKey(MethodInfo fInfo) {
  return fInfo.DeclaringType.FullName + "+" + fInfo.Name;
}
```

With these helper functions, you can now memoize any existing function, or even one you create
on-the-fly. Here are a few examples:

```
static void AlgorithmWithSquares( ) {
  var memoizedSquare = Functional.Memoize<int, int>(SquareSimple);
  var memoizedLambdaSquare = Functional.Memoize<int, int>(x => x * x);
  var memoizedDelegateSquare =
    Functional.Memoize(
    delegate(int x) {
      return x * x;
    });
}
```

Deep Memoization

There is one problem with the memoization techniques that have been shown so far: they only
work for functions with one parameter. When more than one parameter is used, the data structures
needed for the memory get complex very quickly — dictionaries nested within dictionaries.

Shouldn't curried functions solve this problem? Have a look at this piece of code:

```
static Func<P, R> LoggingMemoize<P, R>(Func<P, R> f) {
  var memory = new Dictionary<P, R>( );

  return arg => {
    if (!memory.ContainsKey(arg)) {
      Console.WriteLine("Memory doesn't have result for {0}, calling function... ",
arg);
      memory[arg] = f(arg);
      Console.WriteLine("  ... memoizing result {0}", memory[arg]);
      return memory[arg];
    }
    else {
      Console.WriteLine("Returning result {0} for {1} from memory", memory[arg],
arg);
      return memory[arg];
    }
  };
}

static void FirstTryMultipleParameters( ) {
  Func<int, Func<int, int>> add = x => y => x + y;
```

```
        var memoizedAdd = LoggingMemoize(add);
        Console.WriteLine("Adding 10 + 3: {0}", memoizedAdd(10)(3));
        Console.WriteLine("Adding 10 + 4: {0}", memoizedAdd(10)(4));
        Console.WriteLine("Adding 10 + 3: {0}", memoizedAdd(10)(3));
    }
```

This is a variation of the `Memoize` function shown previously, with extra code that produces some helpful debugging to visualize exactly what's going on. The function `FirstTryMultipleParameters` executes several memoized add operations. The second call should reuse the result for the parameter 10, which has been passed in before, and the third call replicates the entire parameter list from the first. The function `add` is curried, so it only takes one parameter. Here is the console output from a run of `FirstTryMultipleParameters`:

```
Memory doesn't have result for 10, calling function...
   ... memoizing result System.Func`2[System.Int32,System.Int32]
Adding 10 + 3: 13
Returning result System.Func`2[System.Int32,System.Int32] for 10 from memory
Adding 10 + 4: 14
Returning result System.Func`2[System.Int32,System.Int32] for 10 from memory
Adding 10 + 3: 13
```

What does this show? The first parameter is memoized correctly, so the function returned by the first level of the curried function isn't created again on further calls. But the value for the second parameter isn't memoized at all — there is no debug output pertaining to the values 3 or 4. It becomes quite clear in the "expanded" code that the `memoizedAdd` function represents:

```
x => {
  if (!memory.ContainsKey(x)) {
    memory[x] = y => x + y;
    return memory[x];
  }
  else {
    return memory[x];
  }
```

Looking at this abstract piece of code, you can see what a fully memoized version of the function would have to look like:

```
x => {
  if (!memory.ContainsKey(x)) {
    memory[x] = Memoize(y => x + y);
    return memory[x];
  }
  else {
    return memory[x];
  }
```

Armed with this idea, here's another try at the test function:

```
private static void ManualMultipleParameters( ) {
  Func<int, Func<int, int>> memoizedAdd =
    LoggingMemoize<int, Func<int, int>>(x => LoggingMemoize<int, int>(
      y => x + y));
  Console.WriteLine("Adding 10 + 3: {0}", memoizedAdd(10)(3));
  Console.WriteLine("Adding 10 + 4: {0}", memoizedAdd(10)(4));
  Console.WriteLine("Adding 10 + 3: {0}", memoizedAdd(10)(3));
}
```

Here's the output from this function:

```
===== Manual multiple parameters
Memory doesn't have result for 10, calling function...
  ... memoizing result System.Func`2[System.Int32,System.Int32]
Memory doesn't have result for 3, calling function...
  ... memoizing result 13
Adding 10 + 3: 13
Returning result System.Func`2[System.Int32,System.Int32] for 10 from memory
Memory doesn't have result for 4, calling function...
  ... memoizing result 14
Adding 10 + 4: 14
Returning result System.Func`2[System.Int32,System.Int32] for 10 from memory
Returning result 13 for 3 from memory
Adding 10 + 3: 13
```

Of course, it is far from convenient to memoize functions in this way. At the same time, the type safety of generic functions in .NET makes it difficult to write a helper that performs nested memoization automatically. It is possible with the help of a bit of reflection, and the result is the function `Functional.DeepMemoize`, which is part of FCSlib. Here it is, together with a little helper:

Available for download on Wrox.com

```
private static MethodInfo deepMemoizeMethodInfo;
private static MethodInfo DeepMemoizeMethodInfo {
  get {
    if (deepMemoizeMethodInfo == null) {
      deepMemoizeMethodInfo = typeof(Functional).GetMethod(
        "DeepMemoize", BindingFlags.Public | BindingFlags.Static);
    }
    return deepMemoizeMethodInfo;
  }
}

public static Func<P, R> DeepMemoize<P, R>(this Func<P, R> f) {
  return arg => {
    MethodInfo fInfo = f.Method;
    string memoryKey = GetDefaultMemoryKey(fInfo);
    var memory = Memoizer<P, R>.GetMemory(memoryKey);
    if (!memory.HasResultFor(arg)) {
      R result = f(arg);
      Type resultType = typeof(R);
      if (typeof(System.Delegate).IsAssignableFrom(resultType)) {
```

```
        Type[] parameterTypes = resultType.GetGenericArguments( );

        MethodInfo typedDeepMemoizeMethod =
          DeepMemoizeMethodInfo.MakeGenericMethod(parameterTypes);
        R memoizedResult = (R) typedDeepMemoizeMethod.Invoke(
          null, new object[] { result });
        memory.Remember(arg, memoizedResult);
      }
      else
        memory.Remember(arg, result);
    }
    return memory.ResultFor(arg);
  };
}
```

code snippet Functional.cs

The need to resort to reflection is a a drag on performance. The memoization step is made only once, but at least some of the code that utilizes reflection is executed on each function call. Since .NET 3.5, it is possible to change this algorithm in part by introducing expression trees for the invocation step. However, the result is a much more complex algorithm, and reflection still needs to be used to analyze the nesting of the function on each level and to deal with the generic types.

Looking at the deep memoization technique, it seems like the overhead of the data structures involved with multiple parameters grows very quickly. That is certainly true, and there is no real alternative that would be as manageable and at the same time more efficient. For comparison purposes, here is an implementation that memoizes a function with two parameters, which is not in curried format:

```
public static Func<P1, P2, R> Memoize<P1, P2, R>(Func<P1, P2, R> f) {
  var memory = new Dictionary<P1, Dictionary<P2, R>>( );
  return (a, b) => {
    Dictionary<P2, R> aMemory;
    bool created = false;
    if (!memory.ContainsKey(a)) {
      aMemory = new Dictionary<P2, R>( );
      created = true;
    }
    else
      aMemory = memory[a];

    if (created || !(aMemory.ContainsKey(b))) {
      var result = f(a, b);
      aMemory[b] = result;
      return result;
    }
    else
      return aMemory[b];
  };
}
```

This function is not part of FCSlib, it is just meant as an example. Even though the function has only two parameters, it is already obvious that the logical structure of the data-handling code gets more complex because multiple layers have to be handled in one algorithm. If you drop the type safety and access the dictionaries as being equal on all levels, you might be able to use recursion to eliminate some complexity, but the most important point doesn't change: the number of lookups that need to be performed to get to the correct nested dictionary still depends on the number of parameters you are handling.

Overall, performance considerations are just one of the things you must keep in mind when using memoization.

Considerations on Memoization

These are some general considerations for and against memoization, as well as the details of its optimal implementation for any given scenario.

Data Types for the Cache

The examples shown in this chapter all use the standard .NET `Dictionary<K,V>` type for the cache. This has been done mainly for simplicity. `Dictionary` has good lookup performance (although you may want to consider a hash-based data structure for even more efficiency), and the fact that it's a mutable data structure is also useful for the purpose. At the same time, it is not thread safe, which can be a major problem.

The use of immutable data structures for caching is a possibility. It makes the cache thread-safe as long as it doesn't have to be changed. When changes occur, immutable data structures change the perspective on the changes. That is, a data structure may not change internally, but a new view of it is constructed externally. It is quite easy to encapsulate the handling of the caches so that locks can be applied effectively, but immutable data structures might enable lockless operation. These steps haven't been made for the implementation of FCSlib.

Cache Expiry

Another characteristic of the implementation in this chapter is that the caches aren't very flexible — they can only grow when new elements are added. It can be useful to implement an interface to the cache that allows you to remove elements, for two reasons:

➤ Indefinite growth of caches over long periods of time can be prevented.

➤ It becomes possible to use memoization with functions that are not pure.

The first reason is quite obvious. Remembering every single result that a function calculates for the duration of an application run is not always the best strategy. Of course, a particular instance of a function doesn't have to be memoized for the length of an application run, so scoping can be one approach to keep memory use within bounds.

The second reason should be handled with a lot of care because using memoization with non-pure functions cannot be recommended lightly. But there are cases where such an approach can be useful — for instance, when dealing with persistent data from databases, or data that is being received through network connections. In those cases, a caching approach like memoization is still a promising strategy, when coupled with careful expiry of outdated cache elements.

Depending on considerations of the algorithm, an automated cache cleanup can be very useful based, for instance, on a high-water mark applied to the number of elements in the cache or on a certain time that can elapse before an element is regarded as outdated.

SUMMARY

The need for strategies to remember previous results of computations is not specific to functional programming. However, with lazy evaluation mechanisms and the general guideline of calling functions as much as possible, it is especially important in functional programming to have caching technology easily available. Precomputation and memoization are two techniques of storing calculated data before and after it's first needed.

11

Calling Yourself

In functional programming languages, recursion is a tool with a lot of tradition. Many of the original functional languages didn't have any loop constructs, and recursion was used for all cases where looping is typically used in imperative languages. Even though some functional languages have extended syntax today that allows for imperative looping, recursion is, for many programmers, still the preferred approach.

RECURSION IN C#

The use of recursive algorithms in C# is restricted because for recursive function implementations, support for tail call optimization is something you want to rely on (see more about this in the next section). It is nevertheless important to understand the ideas of recursion. Doing so makes it easier to understand the limits of what can be done functionally in C#. And the transfer of algorithms from functional languages requires a good understanding of recursion — the result can often be worthwhile even if slightly different approaches have to be used in C#.

The following implementation of a factorial function is a simple first example of recursion:

```
static int RecFact(int x) {
  if (x == 0)
    return 1;
  return x * RecFact(x - 1);
}
```

The factorial of a positive integer is defined as the product of all positive integers smaller or equal to that integer. So, the factorial of 3 (written `3!`) is `3! = 1 * 2 * 3 = 6`. The factorial of 4 is `4! = 1 * 2 * 3 * 4 = 24`. As you can see, there's overlap in the calculations of those factorials. The factorial of any number n — `fact(n)` — can also be defined as n `* fact (n - 1)`. For instance, `fact(3) = 3 * fact(2)`. And `fact(4) = 4 * fact(3)`.

The example implementation mirrors that simple rule precisely; the default return value of the function `RecFact` is x `* RecFact(x - 1)`. The function `RecFact` is defined in terms of itself, which is the important defining factor for direct recursion (there's also indirect recursion, which is explained later in this chapter).

```
if (x == 0)
   return 1;
```

This is called the base case of the recursion. Recursions usually have a base case, although it's not always as simple as this. The base case defines the end of the recursion chain. Every time the recursive function calls itself, it changes the parameters of the call a bit, compared to the previous invocation. Assuming the function is pure in a functional sense, this change of the parameters is essential because otherwise the recursive calls would simply result in an infinite loop. If the recursion is supposed to have a deterministic end, there must be a way for the state of the function, call by call, to converge toward the base case.

The example base case is simple. The factorial of 0 is defined to be 1, and the modification of the parameter value is that it is decremented by 1 in each invocation. Assuming that the parameter is a positive integer to begin with (which isn't checked in this implementation, which is therefore somewhat unsafe), it is obvious that at some point, the parameter is going to be 0 and the chain of recursive calls is going to unwind itself.

Here's an overview of the states the function goes through to calculate the factorial of 3:

```
int result = RecFact(3);
Call: RecFact(3) => x = 3
  Is x == 0? => No
    return 3 * RecFact(2)
    Call: RecFact(2) => x = 2
      Is x == 0? => No
        return 2 * RecFact(1)
        Call: RecFact(1) => x = 1
          Is x == 0? => No
            return 1 * RecFact(0)
            Call: RecFact(0) => x = 0
              Is x == 0 => Yes
                return 1
            return 1 * 1 => 1
        return 2 * 1 => 2
    return 3 * 2 => 6
result = 6
```

The implementation of the functionality as a recursive function is clear, simple, and elegant, and its relation to the mathematical definition of a number's factorial is obvious. These considerations are often behind decisions to implement algorithms recursively, more so than performance considerations, for example. In most imperative languages, a loop-based implementation of the factorial is more efficient because it eliminates the need for function calls and returns from those calls. Some imperative language compilers can recognize specific cases of recursion and convert them into loops when applicable. The C# compiler doesn't do this and it's highly unlikely it ever will, because the C# team leaves most optimizations to the JIT (just-in-time) compiler. Unfortunately it has been stated that the optimizations the JIT compiler does have have been left undocumented intentionally to prevent you from relying on them.

Functional languages tend to value the simplicity and elegance of an implementation more highly than pure performance. In newer times, optimizations have eliminated much of the performance advantages that an explicit loop implementation may have had in the past; on the other hand, imperative languages also see a trend toward a greater focus on ease of implementation, readability of code, flexibility of execution environments like the .NET Framework, and so on.

TAIL RECURSION

One of the most important developments that makes it possible to implement all iterative algorithms with the help of recursion instead of explicit loop constructs is tail call optimization. This was first made mandatory in the programming language Scheme, a dialect of LISP.

The first part of the call sequence for the factorial calculation has recursive calls into `RecFact` only. There is never (for as long as x is still greater than 0) any return out of the function. When the unwinding process starts, the sequence is followed in reverse order by the return statements and each return takes the sequence back to the previous instance of a `RecFact` call. This return is important because every time a value is returned by one of the inner calls, its result must first be multiplied with the value of the current x, before the result of that calculation can be returned yet another level up the hierarchy.

For instance, at some point x is 2. There is a call to `RecFact` with a parameter of 1. Only when the result of the `RecFact(1)` call is known can the calculation of 2 * (that result) be performed. If the algorithm is implemented as shown, the fact that recursion results in this precise execution order is what makes things work, what makes the function return the correct value in the end.

The downside of having to navigate out of the entire call hierarchy step by step is that there must be a record of the place that each return must go back to, and also the state of all local variables in that place. The precise implementation of this logic may vary from language to language, but usually it involves a stack where return addresses are stored each time another function (or another instance of one function) is called, and during unwinding these return addresses are removed from the stack in reverse order. There are two issues with this: first, both a function call and a return are somewhat more expensive than a straight "jump" because the required stack operations take time. Second, stack space is limited, usually artificially, but eventually by the amount of available memory in the system.

Some recursive functions implement a tail call. A tail call is a call that happens at the end of the function execution, so that a return to the call site after the tail call is not necessary. The tail call may produce a result (in which case the call site is typically a `return` statement itself), or it can just be the last call that will be executed in a function. If the tail call is to the function itself, the function is said to be tail recursive. Here's an example of a recursive tail call without a return value:

```
static void Recurse(int x) {
  Console.WriteLine("Value: " + x);
  if (x == 100000000)
    return;
  Recurse(x + 1);
}
```

Nothing happens after the tail call. This example iterates to 100000000, which is a bit too much to show in a sequence in this book — what's more, if you run it as a 32-bit application, you can observe a `StackOverflowException` ending the program run:

```
...
Value: 32189
Value: 32190
Value: 32191
Value: 32192
Value: 32193
Value: 32194
Value: 32195

Process is terminated due to StackOverflowException.
```

Here's what the sequence would be like if it only iterated to 4:

```
Main Program
  Recurse(1)
    Is x == 4? => No
    Recurse(2)
      Is x == 4? => No
      Recurse(3)
        Is x == 4? => No
        Recurse(4)
          Is x == 4? => Yes
        Recurse(3) => nothing happens…
      Recurse(2) => nothing happens…
    Recurse(1) => nothing happens…
Back in the main program
```

It is easy to see that in this case it would also be possible to follow the sequence without changing the outcome of any of the function calls:

```
Main Program
  Recurse(1)
    Is x == 4? => No
    Recurse(2)
      Is x == 4? => No
      Recurse(3)
        Is x == 4? => No
        Recurse(4)
          Is x == 4? => Yes
Back in the main program
```

The sequence skips the steps of going back through the call iterations. This is the idea of tail call optimizations. A compiler could recognize cases where tail calls are being performed (the recursive call is the last thing that happens in a function). In such cases, stack manipulation operations do not have to be performed, and an eventual return can be interpreted as a direct jump back to the original initiation point of the entire call sequence. Optimization takes away a lot of the overhead of function calls and eliminates the issue of stack overflows when call sequences are long.

The situation regarding tail call optimization on the .NET platform and in the C# language is a bit confusing. The CLR (Common Language Runtime) supports tail call optimization through a special `tail` instruction in IL. The C# compiler doesn't generate that instruction, although the F# compiler does, for example. The execution infrastructure of the .NET environment offers a second point where this kind of optimization can be performed, which is the JIT compiler that translates IL into native assembly code. When JIT compiler optimizations are switched on, by default only in Release build mode in Visual Studio, the 64-bit JIT compiler can perform its own tail call optimizations, but unfortunately the 32-bit JIT compiler can't. In some ways, having the JIT compiler make this step is a good thing because it covers all .NET languages equally. But the fact that the 32-bit and 64-bit versions behave differently makes it quite unfortunate that C#, unlike F#, doesn't have language level support for tail call optimization.

ACCUMULATOR PASSING STYLE

Accumulator passing style offers one approach to structuring a recursive algorithm so that it employs tail calls in situations where the easiest possible implementation would not do so. Consider this function:

```
static int CalcLengthSimple<T>(FCSColl::List<T> list) {
  return list.IsEmpty ? 0 :
    1 + CalcLengthSimple(list.Tail);
}
```

A special `List<T>` class, which will be described in more detail in Chapter 16, is used here. The important thing to know now is that it has two properties: `Head`, which contains the first element of the list, and `Tail`, which is an instance of `List<T>`. `List<T>` refers to the entire "rest of the list" — that is, all the elements with the exception of the one in `Head`.

The example recursive function calculates the length of the list using the fact that the length can be defined as one element plus the length of the remaining list, as returned by the `Tail` property. The base case of this recursion is the empty list, which has a length of 0. The implementation is not tail recursive, because the return value of each recursive call is used in the addition expression.

Now look at this alternative implementation:

```
static int CalcLengthAccumulator<T>(FCSColl::List<T> list, int accumulator) {
  return list.IsEmpty ?
    accumulator :
    CalcLengthAccumulator(list.Tail, accumulator + 1);
}
```

The function signature has changed to include the additional parameter `accumulator`. This parameter, in a way, takes on the job of the return value. In each iteration of the function, the `accumulator` contains the length of the list, as far as calculated to that point. As long as the list is not found to be empty, a recursive call is performed, the `accumulator` is incremented and the remainder of the list is passed. At some point down the chain, that remainder will be found to be empty, and the value in the `accumulator` is returned as the end result.

In this implementation, the recursive call to `CalcLengthAccumulator` is a tail call because there is nothing else that happens once that call returns. Of course the `accumulator` needs to be seeded on the initial call, like this:

```
int length = CalcLengthAccumulator(list, 0);
```

That a seed for the `accumulator` is needed by the function, and that the seed should be zero for a valid result, can be regarded as an implementation detail, which should not be visible to an outside caller. It is possible to create a wrapper implementation, which uses an inner function for the recursion. Here is how:

```
static int CalcLengthAccWrapper<T>(FCSColl::List<T> list) {
  Func<FCSColl::List<T>, int, int> accumulator = null;
  accumulator =
    (l, acc) => l.IsEmpty ? acc : accumulator(l.Tail, acc + 1);
  return accumulator(list, 0);
}
```

To make the lambda expression recursive, use the trick of assigning `null` to the `accumulator` variable first, and then redefining it while referring to itself under the variable name.

The `accumulator` lambda expression has the same implementation as the function `CalcLengthAccumulator` in the previous example, but it is now hidden inside a wrapper function with the same signature as the initial `CalcLengthSimple` function. `accumulator` is a tail-recursive function and can therefore benefit from any tail call optimization that may be performed by a compiler.

Finally, for comparison purposes, here is an implementation of the factorial calculation using `accumulator` passing style:

```
static int RecFactAcc(int x) {
  Func<int, int, int> acc = null;
  acc = (val, accVal) => val == 0 ? accVal : acc(val - 1, accVal * val);
  return acc(x, 1);
}
```

CONTINUATION PASSING STYLE

Continuation passing style (CPS) is a technique that can be used for the same purpose as `accumulator` passing style: allowing the implementation of recursive algorithms using tail calls. CPS can often result in rather mind-bending logic, but it can be worth it because you can restructure complex algorithms to use tail calls. The examples in this section are not going to take things too far because the restrictions with tail call optimization mean that recursion in C# will never be the all-encompassing tool it is in full functional languages, but they should be enough to get you started in your own efforts. (There is a lot of information on CPS out there and there's much you can do with it beyond recursion, if you want to pursue this topic further.)

For a simple introduction, look at this function:

```
static int Times3(int x) {
  return x * 3;
}
```

The obvious task that the function performs is that of multiplying the input value by 3. The not-so-obvious task is in the return statement. Implementing a function this way is so natural that you almost don't notice yourself doing it, but the step of returning the value with a return statement has consequences to the overall structure of algorithm implementation. For instance, to calculate the result of 5 times 3 and output the result on the console, this is what you would do:

```
Console.WriteLine(Times3(5));
```

The point is that you're chaining your calls together by nesting them due to the way return values work syntactically in C#. This is intuitive in a mathematical sense, but from the sequential point of view common to imperative languages, it isn't intuitive at all — the innermost part of the overall expression is actually calculated first, then the outermost part.

The continuation in the term continuation passing style is meant to be the "rest of the calculation," or even the "rest of the process" in the context of a larger algorithm, at any given point in a process or calculation. So, at the point where you are calculating the result of 5 times 3, the continuation would be the operation that outputs that result on the console.

For example, here's an expression that has more than one step in itself: `a * (b + c)`. Using function call syntax, you can write this as `Mult(a, Add(b, c))` in C#. Outputting the result (as a placeholder for any operation that utilizes the result once it's calculated) is an additional step. The sequence of steps is as follows:

1. Add b and c.

2. Multiply the result by a.

3. Output the result.

At the point where step 1 is being performed, the continuation is the sequence of steps 2 and 3. At the point where step 2 is performed, the continuation is step 3.

Implementing the `Times3` function in continuation passing style means passing the function an argument that represents the continuation. In reality, even functions that use CPS can usefully have return values, but for this example the return statement is going to be replaced by a call to the continuation. Here's the implementation:

```
static void Times3CPS(int x, Action<int> continuation) {
  continuation(x * 3);
}
```

The call that calculates the result of 5 times 3 and outputs the result is changed as well:

```
Times3CPS(5, x => Console.WriteLine(x));
```

For a slightly more complicated example, here's a function that uses the special List<T> class to calculate the sum of all elements in the list:

```
static int SumRecursive(FCSColl::List<int> list) {
  return list.IsEmpty ? 0 :
    list.Head + SumRecursive(list.Tail);
}
```

The logic is the same as before for the length calculation: the sum of all elements in the list is equal to the first value plus the sum of all remaining values, with the empty list as the base case for which the sum of its elements is zero. This function is not tail recursive; the purpose of using CPS is to make the implementation tail recursive.

To begin a CPS implementation, you can once more replace the return statement in the implementation with a call to a continuation. The problem is the definition of the continuation. At any given point in the sequence, what is the "rest of the process?" If your list is [1,2,3,4], you've started from the left and you're now looking at element 2, the "rest of the process" would be "add 3 and 4 to my current result." Correct, but there is no current result in the pattern used by CPS. In contrast to accumulator passing style, there is no parameter that represents the result of the calculation process directly.

What you have is a function, and from one step to the next you can modify what this function does. How do you do this? Replace it with a new function that adds some logic and then calls the old function.

Imagine the first call to the Sum function from your main program. Similar to the Times3 example, you should be able to write a call to your hypothetical CPS implementation that looks like this:

```
var list = new FCSColl::List<int>(1, 2, 3, 4, 5);
SumCPS(list, sum => Console.WriteLine(sum));
```

The continuation you pass into this first call expects the final result of the calculation in order to utilize it further. Inside the function SumCPS, on that first call, you need to have a recursive call to SumCPS, and you need to modify the parameters, as you've seen before, to make the recursion converge toward its base case. Finally, you need to take the purpose of the function into account, the actual task performed by the function, when you consider these parameter modifications.

For the list parameter, the modification is obvious: each time you get a list passed in, you check it to see whether it's empty, which means that you've reached the base case. If it's not empty, you split it into its head and its tail by accessing the respective properties. For the recursive call, you pass list.Tail as the new list, thereby iterating through the elements in the list.

For the continuation parameter, you have a function that expects the end result of the calculation, that is, the result of the calculation 1 + 2 + 3 + 4 + 5. Right now you're on the first element, 1, which is accessible in list.Head. In order to make a modification to the continuation function, you need to define a new one that is a logical step in the chain. If the function you have expects the result of 1 + 2 + 3 + 4 + 5 and you're currently looking at the value 1, then that logical step is to create a function that expects the result of 2 + 3 + 4 + 5, adds the 1 that you currently have and passes the end result into the "old" continuation. Here's such a function:

```
x => oldContinuation(x + list.Head)
```

The full implementation of the new SumCPS function follows:

```
static void SumCPS(FCSColl::List<int> list, Action<int> cont) {
  if (list.IsEmpty)
    cont(0);
  else
    SumCPS(list.Tail, x => cont(x + list.Head));
}
```

This implementation is tail recursive, since the recursive call is the last thing that happens in the function.

It helps to look at the sequence of calls for a sample scenario. To keep things brief, assume you're passing in a short list:

```
var list = new FCSColl::List<int>(1, 2, 3);
SumCPS(list, sum => Console.WriteLine(sum));

Call 1: SumCPS([1,2,3], x=>Output(x))
Call 2: SumCPS([2,3], x=>Output(x+1))
Call 3: SumCPS([3], x=>Output((x+1)+2))
Call 4: SumCPS([], x=>Output(((x+1)+2)+3))
Call 4: Output(((x+1)+2)+3), with x = 0
Result: 6 written on the console
```

Based on this example, it is simple to make a few modifications. First, it would be more convenient to call the function in the usual style in C# if it had a return value. Here's the necessary change:

```
static int SumCPS(FCSColl::List<int> list, Func<int, int> cont) {
  return list.IsEmpty ?
    cont(0) :
    SumCPS(list.Tail, x => cont(x + list.Head));
}
```

On this level, both the SumCPS function itself and the continuation function have been given a return type, and so the value of the overall calculation ends up being returned as the result of the first outer call into the function. In the initial call, this means you also have to change the continuation you pass in, so the call looks like this:

```
int sum = SumCPS(list, x => x);
```

The last function in the chain of continuations that is built up during the recursion just returns the value.

A final modification is to create a wrapper function, similar to the example in accumulator passing style. This hides the implementation details from the outside caller, using a nested function for the recursion with CPS.

```
static int SumCPS(FCSColl::List<int> list) {
  Func<FCSColl::List<int>, Func<int, int>, int> recursor = null;
  recursor = (l, cont) =>
    l.IsEmpty ?
    cont(0) :
    recursor(l.Tail, x => cont(x + l.Head));
  return recursor(list, x => x);
}
```

INDIRECT RECURSION

So far, all of the recursion examples have had one thing in common: one single function involved that called itself, which is called *direct recursion*. There is also *indirect recursion*, where several functions depend upon one another. For instance, function A calls function B, which calls function C. If function C, under any circumstances, calls back to function A, this is a case of indirect recursion.

There is a simple case of indirect recursion called *mutual recursion*. It involves only two functions that depend upon one another. In reality, the logic behind the dependency can be quite complex. Nonetheless, here's an example that involves odd and even numbers:

```
static bool IsOdd(int number) {
  return number == 0 ? false : IsEven(Math.Abs(number) - 1);
}

static bool IsEven(int number) {
  return number == 0 ? true : IsOdd(Math.Abs(number) - 1);
}
```

As you can see, the definition of an odd integer is this: if the number is zero, it is a known fact that the number is not odd. Otherwise, the number is odd if the number before it is even. The definition of an even number is exactly the other way around: zero is known to be even, otherwise a number is even if the number before it is odd.

The two functions IsOdd and IsEven depend upon each other; they are therefore called mutually recursive. The example scenario also has two different base cases that are checked in the two functions. Obviously, this can get quite complex — if you employ code using an approach like this, don't forget the general idea of providing a concise and clean implementation!

Cases of indirect recursion that involve more than just two functions can be found quite easily. Consider this XML code:

```
<?xml version="1.0" encoding="utf-8" ?>
<form>
  <group>
    <label>Enter your login information</label>
```

```
      <group>
        <label>Name</label>
        <edit />
      </group>
      <group>
        <label>Password</label>
        <edit />
      </group>
    </group>
    <checkbox>Remember me</checkbox>
    <group>
      <button>OK</button>
      <button>Cancel</button>
    </group>
  </form>
```

This is a representation of a piece of UI — a form with a few UI elements, grouped together using group elements. The complete code represents a login dialog. The important point is in the structure: the groups can contain other elements, and they are elements themselves, so they can be contained inside other groups. This is an example of data that can be stored in recursive data structures. Here are a few classes that represent a structure like that in the XML code:

```
public class Element { }
public class ContentElement : Element {
  public string Content { get; set; }
}
public class Group : Element {
  public List<Element> Elements { get; set; }
}
public class Form : Group { }
public class Label : ContentElement { }
public class Checkbox : ContentElement { }
public class Button : ContentElement { }
public class Edit : ContentElement { }
```

The recursion happens in the Group class, which has a collection of Elements, which can in turn be Groups. The code to read the XML from a file and parse it into a class instance hierarchy to represent the content is this:

Available for download on Wrox.com

```
static void ReadUI( ) {
  XmlDocument doc = new XmlDocument( );
  doc.Load("ui.xml");
  var elementTree = BuildElementTree(doc.DocumentElement);
}

static Element BuildElementTree(XmlNode xmlNode) {
  switch (xmlNode.Name) {
    case "form":
      return BuildForm(xmlNode);
    case "group":
      return BuildGroup(xmlNode);
    case "label":
```

```
          return BuildLabel(xmlNode);
        case "checkbox":
          return BuildCheckbox(xmlNode);
        case "button":
          return BuildButton(xmlNode);
        case "edit":
          return BuildEdit(xmlNode);
        default:
          return null;
      }
    }

    private static Element BuildEdit(XmlNode xmlNode) {
      return new Edit { Content = xmlNode.InnerText };
    }

    private static Element BuildButton(XmlNode xmlNode) {
      return new Button { Content = xmlNode.InnerText };
    }

    private static Element BuildCheckbox(XmlNode xmlNode) {
      return new Checkbox { Content = xmlNode.InnerText };
    }

    private static Element BuildLabel(XmlNode xmlNode) {
      return new Label { Content = xmlNode.InnerText };
    }

    private static Element BuildGroup(XmlNode xmlNode) {
      return new Group { Elements = BuildList(xmlNode.ChildNodes) };
    }

    private static Element BuildForm(XmlNode xmlNode) {
      return new Form { Elements = BuildList(xmlNode.ChildNodes) };
    }

    private static List<Element> BuildList(XmlNodeList xmlNodeList) {
      var result = new List<Element>( );
      foreach (XmlNode node in xmlNodeList)
        result.Add(BuildElementTree(node));
      return result;
    }
```

Code snippet Program.cs

There is nothing complicated about this. The structure of the functions and the calls between them mirror the recursive nature of the data structures, and the recursion is indirect because no function ever calls itself. The recursion happens, for instance, when BuildElementTree calls BuildGroup, which calls BuildList, which calls BuildElementTree. One interesting thing in this example is that there doesn't seem to be an explicit base case. The base case is implicit: if all elements underneath the root node in the XML code have been handled, the algorithm ends. In cases where recursion is driven by data this is quite common. The amount of data that is available for reading by your program is always finite, and the end of the data stream signals the end of any reading algorithm (albeit perhaps temporarily).

SUMMARY

This chapter has shown how powerful recursion is as a structural algorithmic approach. However, C# is not the perfect environment for recursion due to the limitations of the C# and JIT compilers where tail call optimizations are concerned. You can still benefit from recursive algorithms whenever the depth of nested calls is rather shallow — a good recommendation to imperative programmers, because many algorithms can be stated more elegantly with the help of recursion.

12

Standard Higher Order Functions

Higher order functions are a pillar of functional programming. They are functions that either take other functions as parameters or return other functions as values. The latter case also implies that new functions might have been created dynamically before being returned.

Many well known languages support these concepts only partially. For instance, in C it is possible to pass around function pointers, and there's even a certain extent of type safety guaranteed. But the language doesn't support the creation of dynamic new functions. The same was true for the C# language in version 1, where typed delegates were allowed to pass functions back and forth. Only C# 2.0 brought anonymous methods, with the syntactical addition of lambda expressions in C# 3.0.

The term *standard higher order functions* is not a scientific one, it's just a convenient expression that describes a set of three especially well known higher order functions: `Map`, `Filter`, and `Fold`. These functions are available in many languages, or rather in the runtimes supporting these languages. Even .NET delivers versions of them in the LINQ libraries in .NET 3.5 — more about that at the end of this chapter. Each of the functions works against a list of elements and uses another function, which can be passed in by the caller, to perform some operation with the elements.

The following sections describe how `Map`, `Filter`, and `Fold` work, and how they are implemented in FCSlib. You will find practical use cases of these functions throughout the book.

APPLYING OPERATIONS: MAP

The `Map` function is quite simple — but then that's the nature of the standard higher order functions; that's what makes them the great building blocks they are in functional programming. `Map` takes a list of elements and a function to call with each element in turn. Then it constructs a new list from the results of the function calls and returns that new list.

Using iterators in C#, `Map` can be implemented lazily. Here is the implementation from FCSlib:

```
static IEnumerable<R> Map<T, R>(Converter<T, R> function, IEnumerable<T> list)
{
  foreach (T sourceVal in list)
    yield return function(sourceVal);
}
```

The `Converter<T, R>` delegate type is a function that receives a parameter of type `T` and returns an element of type `R`. The name `Converter` can be a bit misleading, since the function doesn't necessarily convert anything. It might just as well extract something, which is a major use case of the `Map` function. For example, given a list of objects, `Map` can be used to extract a particular property from each of the objects:

```
var people = new List<Person> {
  new Person {Name = "Harry", Age = 32},
  new Person {Name = "Anna", Age = 45},
  new Person {Name = "Willy", Age = 43},
  new Person {Name = "Rose", Age = 37}
};
var names = Functional.Map(p => p.Name, people);
```

Of course, actual calculations can be performed just as easily:

```
var squares = Functional.Map(i => i * i, Enumerable.Range(1, 10));
```

Using Criteria: Filter

`Filter` is a function that applies criteria to elements in a list. The criterion is a function itself and it is called for each of the elements in the source list. The resulting list contains only those elements for which the criterion function returned a positive result. The implementation of `Filter` which is part of FCSlib looks like this:

```
public static IEnumerable<T> Filter<T>(Predicate<T> predicate,
  IEnumerable<T> list) {
  foreach (T val in list)
    if (predicate(val))
      yield return val;
}
```

Just like `Map`, `Filter` uses a special delegate type, in this case, `Predicate<T>`. This type accepts a parameter of type `T` and returns a `bool`. Again, the implementation is lazy.

Based on the list "people" shown in the previous section, `Filter` can be used to find all those people who are over 40:

```
var over40 = Functional.Filter(p => p.Age >= 40, people);
```

Accumulating: Fold

`Fold` is really a family of functions that covers a number of different use cases. The most important ones are the left and the right fold. There are two main differences between left and right fold, and only one of these is relevant in the FCSlib implementation. More on this a bit later, after you've seen the simpler left fold.

 In this section, the term `Ftype="note"old` *will sometimes be used to mean "the family of Fold functions."*

The function that folds left is called `FoldL`. It takes three parameters: an accumulation function, a start value and a list. In contrast to the other higher order functions you have seen so far, it doesn't return a list as its result. It returns just one value, which is where the name comes from: it folds the list into one, using some kind of accumulation.

To accumulate the list, the function iterates over the elements and calls the accumulator with two values: the result from the previous run and the current element from the list. On the first run there is no previous result, so the start value is passed instead.

Here is the implementation from FCSlib:

```
public static R FoldL<T, R>(Func<R, T, R> accumulator, R startVal,
  IEnumerable<T> list) {
  R result = startVal;
  foreach (T sourceVal in list)
    result = accumulator(result, sourceVal);
  return result;
}
```

A simple call to sum up some values might look like this:

```
var sumOf1to10 = Functional.FoldL((r, v) => r + v, 0,
  Enumerable.Range(1, 10));
```

The expression `(r, v) => r + v` is the accumulator in this example. It takes the previous result `(r)` and the next value `(v)` and returns the result of adding the two. The second parameter `0` is the start value, which must be zero, of course, to calculate a sum.

The start value is always important when using any `Fold`. This is immediately obvious if you think about other accumulations you could use. For instance, if you wanted to multiply the entire sequence instead of adding, you would have to start from `1`:

```
var productOf1to10 = Functional.FoldL((r, v) => r * v, 1,
  Enumerable.Range(1, 10));
```

For more complex applications, the choice of a good start value is often key. `Fold` is extremely powerful and a surprising number of algorithms can be implemented on its basis.

The following lines calculate the average age of the people in the sample list above. The acculumlator is written to work with two values instead of just one:

```
var acc = Functional.FoldL(
  (r, v) => Tuple.Create(r.Item1 + v.Age, r.Item2 + 1),
  Tuple.Create(0, 0),
  people);
var averageAge = (double) acc.Item1 / (double) acc.Item2;
```

This implementation uses the new tuple types in .NET 4.0.

It has been said before that `Fold` differs from `Map` and `Filter` in that it returns just one value. This statement wasn't as precise as it should be. Correctly it would have to be: `Fold` takes a list of values of type A and returns one value of type B. A and B can be the same (as in the sum and multiply examples) or they can be different (as they were in the average example). Confusingly, B might actually be a list type. Look at this:

```
var cloneList = Functional.FoldL((r, v) => r.Cons(v),
  FCSColl::List<int>.Empty, Enumerable.Range(1, 5));
```

This example uses the immutable list data type from FCSlib. The reason is just that the syntax is more concise this way, since the `Cons` operation, which adds an element to the list, returns the new list instead of making a change in place. The point is that the result type of `Fold` is a list in this case.

Finally, to deliver more proof of how powerful the `Fold` function is, here are implementations of `Map` and `Filter` on the basis of `FoldL`:

```
public static IEnumerable<R> FoldMap<T, R>(Converter<T, R> converter,
  IEnumerable<T> source) {
  return Functional.FoldL(
    (r, v) => r.Append(new FCSColl::List<R>(converter(v))),
    FCSColl::List<R>.Empty, source);
}

public static IEnumerable<T> FoldFilter<T>(Predicate<T> predicate,
  IEnumerable<T> source) {
  return Functional.FoldL(
    (r, v) => r.Append(predicate(v) ?
      new FCSColl::List<T>(v) :
      FCSColl::List<T>.Empty),
    FCSColl::List<T>.Empty, source);
}
```

Now it's time to get back to the difference between left and right folding. Have another look at a simple sum calculation:

```
Func<int, int, int> acc = (r, x) => r + x;
var sum = Functional.FoldL(acc, 0, Enumerable.Range(1, 5));
```

As you know, the function calls the accumulator first with the start value and the first value from the list. Then it calls the accumulator again, with the result from the first time and the next value from the list. The overall result of the calculation is this:

```
acc(acc(acc(acc(acc(0, 1), 2), 3), 4), 5)
```

Obviously, the sequence of numbers is added up in a particular order — from left to right. In this case where all numbers are being added, the order doesn't actually matter, because the operator in question, the addition operator, is associative.

Using right folding, the expression changes to this:

```
acc(1, acc(2, acc(3, acc(4, acc(5, 0)))))
```

If the operation that is being applied by the accumulator is non-associative, then it is important to have the choice between left and right folding.

From a technical point of view, there are two differences between left and right folding. First, the sequence of applying the accumulator starts from the end of the sequence that is being passed in. Second, the order of parameters passed in to the accumulator changes — with left folding, the result of previous computation was passed first, with right folding it's passed second. The second point is really more a convention than a necessity, but since that convention is being followed in the vast majority of right folding implementations, this book follows it as well.

FCSlib implements `FoldR` on the basis of `FoldL` and another helper function called `Reverse`. Here are these two functions:

```
public static IEnumerable<T> Reverse<T>(IEnumerable<T> source) {
  FCSColl::List<T> stack = FCSColl::List<T>.Empty;
  foreach (T item in source)
    stack = stack.Cons(item);
  while (stack != FCSColl.List<T>.Empty) {
    yield return stack.Head;
    stack = stack.Tail;
  }
}

public static R FoldR<T, R>(Func<T, R, R> accumulator, R startVal,
  IEnumerable<T> list) {
  return FoldL((r, x) => accumulator(x, r), startVal,
    Functional.Reverse(list));
}
```

The accumulator accepted by FoldR has its parameter order changed according to the convention described before. FoldR simply swaps round the parameters with the help of a wrapper before calling FoldL, and it reverses the list so it's effectively processed from the end.

In many programming languages that are more focused on functional programming than C# is, there are other important differences between left and right folding. Most of these languages support tail recursion, which unfortunately isn't available in C#.

 There is support for tail recursion on the IL level in .NET. This is leveraged by the F# compiler, but not by the C# compiler. You can find more information about recursion in Chapter 11, if you need a refresher.

Look at the following two recursive implementations of FoldL and FoldR:

```
public static R FoldLRec<T, R>(Func<R, T, R> acc, R start,
  FCSColl::List<T> list) {
  if (list == FCSColl::List<T>.Empty)
    return start;
  return FoldLRec<T, R>(acc, acc(start, list.Head), list.Tail);
}

public static R FoldRRec<T, R>(Func<T, R, R> acc, R start,
  FCSColl::List<T> list) {
  if (list == FCSColl::List<T>.Empty)
    return start;
  return acc(list.Head, FoldRRec(acc, start, list.Tail));
}
```

This implementation is, of course, specific to the List class in FCSlib, but the main problem is the lack of tail recursion support — both these functions quickly run out of stack space when the lists get too large. Nevertheless, it is quite easy to see that the FoldLRec function would be tail recursive if C# supported it. Since it doesn't do anything after the recursive call to itself, a return into the function itself is clearly not necessary.

In languages that support tail recursion, this is a big advantage for the left folding function, because it can be implemented to benefit from tail recursion.

Finally, some languages that support lazy evaluation have a certain benefit in the case of right folding, because the laziness means that the call into the accumulator isn't actually performed before the result is "needed." As a consequence, the right folding function can be called on infinite lists — of course it can never return a result, but in contrast to the left folding function it doesn't hang in an infinite loop immediately.

As additional illustration of the call order difference between left and right folding, here's some sample code based on the recursive implementations, which has been instrumented to output info about the order of calls:

Available for download on Wrox.com

```csharp
public static R FoldLRecD<T, R>(Func<R, T, R> acc, R start,
  FCSColl::List<T> list) {
  Console.Write("flr(acc, {0}, {1})", start, list);
  if (list == FCSColl::List<T>.Empty) {
    Console.WriteLine(" ... returning {0}", start);
    return start;
  }
  else
    Console.WriteLine();
  return FoldLRecD<T, R>(acc, acc(start, list.Head), list.Tail);
}

public static R FoldRRecD<T, R>(Func<T, R, R> acc, R start,
  FCSColl::List<T> list) {
  Console.Write("frr(acc, {0}, {1})", start, list);
  if (list == FCSColl::List<T>.Empty) {
    Console.WriteLine(" ... returning {0}", start);
    return start;
  }
  else
    Console.WriteLine( );
  return acc(list.Head, FoldRRecD(acc, start, list.Tail));
}

...

Console.WriteLine("Fold Left Recursive ==========================");
var onetothree = new FCSColl::List<int>(Enumerable.Range(1, 3));
Func<int, int, int> accD = (r, x) => {
  int sum = r + x;
  Console.WriteLine("accD({0}, {1}) ... returning {2}", r, x, sum);
  return sum;
};
var resultL = FoldLRecD(accD, 0, onetothree);
Console.WriteLine(resultL);

Console.WriteLine("Fold Right Recursive ==========================");

Func<int, int, int> accRD = (x, r) => {
  int sum = r + x;
  Console.WriteLine("accRD({0}, {1}) ... returning {2}", r, x, sum);
  return sum;
};
var resultR = FoldRRecD(accRD, 0, onetothree);
Console.WriteLine(resultR);
```

Code snippet Program.cs

The output of this sample looks like this:

```
Fold Left Recursive ==========================
flr(acc, 0, [1, 2, 3])
accD(0, 1) ... returning 1
```

```
flr(acc, 1, [2, 3])
accD(1, 2) ... returning 3
flr(acc, 3, [3])
accD(3, 3) ... returning 6
flr(acc, 6, []) ... returning 6
6
Fold Right Recursive ============================
frr(acc, 0, [1, 2, 3])
frr(acc, 0, [2, 3])
frr(acc, 0, [3])
frr(acc, 0, []) ... returning 0
accRD(0, 3) ... returning 3
accRD(3, 2) ... returning 5
accRD(5, 1) ... returning 6
6
```

Even though the algorithms used by the FCSlib implementations of these functions are different, the sample demonstrates nicely how the accumulator is applied to the list elements in different orders.

MAP, FILTER, AND FOLD IN LINQ

The functionality of Map, Filter, and Fold is very similar to that offered by SQL for relational database systems. The following example sets up some relational structured data in nested collections and queries those of the orders that have a total value greater than 5.00. This type of query uses all three higher order functions that were shown in this chapter:

```
var rubberChicken = new Product {
  Name = "Rubber chicken", Price = 3.99m };
var pulley = new Product { Name = "Pulley", Price = 0.99m };
var bread = new Product { Name = "Bread", Price = 0.89m };
var butter = new Product { Name = "Butter", Price = 1.19m };

var orders = new List<Order> {
  new Order{ Date = DateTime.Now.Date,
    Lines = new List<OrderLine>{
      new OrderLine{Product = rubberChicken, Count=3},
      new OrderLine{Product = pulley, Count = 3}
    }
  },
  new Order{ Date =
    DateTime.Now.Date.Subtract(new TimeSpan(1,0,0,0)),
    Lines = new List<OrderLine>{
      new OrderLine{Product = bread, Count=1},
      new OrderLine{Product = butter, Count = 1}
    }
  }
};

var ordersWithValueGreater5 =
  Functional.Filter(v => v.Value > 5.00m,
```

```
Functional.Map(o => new {
  Date = o.Date,
  Value = Functional.Fold(
    (r, v) => r + v.Product.Price * v.Count,
    0m, o.Lines)
}, orders));
```

In .NET 3.5, Microsoft picked up on this concept and delivered LINQ. This package contains methods very similar to the `Map`, `Filter`, and `Fold` implementations you've seen. In LINQ, `Map` is called `Select`, `Filter` is called `Where`, and `Fold` is called `Aggregate`. Due to this naming, the functions are even closer to their SQL equivalents and Microsoft clearly wants to focus on this.

For completeness it should be said that LINQ contains a whole lot more than just these three functions. There are lots of other higher order functions, there's integrated language syntax, and there's the great expression-based "translation" system that allows queries to execute against different back ends transparently.

Using LINQ, the previous query could be written in two different ways:

```
var ordersWithValueGreater5Linq1 =
  orders.Select(o => new {
    Date = o.Date,
    Value = o.Lines.Sum(ol => ol.Product.Price * ol.Count)
  }).Where(t => t.Value > 5.00m);

var ordersWithValueGreater5Linq2 =
  from t in
    from o in orders
    select new {
      Date = o.Date,
      Value = o.Lines.Sum(ol => ol.Product.Price * ol.Count)
    }
  where t.Value > 5.00m
  select t;
```

LINQ being as data-centric as it is, many programmers don't realize that the functions `Select`, `Where`, and `Aggregate` are really the equivalent of `Map`, `Filter`, and `Fold`.

There is one main difference between the LINQ implementations and the FCSlib ones: the parameter order. In the context of LINQ, Microsoft had to make these functions extension methods, which makes for a nice chaining syntax, as demonstrated in the `ordersWithValueGreater5Linq1` example. But extension methods are restricted in the way that the first parameter must always be of the type that is being extended, in this case `IEnumerable<T>`. Most languages and runtimes with a functional background use a different parameter order, listing the algorithm — that is, the function that is passed in first and the list last.

The reason for this ordering preference lies in partial application. Parameter order is somewhat important for partial application, because it always works from left to right — Chapter 8 has more information on this in the section "Why Parameter Order Matters."

The choice in the case of a function like Map is whether you are more likely to be applying a certain Map call to the same algorithm, but different lists, or to the same list with different algorithms. The usual choice is to focus on the algorithm, but with LINQ Microsoft had to put the list first.

STANDARD HIGHER ORDER FUNCTIONS

Many of the applications of the higher order functions described in this chapter could be replaced by simple algorithms. The functions themselves aren't very complicated, and in some instances it doesn't seem immediately obvious why it might be a good idea to use the standard functions instead of explicit loops or other imperative constructs.

Standardizing functional building blocks has many purposes, and just one of them is the obvious saving of programmer time that results from not having to write similar algorithms over and over again.

Try to think of standard higher order functions in the context of patterns. Design patterns in object oriented programming rarely have anything of major importance to offer for an experienced programmer. It is likely that most programmers have used a certain pattern, or a variation thereof, to solve a problem before, without ever being aware that somebody had written a description of it down and given it a name. But the knowledge of patterns and their names allows their discussion, arguing for and against them, listing good and bad use cases. Why do scientists decide to call a particular kind of blue rock a Lapis Lazuli? Because they want to talk about it to other scientists.

Defining and using standard higher order functions creates a certain expectation coupled with ease of understanding. If you read a piece of code and you see a call to a function called Map or Fold, you don't need an explanation to understand in general terms what's happening there. You can move on and try to understand the really specific parts of the algorithm. From this perspective, these functions form an important part of functional modularization.

SUMMARY

There is nothing complex about the implementation of Map, Filter, or Fold, but they can solve almost arbitrarily complex problems. This fact, coupled with the effect of easy pattern recognition for other programmers, should give you food for thought when you find yourself writing algorithms with loops next time — perhaps a few cleverly applied standard higher order functions would be a better approach? It is also a good idea to use these functions as starting points for your own general purpose helpers!

13

Sequences

WHAT'S IN THIS CHAPTER?

➤   Understanding list comprehensions

➤   Creating iterators functionally

➤   Working with ranges

Sequences of data are an important encapsulation of the information computer programs need to do their work. Whether they come from databases or other types of storage, or whether they are calculated, entered, or otherwise retrieved, a programming language needs ways of representing such sequences, passing them around, and reading and manipulating them.

UNDERSTANDING LIST COMPREHENSIONS

The notion of lists is deeply embedded in many programming languages. This is quite natural because computers are good at repetitive tasks. A lot of algorithms evolve around executing certain calculations, in the widest possible sense of the word, over lists of data.

In imperative languages, the importance of lists usually leads to the inclusion of array features in the language syntax, while more complex as well as flexible list types are typically implemented in libraries.

Initialization syntax support that works with many different lists was added to C# in version 3.0. Unfortunately, this support isn't very clean because the language uses an arbitrary mechanism to find out whether this syntax is supported for a given type, and to actually add the elements. For instance, the type has to implement the interface `IEnumerable` and it needs to have an `Add` method. `IEnumerable` isn't needed at all for the purpose of adding elements to the collection, and `Add` is a member of a different interface in most of the standard .NET collections. On the other hand, even if a class has a constructor that takes an `IEnumerable` as a parameter, it is not used by the mechanism, resulting in potential performance drawbacks.

The initialization syntax for array types has been available in C# since version 1.0, and it works differently. The mechanism outlined here is the somewhat more flexible initialization syntax supported since C# 3.0.

List comprehensions in functional languages are all about initializing collections. Often there are several different kinds of list comprehensions, with slight syntactic differences, to create lists, sequences, and sometimes other similar constructs. For example, in F# the syntax [<expression>] creates a list, whereas {<expression>} creates a sequence.

In .NET terms, a sequence is an iterator; in other words, an implementation of the IEnumerable interface. Iteration over the values in the sequence happens step by step, which means that values can be calculated, retrieved, or otherwise manufactured one by one when they are requested "from the outside." The advantage of sequences is mainly in this lazy evaluation approach, where the basic sequence doesn't make any assumptions about the way it is going to be used. Sequences can be empty, endless, or somewhere in between, and a caller can't calculate the total length of a sequence without retrieving all its elements.

A list, on the other hand, is a collection of elements that exist in memory and can be readily read, typically using direct indexed access — still according to general .NET terminology. Obviously, a list can be constructed from a sequence at any time, and for some algorithms this is necessary. For instance, a sequence of numbers can't be sorted fully without retrieving all values from the sequence.

In C# it is impossible to extend the language for advanced list comprehension support, but that doesn't change the importance of the use cases covered by list comprehensions in languages that have them. Since C# 2.0, it has been possible to use iterators to create sequences of numbers based on algorithms, but typically the minimum requirement for a sequence is still a function that implements the algorithm. The yield return statement that's needed for iterators is not available in anonymous methods or lambda expressions, so the creation of sequences on-the-fly is not something that is natively covered.

A FUNCTIONAL APPROACH TO ITERATORS

An iterator function can be generic, which is an approach that most of LINQ functions use to work with arbitrary types. Using the ideas of higher order functions, then, a very flexible function to create sequences can be constructed:

```
public static IEnumerable<T> Sequence<T>(Func<T, T> getNext,
  T startVal, Func<T, bool> endReached) {
  if (getNext == null)
    yield break;
  yield return startVal;
  T val = startVal;
  while (endReached == null || !endReached(val)) {
```

```
        val = getNext(val);
        yield return val;
    }
}
```

Take your time to read through the Sequence function; it's not really complicated. (If you need a reminder on how exactly iterators work, you can find that information back in Chapter 5.)

With the introduction of iterators in C# 2.0, Microsoft made the important move from the classes that are needed to implement the .NET iteration interfaces to functions, which are a much more natural context for functionality that iterates over data according to some algorithm. Creating a higher order function that externalizes important parts of the algorithm is an obvious next step, and that's what the Sequence function represents. As a result, it is now easy to create arbitrary sequences using function calls:

```
var oddNumbersFrom1To19 =
  Functional.Sequence(x => x + 2, 1, x => x >= 19);

var squares =
  Functional.Sequence(x => x * x, 2, x => x >= 10000);

var fibonacci =
  Functional.Sequence(
    x => x.Item2 == 0 ? Tuple.Create(0, 1) :
      Tuple.Create(x.Item2, x.Item1 + x.Item2),
    Tuple.Create(0, 0), null).Select(t => t.Item2).Take(20);
```

The first two examples, oddNumbersFrom1To19 and squares use simple data types (int), simple calculation expressions, and an absolute end check. This is a common type of sequence, which resembles the "sequences" regularly used in loop constructs in imperative languages. The syntax is different, but the elements that are needed by the Sequence function are very similar to those used for the for loop in C# and other languages.

The third example, fibonacci, differs from the others in several ways. The data type used in the iterations is more complex, and the end checking expression has been left out entirely, resulting in an endless sequence. The resulting sequence is then combined with extension methods, which extract the relevant element from the Tuples and restrict the sequence to a certain number of elements.

RANGES

Many use cases for sequences are based on simple calculations and conditions, and the syntax required to use the Functional.Sequence function in these cases is still a bit more complicated than it has to be for simple things. The answer to this is the Range, which is a name for a type of sequence that has a start and an end and typically uses simple data types. These are not restrictions as such, since FCSlib ranges support overriding all these elements with custom ones, resulting in an alternative syntax for sequences — but the idea is that for common use cases, things are going to be easier through the use of a particular predefined range type.

Range<T> is a class defined in the `FCSlib.Data` namespace. There are implementations of ranges on the Internet that don't use classes at all, but their disadvantage is that they cannot be used (as easily) for certain functionality like checking whether a particular value is within the range or not. Here are the first few lines of the class Range<T>:

```
public class Range<T> : IRange<T> {
  public Range(T start, T end, Func<T, T> getNext, Comparison<T> compare) {
    this.start = start;
    this.end = end;
    this.compare = compare;
    this.sequence = Functional.Sequence<T>(getNext, start,
      v => compare(getNext(v), end) > 0);
  }

  public Range(T start, T end, Func<T, T> getNext) :
    this(start, end, getNext, Compare) { }

  private static int Compare<U>(U one, U other) {
    return Comparer<U>.Default.Compare(one, other);
  }
}
```

Range<T> is based on a sequence, and given the start and end values for the range as well as functions to retrieve the next element in the sequence and to compare two values, that underlying sequence is constructed automatically. There is also a constructor that doesn't take a comparison delegate, and in this case comparison is automatically performed through the `Comparer<T>` mechanism.

Finally, the class contains these three functions:

```
IEnumerator<T> IEnumerable<T>.GetEnumerator( ) {
  return sequence.GetEnumerator( );
}

IEnumerator IEnumerable.GetEnumerator( ) {
  return ((IEnumerable<T>) this).GetEnumerator( );
}

public bool Contains(T value) {
  return compare(value, start) >= 0 && compare(end, value) >= 0;
}
```

Range<T> takes its implementation of IEnumerable<T> from the sequence, which is an example of using composition (in the object oriented design sense of the word). Contains implements a piece of functionality that simple sequences, which are represented by IEnumerable<T> alone, can't offer: the capability to check whether a given value is within the range or not. There are good and bad points about basing this on the comparison implementation — Contains doesn't require the whole sequence to be retrieved (or even any part of it), but on the other hand the function can't tell whether any given value will actually end up being part of the range based on the getNext implementation.

To complete the description of the `Range` functionality, there is also a static non-generic class `Range`, which provides a number of convenience functions to construct ranges for simple data types. There are also `Create` functions in this class that duplicate the functionality provided by the constructors in `Range<T>`. As a result, ranges can always be created by a call to `Range.Create`, with a variety of different parameters. The class `Range` defines standard `getNext` functions for all the standard numeric .NET data types as well as `char` and `DateTime`.

Here are some examples of ranges, some of them reproducing the same content as the previous sequence examples:

```
var oneToTen = Range.Create(1, 10);

var oddNumbersFrom1To19Range =
  Range.Create(1, 19, x => x + 2);

var squaresRange =
  Range.Create(2, 10000, x => x * x);

var fibonacciRange =
  Range.Create(Tuple.Create(0,0),Tuple.Create(0,5000),
    x => x.Item2 == 0 ? Tuple.Create(0, 1) :
      Tuple.Create(x.Item2, x.Item1 + x.Item2),
      (one,other) => one.Item2 - other.Item2);
```

The results are mixed. The simple sequence types benefit greatly from the simplified syntax, while the example for the Fibonacci sequence looks even more complicated than previously because an end value as well as the comparison function must be specified explicitly.

Based on the ranges just defined, here are two calls to the `Contains` function:

```
if (oneToTen.Contains(5))
  Console.WriteLine("oneToTen contains 5");
if (oddNumbersFrom1To19Range.Contains(10))
  Console.WriteLine("oddNumbersFrom1To19Range contains 10");
```

To prove the point that was made earlier, both these conditions evaluate to `True`, although in the second case the number 10 is not actually part of the sequence, which contains odd numbers only. This is not considered a bug, but rather a detail of the implementation.

It is hard to leave the impression of a real revelation when describing the functionality to create sequences of values easily. At the same time, for developers who look at fully functional languages for the first time, one of the most confusing details is often the absence of many control structures that are taken for granted in imperative languages, in particular various kinds of loops. The easy availability of sequence construction expressions is one half of the explanation for this! (The other half of that explanation is recursion, described in Chapter 11.) For instance, these two loops perform the same actions:

```
Range.Create(1, 3).Each(x => Console.WriteLine(x));

for (int i = 1; i <= 3; i++)
  Console.WriteLine(i);
```

The `Each` function is an extension method in FCSlib, which takes a delegate to call for each of the values in a sequence. Its usage signature is very similar to the `Parallel.ForEach` function in Microsoft's Parallel Extensions for .NET 4.0, which might be one reason to prefer this over the language standard for loop syntax. In any case the analogy should be clear — sequences and ranges in conjunction with higher order functions perform many of the same jobs that are covered by explicit looping constructs in imperative languages.

RESTRICTIONS

There are two types of practical restrictions on the use of sequences and ranges in C#. The first type is simply a syntactic one, since complex creation logic results in function calls that aren't easy to read or understand anymore.

The second type also has to do with the more complex of cases, but it is performance oriented. The Fibonacci examples give an indication of this because they require a data type with two elements to be used. Construction of a sequence using the functional approach requires the previous value to be passed in as the basis of the calculation for the next value. This always involves a certain overhead, which can quickly become prohibitive when the sequence is very long, or when calculations require several values to do their work. Of course there's the general saying about how premature optimization is usually not a good idea, but because the syntactic issues typically go hand in hand with the ones in the performance area, this forms a natural boundary for the application of functional iterators in C#.

With this in mind, the Fibonacci sequence could be written as an explicit iterator like this:

```
static IEnumerable<int> FibonacciExplicit(int max) {
  int first = 0;
  int second = 1;
  do
  {
    yield return first;
    int temp = first;
    first = second;
    second += temp;
  } while (max >= first);
}
```

As a better alternative, you could use a different approach by creating an endless sequence implementation, and then limit it externally with the `TakeWhile` helper function:

```
static IEnumerable<int> FibonacciExplicit( ) {
  int first = 0;
  int second = 1;
  while (true) {
    yield return first;
    int temp = first;
    first = second;
```

```
            second += temp;
          }
     }

...

   foreach (var item in Functional.TakeWhile(x => x <= 5000, FibonacciExplicit( ))) {
   ...
   }
```

This would be considered better because it is based on smaller and "cleaner" building blocks — the responsibility of the Fibonacci function is just to return the sequence numbers, while it is left to the separate helper `TakeWhile` to limit the sequence as needed.

It's hard to argue that the readability is greatly improved by using a hand-coded sequence (a perfectly readable implementation requires recursion), but it is obvious that there are no temporary data structures being used in this example. There are cases where this is an important distinction; one example of this can be found in Chapter 18.

SUMMARY

Handling of sequences in .NET is easy due to the native support for the lazy interfaces `IEnumerable` and `IEnumerable<T>`. The compiler offers special support for sequence generation since C# version 2.0, but the use of functional approaches still improves the syntax considerably. Unfortunately there's no compiler support for "real" list comprehensions, so the syntax often remains a bit clumsy and there are limits for the applicability of sequence generation approaches.

14

Constructing Functions from Functions

WHAT'S IN THIS CHAPTER?

➤ Function composition

➤ Partially applying algorithms

➤ Combining function construction techniques

Function construction is an important topic in functional programming. Functions are the only existing building blocks that make up application code in pure functional languages. They are reusable elements, comparable to classes in an object oriented language. Of course, to reuse an element, whether it's a function or a class, it is necessary to be able to put pieces together to form a new creation. For this purpose, object oriented languages typically use inheritance, in all its various shapes.

In functional languages, there are two main techniques that can be used to create new functions from existing ones: partial application, which was discussed in Chapter 8, and composition, which is the topic for the next section. These techniques can also be combined, which allows programmers to maximize the reuse potential of existing functions.

COMPOSING FUNCTIONS

The idea of composition is based on a very simple thought. Using an example of simple calculations, consider these lines of code:

```
int a = 10;
int b = a * 3;
int c = b + 27;
```

The first line assigns a value to a. The second line calculates b from a, by applying a calculation. Finally, the third line calculates c from b, again by applying a calculation. Instead of performing these calculations directly, you could create functions like this:

```
int CalcB(int a) {
  return a * 3;
}

int CalcC(int b) {
  return b + 27;
}

int a = 10;
int b = CalcB(a);
int c = CalcC(b);
```

In any real-world application, it is quite likely that you would have helper functions similar (in structure, not in the calculations themselves!) to CalcB and CalcC. Now imagine you have a particular algorithm somewhere in your application that starts with a values and needs to calculate c values from them — in other words, you're not interested in b at all. There are several things you could do now. For instance, you could create a new function CalcCfromA:

```
int CalcCfromA(int a) {
  return a * 3 + 27;
}
```

That is not a very good idea because you might need the original functions elsewhere, and of course it's generally a good guideline to separate functionality as much as possible, which leads to several small functions that each do just one thing. Instead, you could implement the function like this:

```
int CalcCfromA(int a) {
  return CalcC(CalcB(a));
}
```

This is much better, and you will see in a moment that this is very close to what composition does, too. Composition goes one step further, though, by allowing you to create the new function in the context where you really need it instead of at the class level, as the previous example steps assume. To reuse the function locally, within a particular algorithm that needs it, you could create an anonymous function instead:

```
Func<int, int> calcCfromA = a => CalcC(CalcB(a));
```

FCSlib contains a helper function called Compose that automates this step. Here it is:

```
public static Func<TSource, TEndResult>
  Compose<TSource, TIntermediateResult, TEndResult>(
    this Func<TSource, TIntermediateResult> func1,
    Func<TIntermediateResult, TEndResult> func2) {
  return sourceParam => func2(func1(sourceParam));
}
```

In the function body, you can easily identify the line that looks exactly like the lambda expression calcCfromA. Compose takes two functions that fit the descriptions of CalcB and CalcC in this example and chains them together, returning a new function that performs the two steps in one.

Using Compose, CalcB and CalcC can be combined like this:

```
var calcCFromAauto = Functional.Compose<int, int, int>(CalcB, CalcC);
```

Once more, type inference in C# is unfortunately not good enough here, so you need to pass in the type parameters explicitly for this example:

```
Func<int, int> calcB = a => a * 3;
Func<int, int> calcC = b => b + 27;
var calcCFromA = Functional.Compose(calcB, calcC);
// Alternatively:
var calcCFromA_ = calcB.Compose(calcC);
```

If the two functions are themselves lambda expressions, this is not necessary.

The most important thing when working with functional composition is to keep the types aligned correctly. In this example, that's quite simple because all the parameter and return types in question are int. In the implementation in FCSlib, you can imagine a pipeline being constructed. The first function passed into Compose (calcB) has a certain parameter type (int), which will also be the parameter type of the resulting combined function. The result type of calcB is int, which has to match with the parameter type of the second function passed into Compose (calcC) — again, this is int. Finally, the result function will also have a result type of int because that's the result type of calcC.

Functional languages often have an operator specifically for composition, which is unfortunately impossible in C#. When reading source code in other languages, always remember that they don't all use the same semantics. In F#, there are two composition operators. One of them works similarly to the C# implementation described here:

```
let calcCFromA = calcB >> calcC
```

In Haskell, on the other hand, the notion of the pipeline that works from left to right is not used, so the example is the other way around:

```
calcCFromA = calcC . calcB
```

Both languages make it extremely easy to perform this step, but the order of combining the functions isn't necessarily the same as in the FCSlib C# implementation.

FCSlib has a number of overloads for the Compose function, which differ in two ways. First, the first function in the chain can have an arbitrary number of parameters. All other functions in the chain can only have one parameter, of course, since they need to take the value as input that has been returned by the previous function in the chain. Second, the last function in the chain can be an Action instead of a Func. In this case, the resulting function will be an Action as well, without an overall return value.

The overloads for different parameter counts on the first function use Func<T, R>, Func<T1, T2, R> ... Func<T1, ..., R> as their types. There are no overloads that take, explicitly, the nested Func types that represent curried format functions. That's because the basic type Func<T, R> covers these cases — in the case of curried format functions, the generic type parameter R is in itself a Func type.

ADVANCED PARTIAL APPLICATION

Partial application was covered to some extent in Chapter 8, but the use cases that were described there were rather simple. In the overall context of function construction, partial application deserves a bit more attention.

To remind you, currying is the conversion step from a multi-parameter function to a chain of single-parameter functions. It enables partial application, the technique of passing less than the complete set of parameters to a function in curried format, in order to create new functions out of existing ones.

Chapter 12 showed the standard higher order functions, and applying partial application to these functions creates many interesting opportunities. These functions tend to receive an algorithm as one of their parameters, in the form of an anonymous function, which they continue to apply to a list of elements. Partial application makes it easy to create very useful helper functions on the basis of these higher order functions, by applying the algorithm first and leaving the data to work against for later. Here's a simple example of a function to square all the integer values in a sequence:

```
var curriedMap =
  Functional.Curry<Converter<int, int>,
    IEnumerable<int>, IEnumerable<int>>(Functional.Map<int, int>);

var squareList = curriedMap(x => x * x);

var list = new int[] { 2, 3, 4 };
var squaredList = squareList(list);
foreach (var item in squaredList)
  Console.Write("{0} ", item);
Console.WriteLine( );
```

The curried Map function is created using the Functional.Curry helper function. Unfortunately, the call isn't simple. Restrictions of the C# language make this much harder than it should be because anonymous functions can't be generic (hence the pre-typing of Functional.Map for int and int) and type inference can't infer the types for the call to the generic Curry method (so the type parameters have to be given explicitly in the call). Read on to see how these issues can be worked around — at least partly.

The next step is the most interesting one here; it creates a new function squareList from curriedMap by applying the first argument. The argument is a lambda expression that performs the actual square calculation. That is the algorithm that was mentioned earlier. squareList is now a function that takes the remaining parameter of the original Map function, which is the sequence of ints to work with. In the sample code, an array of int values is now constructed and passed to squareList, calculating a result list of squared values.

The type inference problem discussed earlier is based on the fact that C# doesn't infer the types of methods. For instance, this simple case is invalid in C#:

```
int Square(int x) {
  return x * x;
}

...

var square = Square;
```

It is perfectly valid, however, to do this:

```
Func<int, int> Square = x => x * x;
var square = Square;
```

There doesn't appear to be a really good reason for this design decision in C#. Something that is sometimes mentioned in discussions on the issue is that the type to infer isn't entirely clear — for instance, in some cases it could be `Expression<Func<int, int>>` instead of `Func<int, int>`. But in the snippet that refers to the fully implemented `Square` function, this is not true because expressions work only with statement-body lambda expressions. There are also lots of cases where type inference just uses a default assumption in the face of other alternatives, so the decision to restrict inference in certain cases for anonymous functions seems quite arbitrary, or at least overly restrictive. It is clear that the C# team is making some decisions to prevent issues with future extensions to the language — such as expressions supporting lambda expressions with any type of body, for instance — but it is also true that other languages have type inference systems that work better than C# in similar cases.

Type inference with anonymous functions works only in cases where the type of the anonymous function has been specified explicitly at least once. It is possible to benefit from this by moving the place where this specification happens away from the code a programmer writes most commonly — into a library that is changed less regularly, for instance. In this vein, FCSlib provides a number of helper functions corresponding to the standard higher order functions (and several others), which return pre-typed delegates for use with currying and partial application.

Using one of those helper functions, the line to create a curried `Map` function to work with `int` types can be rewritten like this:

```
var curriedMap =
  Functional.Curry(Functional.MapDelegate<int, int>());
```

The function `MapDelegate` in FCSlib looks like this:

```
public static Func<Converter<T, R>, IEnumerable<T>, IEnumerable<R>>
  MapDelegate<T, R>( ) {
  return Map<T, R>;
}
```

Using this approach, the code that specifies the type of the anonymous function explicitly is now part of FCSlib, greatly simplifying the calling code.

Now, consider this example, using partial application with the `FoldL` function:

```
var curriedFoldL = Functional.Curry(Functional.FoldLDelegate<int, int>());
var sumList = curriedFoldL((r, v) => r + v)(0);
```

In this example, a new function `sumList` is created from `Functional.FoldL`, by applying both the folding algorithm and the starting value, and leaving open the list parameter.

In contrast to the `Map` function, `FoldL` has three parameters, so the chain of functions returned by `Curry` has three elements: two functions that return another one and one function that returns the final result. In this case, two of these parameters are actually applied immediately, leaving just one open. This makes the format returned by `Curry` slightly inefficient, because it involves intermediate anonymous functions that are not actually used. On the other hand it might make sense to just apply the algorithm, leaving two parameters open:

```
var sumList = curriedFoldL((r, v) => r + v);
var result = sumList(0)(list);
```

Here it is even more obvious — `sumList` is a chain of functions, which results in overhead when called, and also in the somewhat unusual syntax involving two parameter lists.

Currying of functions can be performed for a variety of reasons, and in some cases it is necessary to have the entire parameter list split up into a chain of functions with the same number of elements as the parameter list. But when currying is applied to facilitate partial application, it is regularly unnecessary to have all the elements in the chain. Instead, one or more parameters can be applied directly, without the intermediate full currying. For this purpose, FCSlib provides several overloads of a function called `Apply`. Here's one of those overloads, one that can be used with `FoldL`:

```
public static Func<T2, T3, TR>
  Apply<T1, T2, T3, TR>(Func<T1, T2, T3, TR> function, T1 arg) {
  return (arg2, arg3) => function(arg, arg2, arg3);
}
```

The overloads provided by FCSlib cover different `Func` types as well as `Action` types, with up to nine parameters, and all the cases of applying up to n-1 parameters, where n is the total number of parameters a function has. As a result, it is possible to rewrite the applications of `FoldL` in either of these forms:

```
var sumList = Functional.Apply(
  Functional.FoldLDelegate<int, int>( ), (r, v) => r + v, 0);

var sumList = Functional.Apply(
  Functional.FoldLDelegate<int, int>( ), (r, v) => r + v);
```

The result is the same: a new function that has either one or two parameters applied already, leaving the remaining ones open. In the latter case, the call syntax changes back to the more natural form with just one parameter list:

```
var result = sumList(0, list);
```

Even the example dealing with squaring values in a sequence can benefit from the syntax of the `Apply` call, although performance or overhead considerations are unimportant here because `Map` has only two parameters.

```
var squareList = Functional.Apply(
  Functional.MapDelegate<int, int>( ), x => x * x);
```

COMBINING APPROACHES

In pure functional programming, the two function construction approaches — composition and partial application — are commonly used to create new functions on the basis of existing ones. This is not the only possible approach; there's always the alternative of defining a new function that calls one or more existing functions. Look at this example:

```
Func<int, Func<int, int>> add = x => y => x + y;

var add5PA = add(5);

Func<int, int> add5 = x => add(5)(x);
```

Both the `add5PA` and the `add5` functions make use of the existing `add` function, and define a new function that will add 5 to its one remaining argument. This is a choice that's always available when it comes to functional reuse, and there's no general guideline as to when you should go for one or the other approach.

The main difference is that when using function construction techniques, you typically create a number of intermediate functions that perform part of the task at hand. When functions are constructed for the purpose of reuse within a single function, this might be irrelevant, but when they are created as parts of a larger functional framework, the intermediate functions might be usable in their own right. That is an advantage over the complete redefinition approach because there is no redundancy in the declarations.

The following paragraphs describe a use case for function construction that has been chosen purposefully because it is rather more complex than what you'd typically want to do in C#. It does cover a number of interesting scenarios, though, and an understanding of the techniques in this depth is valuable when it comes to understanding code written in pure functional languages.

The task is quite simple. A function will be constructed that takes two parameters, a sequence of `Customer` objects and an `int` value n. The function will extract from each `Customer` object a field called `SalesVolume`. The resulting sequence is to be sorted in descending order, and then cut off after the first n elements. An average value calculated over the remaining values is to be the result of the function.

To begin, here's an iterator function that returns the sequence of `Customers` that's going to be used in the example:

```
private static IEnumerable<Customer> GetCustomers( ) {
  yield return new Customer { Name = "Harry", SalesVolume = 3462.74m };
  yield return new Customer { Name = "Anna", SalesVolume = 112.9m };
  yield return new Customer { Name = "James", SalesVolume = 1269m };
  yield return new Customer { Name = "July", SalesVolume = 634.86m };
```

```
    yield return new Customer { Name = "Pete", SalesVolume = 17764.29m };
}

internal class Customer {
  public string Name { get; set; }
  public decimal SalesVolume { get; set; }
}
```

A few helper functions need to be constructed. The task of extracting the `SalesVolume` can be implemented with a call to `Map`:

```
var salesVolumes = Functional.Map(c => c.SalesVolume, GetCustomers());
```

To create a function that can perform this task for any given sequence of customers, the extraction algorithm is fixed using partial application, like this using a projection:

```
var salesVolumeExtractor = Functional.Apply(
  Functional.MapDelegate<Customer, decimal>( ), c => c.SalesVolume);
```

At this point, `salesVolumeExtractor` is a function that takes a sequence of `Customer` objects and returns a sequence of `decimal` values representing the `SalesVolume` fields from the `Customers`.

For the purpose of sorting the values in descending order, a function must be constructed that takes a sequence of `decimals` and returns the same type. FCSlib doesn't have any ordering functionality itself, so instead the LINQ function `Enumerable.OrderByDescending` is used. This function takes a parameter to extract a key value, which is not really needed in this case. So here's the `orderer` function that is required:

```
Func<IEnumerable<decimal>, IEnumerable<decimal>> orderer =
  l => Enumerable.OrderByDescending(l, v => v);
```

It would have been possible to create the `orderer` function using currying and partial application, but then an intermediate step would have been needed to swap the parameter order. This implementation seemed the better approach, resulting in more concise code.

The next part is the calculation of an average over a sequence of decimal values. The values in the sequence need to be summed up and then divided by the number of values. It's possible to use the length of the sequence as the value to divide by, but that requires a separate traversal of the sequence. Using a call to `FoldL` with a data type of `Tuple<decimal, decimal>`, you can calculate both values at the same time. Because `Tuple` is an immutable data type, the performance profile of that approach isn't optimal either, but performance optimization isn't the target of this example, so the implementation will use `Tuples` anyway. In functional programming, your focus will typically be on the techniques of creating code efficiently — function construction techniques in this example, along with immutable data structures — as well as the desirable technical consequences of using those techniques, such as the option to parallelize.

An average calculation can be performed like this:

```
var resultTuple = Functional.FoldL(
  (r, v) =>
    Tuple.Create(r.Item1 + 1, r.Item2 + v), // Accumulation
```

```
        Tuple.Create(0m, 0m),                    // Starting value
        sequence);                               // Source sequence
var avg = resultTuple.Item2 / resultTuple.Item1;
```

By applying the first two arguments to `FoldL`, a function is created that takes a sequence at its one remaining parameter and returns a `Tuple` with both the sum of the values and the number of the values. This function can then be composed with a second function that takes a `Tuple` as a parameter and returns the result of dividing `Item2` by `Item1`. Here's the complete function:

```
var avgCalculator = Functional.Compose(Functional.Apply(
    Functional.FoldLDelegate<decimal, Tuple<decimal, decimal>>( ),
        (r, v) => Tuple.Create(r.Item1 + 1, r.Item2 + v), Tuple.Create(0m, 0m)),
          t => t.Item2 / t.Item1);
```

`avgCalculator` is now a function that takes a sequence of decimal values and returns the average of these values.

Using all of these helper functions, plus `Functional.Take`, you can chain together a test call to calculate the average of the top n `SalesVolumes` from a sequence of `Customer`s. Here's what it looks like:

```
var avg = avgCalculator(Functional.Take(3, orderer(
    salesVolumeExtractor(GetCustomers( )))));
```

In the example line, the value n is fixed to 3 and the sequence of customers, which is supposed to become a parameter, is deeply nested in the call. This is the outstanding task: shape the nested construct into a function that can easily be called and reused itself. A call to the resulting function should look like this:

```
var avg = salesVolumeAverage(GetCustomers(), 3);
```

Simple composition takes care of the ordering step after the `SalesVolumes` have been extracted:

```
var getOrderedSalesVolumes = Functional.Compose(salesVolumeExtractor, orderer);
```

`getOrderedSalesVolumes` is now a function that takes a sequence of `Customer` objects and returns a sequence of `SalesVolumes`, sorted in descending order.

The restriction of the sequence to n values is the next step, which `Functional.Take` can perform. Unfortunately, the parameters on this function are in the wrong order, so that it can't be composed with `getOrderedSalesVolume`. Using a curried version of that function, the function `Functional.Swap` can turn around the order of the parameters, so it suits the purpose better.

```
var take = Functional.Swap(Functional.Curry(Functional.TakeDelegate<decimal>( )));
```

At this point, `take` is a function that takes a sequence and returns a function that takes an int n, which returns a sequence with (at most) the first n elements of the original sequence. The preceding sentence does indeed make sense; it is written like that to represent the fact that `take` is a curried function. Its first parameter is a sequence, so it is now possible to compose `getOrderedSalesVolumes`, which returns a sequence, with `take`, which accepts a sequence.

```
var getRelevantSalesVolumes = Functional.Compose(getOrderedSalesVolumes, take);
```

The resulting function, getRelevantSalesVolumes, takes a sequence of Customer objects and returns a new function, which, given an int parameter, returns a sequence of at most n elements, consisting of the top SalesVolumes from the sequence of Customers. In other words, getRelevantSalesVolumes is a curried-format function that takes two parameters, a sequence of Customer objects and an int value n, and returns a sequence of at most the highest n SalesVolume values from the Customer objects.

By uncurrying getRelevantSalesVolumes, a function can be created that has exactly the right signature:

```
var uncurriedGetRelevantSalesVolumes =
  Functional.Uncurry(getRelevantSalesVolumes);
```

Finally, composition can be used again, to combine uncurriedGetRelevantSalesVolumes with avgCalculator. avgCalculator needs an argument that is a sequence of decimal values to calculate an average over, and that's exactly what uncurriedGetRelevantSalesVolumes delivers. Here's the result:

```
var salesVolumeAverage = Functional.Compose(
  uncurriedGetRelevantSalesVolumes, avgCalculator);
```

That's the final result. salesVolumeAverage is now a function that conforms exactly to the call syntax previously discussed:

```
var avg = salesVolumeAverage(GetCustomers(), 3);
```

SUMMARY

This chapter has taken the techniques that are available for function construction to the limit and beyond. Composition and partial application are the tools that enable you to treat functions as building blocks, and while they compare to object oriented techniques with similar purposes, they have their own priorities and advantages. It depends on your work environment and team, your projects and tasks, as well as many other factors, to which extent you'll find yourself using the language techniques described in this chapter. But whatever you decide, you know your options now, and you know where the limits are.

15

Optional Values

WHAT'S IN THIS CHAPTER?

➤ Expressing the lack of values

➤ The implementation of an Option type

Programmers of languages derived from C have long been familiar with null as a representation of "nothing." In spite of common disadvantages that date back as long as the keyword null itself, the concept is still around today. Functional languages have a different heritage when it comes to expressing "nothing" and the approaches used there can also be mirrored in C#.

THE MEANING OF NOTHING

When dealing with data in computers, there is always the dilemma of representing "nothing." This problem is indeed special because in working with data outside the computing world, it's rarely much of an issue. Imagine a printed form on paper, with fields for values. Simply doing nothing — not filling in any one of the fields — results in the field representing nothing, automatically. There are no additional steps to be taken to make it obvious to anybody who reads the form that this field has not been filled in.

For computers, the situation is different, and this goes back to the fact (without going into the physics of it) that any byte in a computer's memory always has a value. That value might start out being quite random, and depending on the memory management system you're working with, it might have a standard default value when it is made available to you as a programmer. But the point remains: there's always a value. There is no built-in way of saying, "This byte contains nothing."

Many imperative languages, and especially those with elements that go back to C, have singled out the value 0 (zero) for the purpose of meaning "nothing." Of course such a value must be distinguishable from all other values that mean "something." I'm sure many of you remember writing algorithms where some integer variable was assigned a magic value of –1 (or something similar) at the start, as a default or starting value. Very generally speaking, the zero value seemed like a good idea under the assumption that memory locations would regularly store pointers to other memory locations, and because a pointer to zero is not a valid pointer in most memory models, it seems quite safe to use for the "nothing" case. To account for those architectures in which zero is, in fact, a valid pointer, the C language introduced the keyword `null` to represent that empty pointer — of course, it wouldn't actually have to be equal to zero on every single platform targeted by the C language, but the concept is the same.

For many use cases the value `null` is obviously less useful. If computers only ever stored pointers to memory locations in all their memory locations, where would that leave you with regard to data? There have to be other data types available to programmers, where bytes are interpreted differently. C had only very few of those, but many later languages came along with lots of data types. The problem of those data types not having a language-supported official value for "nothing" was typically not solved by the language designers.

In C# 2.0 and .NET 2.0, Microsoft introduced *nullable types*. These are essentially a solution to the preceding problem, and they are very similar to the `Option` type implementation that is going to be the subject of the rest of this chapter. Nevertheless, the `Option` type is a slightly more unified approach to the problem, and it also reflects a mechanism that exists in many functional languages. It moves the understanding of "nothing" away from the C-derived null value, which is really quite meaningless in a managed language anyway. In contrast to nullable types, `Option<T>` can be used with reference types as well as value types — there is some potential for confusion in these cases, but the advantages of having a unified system seem to outweigh those.

It should be mentioned that there is a type `Option<T>` in F#, which has been used to an extent as a template for the C# implementation. But to prevent any complaints about copied code, the C# type has been implemented from scratch, to support a similar public API.

IMPLEMENTING OPTION(AL) VALUES

The basic structure of the class `Option<T>` is obvious: in addition to a value of type `T`, it stores a flag that says whether the value has been set. The type is immutable, so it is during construction that this decision is made: does the new instance represent an actual value or "nothing"?

It doesn't make much sense to create loads of new instances of `Option<T>` that all represent "nothing" for any given type `T`. So the "nothing" case is covered by a single instance of the class, which is made available through a public field called `None`. Here's what the class may look like at this point (this is not what is actually in FCSlib; read on for that):

```
public sealed class Option<T> {
  private readonly T value;
  public T Value {
    get { return value; }
  }
```

```
    private readonly bool hasValue;
    public bool HasValue {
      get { return hasValue; }
    }
    public bool IsSome {
      get { return hasValue; }
    }
    public bool IsNone {
      get { return !hasValue; }
    }

    public Option(T value) {
      this.value = value;
      this.hasValue = true;
    }

    private Option( ) {
    }

    public static readonly Option<T> None = new Option<T>( );
}
```

To create an option type instance, the code would look like this now:

```
var intVal = new Option<int>(42);
var intValNothing = Option<int>.None;
```

In both cases it is necessary to specify the actual value type explicitly because type inference doesn't work in these scenarios. It is possible, though, to create a helper function to create instances of Option<T>, and if this uses a generic type parameter on the method instead of the class, it can benefit from type inference. Here's a first version of the class Option (non-generic), incorporating such a helper method:

```
public sealed class Option {
  public static Option<T> Some<T>(T value) {
    return new Option<T>(value);
  }
}
```

This allows you to create instances of Option<T>, which contain values, like this:

```
var intVal = Option.Some(42);
var doubleVal = Option.Some(37.5);
var boolVal = Option.Some(false);
```

With the implementation up to this point, there are still some usability issues. For example, value equality isn't what it should be. Look at this piece of code:

```
var intVal = Option.Some(5);
var intVal2 = Option.Some(5);

if (intVal == intVal2)
  Console.WriteLine("Values are equal");
```

It's a sensible expectation that `intVal` and `intVal2` in this example should be regarded as equal, but in fact they are not. The following methods are needed in the `Option<T>` class to account for the equality:

```
public static bool operator ==(Option<T> a, Option<T> b) {
  return a.HasValue == b.HasValue &&
    EqualityComparer<T>.Default.Equals(a.Value, b.Value);
}

public static bool operator !=(Option<T> a, Option<T> b) {
  return !(a == b);
}

public override int GetHashCode( ) {
  int hashCode = hasValue.GetHashCode( );
  if (hasValue)
    hashCode ^= value.GetHashCode( );
  return hashCode;
}

public override bool Equals(object obj) {
  return base.Equals(obj);
}
```

There are two methods of real relevance here, the `operator ==` implementation and `GetHashCode`. Both take into account the possibility that there might not be any actual values, and then modify the standard object behavior to return the correct results for the option type.

At this point, the whole system is functional (no pun intended). The only major difference to the `Option` type in F# is that due to the more advanced type inference and generalization mechanisms in F#, it's not necessary to include an explicit type when using the `None` value. It would be great to be able to write code like this in C# (written as a unit test for clarity):

```
var intVal = Option.Some(42);
var intValNothing = Option.None;

Assert.IsFalse(intVal == intValNothing);

var list = new List<Option<int>>();
list.Add(Option.Some(5));
list.Add(Option.None);
```

With a few more tricks, this is actually possible. First, the `None` member is introduced to the `Option` class, and the one in `Option<T>` is changed to a private member. This is the final result of the class `Option`:

```
public sealed class Option {
  private Option( ) { }

  public static Option<T> Some<T>(T value) {
```

```
      return new Option<T>(value);
   }

   public static readonly Option None = new Option( );
}
```

Now the `Option<T>` class must be extended, so that `Option` can be used as a compatible type. That's not hard — each `Option` instance must be converted into the corresponding `Option<T>` `.None`. This additional method in `Option<T>` takes care of the conversion:

```
   public static implicit operator Option<T>(Option option) {
      return Option<T>.None;
   }
```

To put this in context, here's the complete final version of the class `Option<T>`:

```
   public sealed class Option<T> {
      private readonly T value;
      public T Value { get { return value; } }

      private readonly bool hasValue;
      public bool HasValue { get { return hasValue; } }

      public bool IsSome { get { return hasValue; } }
      public bool IsNone { get { return !hasValue; } }

      public Option(T value) {
         this.value = value;
         this.hasValue = true;
      }

      private Option( ) { }

      private static readonly Option<T> None = new Option<T>( );

      public static bool operator ==(Option<T> a, Option<T> b) {
         return a.HasValue == b.HasValue &&
            EqualityComparer<T>.Default.Equals(a.Value, b.Value);
      }
      public static bool operator !=(Option<T> a, Option<T> b) {
         return !(a == b);
      }

      public static implicit operator Option<T>(Option option) {
         return Option<T>.None;
      }

      public override int GetHashCode( ) {
         int hashCode = hasValue.GetHashCode( );
         if (hasValue)
            hashCode ^= value.GetHashCode( );
```

```
      return hashCode;
   }

   public override bool Equals(object obj) {
      return base.Equals(obj);
   }
}
```

C# does not support meta-programming, especially not adding keywords to the language. Nevertheless, the discussion in this chapter shows how existing mechanisms can be used to enable syntax for new types of data. Whether the `Option` type is useful enough to use it over the built-in nullable types, you will have to decide for yourself. It will be used in further code in this book, to provide a familiar feel and syntax to those who know functional programming languages.

```
FCSlib contains additional helper methods to construct Option<T> values with
extension methods. Here's a simple piece of code that demonstrates
instantiation and equality checking:// Instantiate some options:
var intOpt1 = new Option<int>(10);
var intOpt2 = 10.ToOption( );
var stringOpt1 = Option.Some("text");
var stringOpt2 = "text".ToOption( );
var noneOpt = Option.None;

// Check for equality:
Console.WriteLine("intOpt1 == intOpt2: " +
   (intOpt1 == intOpt2));                            // True
Console.WriteLine("stringOpt1 == stringOpt2: " +
   (stringOpt1 == stringOpt2));                      // True
Console.WriteLine("intOpt1 == noneOpt: " +
   (intOpt1 == noneOpt));                            // False
Console.WriteLine("stringOpt1 == noneOpt: " +
   (stringOpt2 == noneOpt));                         // False
```

One important advantage of `Option<T>` over `null` and nullable types is the fact that null can be a valid value if you want it to. Instead of using a "special case" value from the same value space as the valid values to denote the invalid case, `Option<T>` provides information separately to distinguish the cases of "having a value" and "not having a value." C# nullable types work in a similar fashion, but only for value types. `Option<T>`, on the other hand, uses the same approach across all types.

FCSlib allows you to distinguish two cases where null is either a valid value or a special case.

```
// A null value can be a valid value:
string nullString = null;
var nullStringOpt1 = nullString.ToOption( );
Console.WriteLine("nullStringOpt1 == noneOpt: " +
   (nullStringOpt1 == noneOpt));                     // False

// Or it can be considered equal to None:
var nullStringOpt2 = nullString.ToNotNullOption( );
Console.WriteLine("nullStringOpt2 == noneOpt: " +
   (nullStringOpt2 == noneOpt));                     // True
```

For clarity, here are the two extension methods `ToOption` and `ToNotNullOption`:

```
public static Option<T> ToOption<T>(this T val) {
  return Option.Some(val);
}

public static Option<T> ToNotNullOption<T>(this T val) where T : class {
  return val != null ? val.ToOption( ) : Option.None;
}
```

SUMMARY

The use of `Option<T>` types instead of null values is a different strategy to handle cases where the absence of information is important. `Option<T>` types are a cleaner approach than null values because there are no differences in their use for value and reference types. They are also more powerful because they take a "metadata" approach to store additional information about a value, thereby enabling the full use of a type's value range, including `null` itself.

Another important argument in favor of `Option<T>` is the possibility of viewing it as a monad, which enables the chaining of operations that work on the type without the need of explicit special case handling. This topic is discussed in depth in Chapter 17.

16

Keeping Data from Changing

WHAT'S IN THIS CHAPTER?

➤ Why change is not always good

➤ Simple immutable data types

➤ Cloning with modifications

➤ Immutable container data structures

➤ Alternatives to immutable data types

That data is changeable, that it actually changes all the time in real life, is usually taken as fact in mainstream imperative programming. But the changeability of data creates many problems, so programmers are questioning that idea. In the world of functional programming, data is traditionally immutable, and data structures tend to be persistent. The term persistent is easily misunderstood because it seems to point at persistence in the sense of storing data in file systems, databases, or similar storage units. It's actually used as an opposite of ephemeral, meaning short-lived or volatile, and should not be understood to imply any storage mechanism for the data.

CHANGE IS GOOD — NOT!

The idea behind persistent data structures is simple. For a particular purpose — perhaps a thread of execution, a process, a function, a single algorithm implementation, in other words, any unit of work (in the literal, not the Martin Fowler sense of the term) — it would be useful to know that the data used by that unit of work couldn't change. That means it couldn't change from the perspective of that unit of work. It might appear to have changed when looked at from a different angle; that's fine. But the unit of work should be able to perform its task from beginning to end with no concern for potential changes to the data it works with. If data structures guarantee that behavior, they are called persistent.

A style of programming that uses only persistent data structures has a lot of practical advantages. To begin with, code is easier to write if no provision has to be made for the case where unexpected things happen in the middle of an algorithm. Simpler code structures result in fewer programming errors, better maintainability, stronger encapsulation, and easier and more error-proof debugging and testing. The whole idea of side-effect free programming, as favored by functional programming in general, is brilliantly supported by the idea of immutable data, and as a result, functions that use immutable data and persistent data structures exclusively are a pleasure to parallelize and modularize without any concern for execution order, locking, and similar typical consequences of imperative programming.

The following sample code shows a typical, albeit simple, implementation of two data container classes, `MutableProduct` and `MutableOrderLine`:

```
public class MutableProduct {
  public string Name { get; set; }
  public decimal Price { get; set; }
}

public class MutableOrderLine {
  public MutableProduct Product { get; set; }
  public int Count { get; set; }

  public decimal GetValue( ) {
    return Product.Price * Count;
  }
}

[TestFixture]
public class EphemeralTests {
  [Test]
  public void TestOrderLineValue( ) {
    var product = new MutableProduct { Name = "Rubber boat", Price = 16.99m };
    var line = new MutableOrderLine { Product = product, Count = 3 };
    Assert.AreEqual(50.97m, line.GetValue( ));
  }
}
```

There is also a simple unit test, which checks that for a given combination of object values, the business logic function `MutableOrderLine.GetValue()` returns the correct result. The example is much simpler than in real business applications, but the details are similar.

FALSE ASSUMPTIONS

The interesting thing about the test in this example is that an assumption is made: "while the process of calculating the `MutableOrderLine` value is in progress, the values of `MutableProduct.Price` and `MutableOrderLine.Count` are not going to change." Within the context of this simple test, the assumption is correct, but outside such an artificial context, this cannot easily be guaranteed. The data structures are declared in such a way that the data contained within them could change at any time. Of course this can only happen in reality if the data is shared across threads running in parallel. In Microsoft's documentation of .NET Framework data types, there is a section that states whether each data type is to be regarded thread safe or not. The data structures that are marked thread safe usually use locking or other access protection/coordination mechanisms to prevent conflicting access.

In the example scenario, the data that is assumed to be consistent throughout the unit of work represented by the `GetValue` function lives in two different objects. The objects themselves could theoretically implement locking on their individual properties, but that wouldn't be sufficient. This algorithm would need locking on the function level, acquiring two separate locks before going about its business of calculating the result. Or perhaps it wouldn't matter whether the old or the new value of a simple field like `Count` is being used. The scenario certainly shows the issues that come up when data is allowed to change. Whether that matters to the program depends on the algorithm itself, and also on the complexity of the data structures. The important point is that a test like that in the example only checks the functionality of the business logic implementation in specific artificial circumstances. If you assume that the data could change — and given the details of the implementation this is an assumption you really should make — then you'd have to make changes to the test as well as either the data structures, the business logic implementation, or both to cover all contingencies.

Being Static Is Good

An alternative to locking and other access control mechanisms is implementing data structures like the preceding data container classes in a way that qualifies them as persistent in the functional programming sense of the word. Here is such an implementation, including the same unit test as before:

```
public class PersistentProduct {
  public readonly string Name;
  public readonly decimal Price;

  public PersistentProduct(string Name, decimal Price) {
    this.Name = Name;
    this.Price = Price;
  }
}

public class PersistentOrderLine {
  public readonly PersistentProduct Product;
  public readonly int Count;

  public decimal GetValue( ) {
    return Product.Price * Count;
  }

  public PersistentOrderLine(PersistentProduct Product, int Count) {
    this.Product = Product;
    this.Count = Count;
  }
}


[TestFixture]
public class PersistentTests {
```

```
[Test]
public void TestOrderLineValue( ) {
  var product = new PersistentProduct("Rubber boat", 16.99m);
  var line = new PersistentOrderLine(product, 3);
  Assert.AreEqual(50.97, line.GetValue( ));
}
}
```

This is an immutable implementation of the data classes, made to allow no changes to the data stored in them after initialization is complete. Compare the individual classes to their mutable counterparts, and note a few interesting details:

➤ The C# keyword `readonly` is used for the data fields. This guarantees that the field values can't change once they have been initially assigned.

➤ The constructor provides the only way of setting the values.

➤ Public fields are being used to store the values. This is quite uncommon these days, with properties being used almost everywhere. Properties could be used, but it is often unnecessary to do so. One of the major reasons to use properties is that they are fully compatible with standard data binding mechanisms as implemented by .NET Windows Forms. But in reality the immutable data explained in this chapter is used for algorithms a lot more than it is for direct UI presentation — for instance, it can't be changed anyway, which takes away a large percentage of the use cases for direct data binding! You have a choice here. In this case I chose to go with public fields because that also facilitates the automatic cloning mechanism described later in this chapter.

➤ The implementation of `GetValue()` hasn't changed at all.

➤ The only difference in the test code is that constructor instead of initialization syntax is used to instantiate the classes.

With the help of a few rather simple changes, all the considerations outlined earlier are now irrelevant. The function `GetValue()` is a unit of work, by the definition of the term introduced in the beginning of this chapter. Within its execution context, the values of `Product.Price` and `Count` cannot change. The data structures used in this second example are therefore persistent.

There are three interesting questions regarding this type of persistent data structure:

➤ When do you call a data structure persistent? For instance, a data structure could refer to another data structure that is not persistent.

➤ What happens if data really needs to change? In the example, you have to assume that a product is going to change its price at some point.

➤ Are persistent data structures always the best answer?

For the answers to these questions, please read on.

A Matter of Depth

When persistence of data structures was explained at the beginning of this chapter, the focus was on the fact that data stored inside them should not appear to change from the perspective of a particular unit of work. The technical implementation chosen in the previous example was that of immutable data types. This is not the only possible way of implementing persistent data structures, but a commonly used one due to its simplicity.

Immutability of data is gradual and there is a distinction between flat and deep immutability. *Flat immutability* means that values on the level of a particular data structure can't be changed. *Deep immutability* means that all of the data structures to which those values refer are also immutable. The data structures in the preceding example satisfy both of those conditions. You could combine PersistentOrderLine with MutableProduct, in which case you'd have a data structure with flat, but not deep, immutability. Generally, deep immutability is preferable, but in practice a combination of data structures can make a lot of sense. As you will see later, it isn't all that hard to implement even complex data structures such as lists with flat immutability. But deep immutability depends rather more on the way these structures are being used — That is, what data you end up storing in them — than on their own implementation. This should suffice to answer the first question.

Cloning

The second question (what happens if data really needs to change?) also has to do with the depth of the "tree" that results from having a network of objects that relate to one another. With immutable objects, the fact that data tends to change occasionally in the real world is modeled with the help of a cloning process. Basically, to apply a change to an object, you create a copy of that object that differs from the original in one or more points. The modified clone can then be used in certain places in your code without affecting existing units of work that are still active and were started with a reference to the old object.

For example, here's how to change the price in an instance of the PersistentProduct class:

```
var chicken = new PersistentProduct("Rubber Chicken", 10.99m);
var discountedChicken = new PersistentProduct(chicken.Name, 8.49m);
```

There are two problems with this approach, which lead to an answer to the third question (are persistent data structures always the best answer?). The first problem is a logical one: if there is a network of related objects and one of them changes in this way, then a potentially large number of other objects needs to be cloned as well. In a simple case:

```
var chicken = new PersistentProduct("Rubber Chicken", 10.99m);

// this orderLine relates to the unchanged chicken
var orderLine = new PersistentOrderLine(chicken, 5);

// now the chicken "changes" - in this case the local reference to the
// "old" chicken is actually dropped
chicken = new PersistentProduct(chicken.Name, 8.49m);

// the old orderline needs to be cloned as well
// (assuming your business logic dictates that the order should be
// updated with the price change)
orderLine = new PersistentOrderLine(chicken, orderLine.Count);
```

You will see later that in the case of persistent container data structures such as linked lists, this logic leads to a certain, possibly large, overhead. Remember that there is a reason why you're perhaps considering the use of this approach to immutable data! When thinking about parallelization, for example, there is always overhead involved when it comes to sharing data between execution contexts. The cloning idea described here incurs its overhead when data manipulation tasks are being performed, whereas algorithms that share data and employ locks incur their overhead at a different point.

A LOOK AT LOCKING

Locking is a mechanism used in multi-threaded code, which protects certain sections of code from being executed concurrently, or at least restricts how exactly concurrent execution can occur.

It has been implied several times in this chapter that locking is not a good approach to the data sharing problem. There are three main considerations behind this statement:

➤ Locking has a cost.

➤ Locking prevents parallelization.

➤ Locking is very hard to get right.

The cost of locking is a certain management overhead of the locked sections of code — in other words, an algorithm that needs to lock data before it can do its work will take a bit longer even if the lock can be acquired right away. This seems irrelevant, but in reality it can accumulate to a considerable overhead if locking is quite fine-grained (when you have a lot of short sections of code that each have their own locking, for instance). You do want locking to be fine-grained because the basic idea of locking is to restrict the degree of parallelization that can happen in a certain section of your code, and having coarse-grained locking means that large parts of your code can never be executed in parallel. That's what's meant by the statement "locking prevents parallelization."

Of course there are not locks that simply prevent parallelization outright. There are different types of locks, some of which allow several readers but just one writer of a piece of information, for example. There are also other means of coordinating shared information such as semaphores, mailboxes, and so on, depending on the precise APIs you're using. That's why it's hard to get locking right: you have to be aware of all the options and structure your code and its algorithms accordingly. The types of locks and other structures you use depend on the code you're writing and what it does, so maintenance is important as well as difficult. Lots of things can go wrong, and special books about parallelization have whole chapters about deadlocks, lock chains, and other sinister special cases. You need to be specific and fine-grained in your efforts, but the result will come at a cost and probably still be coarser than you would like, thereby restricting parallelization to a non-optimal degree.

The idea of trying to work without locks is an interesting one from this point of view. Using immutable data is just one part of a possible solution.

Automatic Cloning

Another problem with cloning is with the syntax of applying cloning in C#. An earlier example showed a new version of the chicken constructed by passing in one old and one new value to the constructor of the class. Unfortunately, it isn't going to be quite that simple in real applications because your data structures will be much more complex, meaning you'll have to pass in lots and lots of constructor arguments that are simply read from the old version of the object just to create a clone with perhaps a single changed value. Unlike many functional programming languages, C# doesn't have syntax support for the creation of a modified clone, which makes cloning cumbersome from a coding and readability point of view.

FCSlib implements some functionality that can be useful to automate the process of cloning to a certain extent, although it comes at a cost. The code doesn't use reflection and it resorts to compiled expression trees to dynamically access property values and construct new objects, but the process of creating a clone with the help of this automated functionality is still much slower than creating the same object manually in C#.

With the help of the library function, the combination of cloned chicken and order line can be constructed like so:

```
var chicken = new PersistentProduct("Rubber Chicken", 10.99m);
var orderLine = new PersistentOrderLine(chicken, 5);

chicken = chicken.CloneWith(new Dictionary<string, object>{
  {"Price", 8.49m}
});
orderLine = orderLine.CloneWith(new Dictionary<string, object>{
  {"Product", chicken}
});
```

The method `CloneWith<T>` is implemented as an extension method:

```
public static T CloneWith<T>(this T source, Dictionary<string, object> newValues) {
  return (T) GetCreator(typeof(T))(source, newValues);
}
```

`GetCreator()` is a function that returns a function to create a new object of a certain type. The returned function takes the source object as an argument as well as the dictionary with new values. Here's the code for `GetCreator()`, including the cache it uses to make things more efficient when the same type is cloned multiple times:

```
static ConcurrentDictionary<Type, Func<object,
  IDictionary<string, object>, object>> creators =
  new ConcurrentDictionary<Type, Func<object, IDictionary<string, object>,
object>>( );

static Func<object, IDictionary<string, object>, object> GetCreator(Type type) {
  return creators.GetOrAdd(type, k => CreateCreator(k));
}
```

When a new creator needs to be generated, the function `CreateCreator` does the heavy lifting:

Available for
download on
Wrox.com

```
static Func<object, IDictionary<string, object>, object> CreateCreator(Type type) {
  var ctors = type.GetConstructors( );
  if (ctors.Length > 1)
    throw new InvalidOperationException(String.Format(
      "Can't clone type {0} because it has more than one constructor.", type));
  var ctor = ctors[0];
  var cparams = ctor.GetParameters( );
  var paramCount = cparams.Length;
  var paramArray = new Expression[paramCount];

  var sourceParam = Expression.Parameter(typeof(object), "s");
  var dictParam = Expression.Parameter(typeof(IDictionary<string, object>), "d");

  for (int i = 0; i < paramCount; i++) {
    ConstantExpression paramName = Expression.Constant(cparams[i].Name);
    paramArray[i] =
      Expression.Convert(
        Expression.Call(
          Expression.Call(GetOptionValueMethod, dictParam, paramName),
          OptionObjectGetValueMethod,
          Expression.Lambda(
            Expression.Invoke(
              Expression.Call(GetAccessorMethod, Expression.Constant(type),
              paramName),
              sourceParam))),
          cparams[i].ParameterType);
  }

  Expression<Func<object, IDictionary<string, object>, object>> exp =
    Expression.Lambda<Func<object, IDictionary<string, object>, object>>(
      Expression.New(ctor, paramArray),
      sourceParam, dictParam);

  return exp.Compile( );
}

static Option<object> GetOptionValue(IDictionary<string, object> dict, string key)
{
  object result;
  if (dict.TryGetValue(key, out result))
    return result.ToOption();
  return Option.None;
}

static MethodInfo getOptionValueMethod;
static MethodInfo GetOptionValueMethod {
  get {
    if (getOptionValueMethod == null) {
      getOptionValueMethod =
        new Func<IDictionary<string, object>, string,
          Option<object>>(GetOptionValue).Method;
    }
```

```
    return getOptionValueMethod;
  }
}

static MethodInfo optionObjectGetValueMethod;
static MethodInfo OptionObjectGetValueMethod {
  get {
    if (optionObjectGetValueMethod == null) {
      optionObjectGetValueMethod =
        typeof(Option<object>).GetMethod("GetValue",
          BindingFlags.Instance | BindingFlags.Public);
    }
    return optionObjectGetValueMethod;
  }
}
```

code snippet CloningExtensions.cs

This is partly very imperative code, a choice that has been made due to the imperative data structures being handled (the parameter array, specifically) as well as for efficiency reasons. The function uses expression trees to construct and compile the actual creation function for the given type. This is much faster than using reflection, and while it may seem confusing initially, it is a more maintainable and easier to read approach.

 For more information on expression trees, see Chapter 7.

Finally, a similar infrastructure exists for the GetAccessor() part of the code, which is already referred to in the preceding code:

```
static ConcurrentDictionary<Type, ConcurrentDictionary<string,
  Func<object, object>>> accessors =
  new ConcurrentDictionary<Type, ConcurrentDictionary<string,
  Func<object, object>>>( );

static Func<object, object> GetAccessor(Type type, string valueName) {
  Func<object, object> result;
  ConcurrentDictionary<string, Func<object, object>> typeAccessors;

  // Let's see if we have an accessor already for this type/valueName
  if (accessors.TryGetValue(type, out typeAccessors)) {
    if (typeAccessors.TryGetValue(valueName, out result))
      return result;
  }

  // okay, create one and store it for later
  result = CreateAccessor(type, valueName);
  if (typeAccessors == null) {
```

```
      typeAccessors = new ConcurrentDictionary<string, Func<object, object>>( );
      accessors[type] = typeAccessors;
    }
    typeAccessors[valueName] = result;

    return result;
  }

  static MethodInfo getAccessorMethod;
  static MethodInfo GetAccessorMethod {
    get {
      if (getAccessorMethod == null) {
        getAccessorMethod = typeof(CloningExtensions).GetMethod(
          "GetAccessor", BindingFlags.Static | BindingFlags.NonPublic);
      }
      return getAccessorMethod;
    }
  }

  static Func<object, object> CreateAccessor(Type type, string valueName) {
    var finfo = type.GetField(valueName);
    var param = Expression.Parameter(typeof(object), "o");
    Expression<Func<object, object>> exp =
      Expression.Lambda<Func<object, object>>(
      Expression.Convert(
      Expression.Field(Expression.Convert(param, type), finfo), typeof(object)),
      param);
    return exp.Compile( );
  }
```

The mechanisms are the same here as already described for GetCreator(). An accessor is a function that accesses a particular value in a source object in an efficient way. Overall, the creator is a compiled piece of dynamically generated code that constructs a new object out of an existing one. It uses a constructor to create the new object. The parameters of the constructor are checked, and the assumption is that the source object has public fields with the same names as the constructor parameters, which is how the connection can be made without any further configuration data.

Overall, this cloning mechanism is just a demonstration. The fact remains that, unfortunately, C# doesn't have any built-in language features to facilitate cloning, and that is a major drawback. Performing cloning manually is not an option that makes for readable code, so automating the process is a useful idea. The automatic mechanism described earlier comes with certain strings attached, like the focus on public fields instead of properties and the somewhat unconventional requirement of corresponding names for those fields and the constructor arguments.

You could write automatic cloning code that implements a variety of different options, but that would make the performance overhead of the automatic method, compared to manual cloning, even more appalling. It is a better idea to use this implementation as a template and create your own, depending on your precise needs and/or the specifications for persistent data types you are comfortable with for your own use.

IMPLEMENTING IMMUTABLE CONTAINER DATA STRUCTURES

The rest of this chapter provides several examples, with explanations, for the implementation of container data structures that are persistent in nature. The algorithms for these implementations are taken from Chris Okasaki's book *Purely Functional Data Structures* (Cambridge University Press). The book contains these algorithms implemented in the functional languages ML and Haskell, and quite a few compromises had to be made in translating to C#.

Linked List

Every programmer has written a singly linked list, and as a programming task usually given to those who are just learning the trade, it can be quite daunting. Part of the reason is that these lists are generally to be implemented in a mutable fashion, which means lots more effort than for a persistent implementation.

The algorithm for the persistent list type isn't hard to understand. It is based on the idea that if a unit of work has been started with a reference of the list in an "old" state, any perceived change to the list should not result in a change from that active unit's point of view. Figure 16-1 shows the three steps for the process of adding elements to the list:

1. The application holds a reference to the list, i.e. the Head element of it, in a variable `list`.

2. A separate unit of work is started and gets a reference to the list according to that current state, which it holds in its own variable `list`.

3. In the outer scope, two new elements are added to the list. The outer scope `list` reference now points to a new `Head` element, but from the perspective of the separate unit of work, the list hasn't changed.

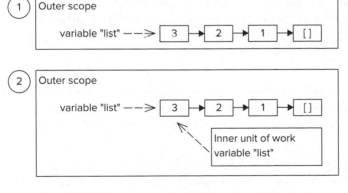

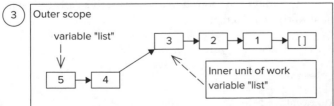

FIGURE 16-1: Persistent list add

A very simple version of the persistent list type looks like this:

```
public class MyListStep1<T> {
  public readonly T Head;
  public readonly MyListStep1<T> Tail;
  public readonly bool IsEmpty;

  public static readonly MyListStep1<T> Empty = new MyListStep1<T>( );

  private MyListStep1( ) {
    IsEmpty = true;
  }

  public MyListStep1(T head, MyListStep1<T> tail) {
    this.Head = head;
    if (tail.IsEmpty)
      this.Tail = MyListStep1<T>.Empty;
    else
      this.Tail = tail;
  }

  public MyListStep1(T head) : this(head, MyListStep1<T>.Empty) { }
}
```

 The name of the class is `MyListStep1` *here, because the download code for this chapter walks through several iterations. In FCSlib, the complete data type is available under the name* `List<T>` *in the namespace* `FCSlib.Data.Collections`.

The list class is generic, so it can work with any type of object you want to store in it. To illustrate the API in this first iteration, here's a line of code that would instantiate a list with two integer items:

```
var list = new MyListStep1<int>(10, new MyListStep1<int>(20,
MyListStep1<int>.Empty));
```

As you can see, the list class itself is actually the type that stores a single item. It uses a field called `Head` for this purpose, which is common naming in functional programming. The rest of the list, from each element's point of view, is called the `Tail`. Eventually, a list is terminated by having an empty list item as its `Tail`. That's it!

There are a lot of extensions you can implement to make the list type a bit easier to use. The first one is a helper function commonly referred to as `Cons` (originating from the Lisp language and the term "construct"). `Cons` takes an element of the data type stored in a list, as well as a list of that same type, and prepends the new element to the list. Here it is:

```
public static MyListStep2<T> Cons(T element, MyListStep2<T> list) {
  if (list.IsEmpty)
    return new MyListStep2<T>(element);
  else
    return new MyListStep2<T>(element, list);
}
```

You can add an instance method into the mix, to make it easier to call Cons:

```
public MyListStep2<T> Cons(T element) {
  return MyListStep2<T>.Cons(element, this);
}
```

With this helper function, the line to create a list with two items now looks like this:

```
var list = new MyListStep2<int>(10).Cons(20);
```

It is possible to make this even easier by supporting conversion of existing .NET collection types and by passing a fixed list of values into a constructor. (You may wonder why the first constructor has both a fixed parameter and a params array — it's because the params array on its own would happily accept an empty parameter list, and by including the one fixed parameter, you require one or more parameters overall.)

```
public MyListStep3(T firstValue, params T[] values) {
  Head = firstValue;
  if (values.Length > 0) {
    MyListStep3<T> newtail = MyListStep3<T>.Empty;
    for (int i = values.Length - 1; i >= 0; i--)
      newtail = newtail.Cons(values[i]);
    Tail = newtail;
  }
  else
    Tail = MyListStep3<T>.Empty;
}

public MyListStep3(System.Collections.Generic.IEnumerable<T> source) {
  T[] sa = source.ToArray( );
  int sal = sa.Length;
  if (sal > 0) {
    Head = sa[0];
    Tail = MyListStep3<T>.Empty;
    for (int i = sal - 1; i > 0; i--)
      Tail = Tail.Cons(sa[i]);
  }
  else
    IsEmpty = true;
}
```

With the help of these two additional constructors, you can now create new lists like this:

```
var list = new MyListStep3<int>(10, 20, 30, 40);

var normalDotNetList = new List<int> { 10, 20, 30, 40 };
var listFromList = new MyListStep3<int>(normalDotNetList);
```

You can see that working with persistent data types is not a black and white decision. Using standard infrastructure like the collection interfaces supplied by the .NET Framework, it is easy to move from one space to the other and back. To facilitate the transfer of information out of your own list type, it makes sense to implement the interface IEnumerable<T> as well:

```
public class MyListStep4<T> : System.Collections.Generic.IEnumerable<T> {

  ...

  public System.Collections.Generic.IEnumerator<T> GetEnumerator( ) {
    for (var element = this; element != MyListStep4<T>.Empty; element =
      element.Tail)
        yield return element.Head;
  }

  System.Collections.IEnumerator System.Collections.IEnumerable.GetEnumerator( ) {
    return this.GetEnumerator( );
  }

...
```

Easy enough, and this allows you to iterate over your own list type, or pass it to the constructor of the .NET standard list type:

```
var list = new MyListStep4<int>(10, 20, 30, 40);

foreach (int i in list)
  Console.WriteLine(i);

Console.WriteLine(list);

var normalDotNetList = new List<int>(list);
```

The second Console.WriteLine line also utilizes a ToString() overload that outputs the entire list, for debugging purposes:

```
public override string ToString( ) {
  var result = "[";
  if (!IsEmpty)
    result +=
    Functional.FoldL1(
      (r, x) => r + ", " + x,
      Functional.Map(x => x.ToString( ), this));
  result += "]";
  return result;
}
```

As examples of more complex algorithms on the list, here are Append and Remove operations. Look at Append first, in an implementation that uses recursion:

```
public static List<T> AppendWithRecursion(List<T> one, List<T> other) {
  if (one.IsEmpty)
    return other;
  return Cons(one.Head, AppendWithRecursion(one.Tail, other));
}
```

Nice and elegant, it demonstrates the simplicity of the algorithm. Of course there's the usual problem with recursion when lists get long: you may see a stack overflow. For that reason, here's another implementation that doesn't look as nice, but doesn't use recursion:

```
public static List<T> Append(List<T> one, List<T> other) {
  if (one.IsEmpty)
    return other;
  List<T> newList = other;

  foreach (var element in one.Reverse( ))
    newList = newList.Cons(element);

  return newList;
}
```

Removing items is much more complicated. You have to move all the items aside that come before the one you want to remove, then drop that item itself, and prepend those items you moved aside. Figure 16-2 illustrates the necessary steps:

1. At this point the application has an outer scope reference to a list with five elements, while a separate unit of work is running with a reference to only three of those elements.

2. From the perspective of the outer scope, the element "3" has been removed. This has resulted in modified clones of "4" and "5" being created, which skip the "3" item, effectively removing it from that point of view. At the same time, the separate unit of work can still see the "3" just as before.

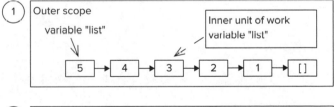

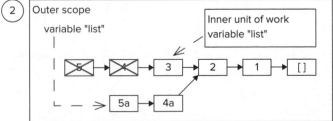

FIGURE 16-2: Persistent list remove

Here's the implementation:

```
public static List<T> Remove(List<T> list, T element) {
  var memory = List<T>.Empty;
  var temp = list;
  while (!temp.IsEmpty &&
```

```
      !System.Collections.Generic.EqualityComparer<T>.Default.Equals(
      temp.Head, element)) {
      memory = memory.Cons(temp.Head);
      temp = temp.Tail;
    }
    if (!temp.IsEmpty) {
      // forget the element itself
      temp = temp.Tail;
      // prepend the items we pushed aside
      foreach (var item in memory) {
        temp = temp.Cons(item);
      }
      return temp;
    }
    else
      // element wasn't found
      return list;
  }
```

All this functionality is implemented in the data type `FCSlib.Data.Collections.List<T>`. It follows here in its entirety to show how quickly and easily you can construct data types that adhere to the ideas of persistent data structures, but that are also fully compatible with standard .NET types. The result of the effort is a list type that has similar call semantics to those simple immutable types described in the first part of this chapter. Making any kind of modification to the list always involves a functional call, and instead of modifying anything in place, a new version of the list is returned by the call.

```
// this is the list I begin with
var list = new FCSColl::List<int>(10, 20, 30);
Console.WriteLine(list);

// adding an item is a function call:
var addedList = list.Cons(40);
Console.WriteLine(addedList);

// removing an item is also a function call:
var removedList = addedList.Remove(20);
Console.WriteLine(removedList);
```

The following code implements an `Order` type with a collection of `OrderLines`, extending the earlier `Product`/`OrderLine` example:

```
public class PersistentOrder {
  public readonly List<PersistentOrderLine> OrderLines;

  public decimal GetValue( ) {
    return Functional.FoldL((r, v) => r + v.GetValue( ), 0m, OrderLines);
  }

  public PersistentOrder(List<PersistentOrderLine> OrderLines) {
    this.OrderLines = OrderLines;
  }
}
```

Because OrderLines is now a persistent data type, the GetValue() calculation, which iterates over all the order lines, executes GetValue() for each of them, and then sums up the results, can do so without danger of data changes during the process.

Queue

Just like the list, the persistent queue data type is based on a clever, albeit quite simple, algorithm. It has two lists internally, "front" and "rear." Figure 16-3 shows a few steps detailing how these two lists work together to add and remove queue items.

1. You'll understand the specific state of the queue with four elements better after you've looked through all the steps. For now suffice it to say that the front list is the "start" of the queue (that is, when you pop off items, this is where they come from) and the rear list is a continuation of the front list, but in reverse order. In other words, if you popped off all the values until the queue was empty, you'd get 1, 2, 3, 4, in that order.

 Figure 16-3 leaves out the [] *empty list from the front and rear lists, for simplicity.*

2. Element 5 has been added to the queue. This works by using Cons on the rear list; the operation itself is called Snoc on the queue. (Yes, that's the reverse of Cons. Yes, really.)

3. Element 1 has been popped off the queue, that is, the Head element of the front list has been dropped.

4. Another element has been dropped from the queue. You may have expected this to result in an empty front list, and that is exactly what happens during this operation. But this special case is caught by the implementation logic of the queue, and the rear list is reversed and used as the new front list (the new rear list is then empty).

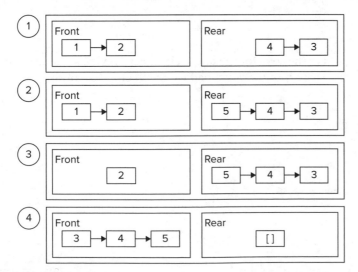

FIGURE 16-3: Persistent queue

Because the queue is based on the persistent list that was previously explained, one thing is immediately obvious: the queue is also a persistent data structure.

Here are the lines of code that would result in the preceding steps:

```
// getting to the step 1 state
var q = FCSColl::Queue<int>.Empty;
q = q.Snoc(11);
q = q.Snoc(1);
q = q.Snoc(2);
q = q.Tail;
q = q.Snoc(3);
q = q.Snoc(4);

// Now we have reached the state the figure shows in step 1
// For step 2, an item is added
q = q.Snoc(5);

// Step 3 removes an item
q = q.Tail;

// Step 4 removes another item
q = q.Tail;
```

In the demo application there is code that outputs the state of the queue after each individual operation. The result looks like this, as expected:

```
[f:[] r:[]]
[f:[11] r:[]]
[f:[11] r:[1]]
[f:[11] r:[2, 1]]
[f:[1, 2] r:[]]
[f:[1, 2] r:[3]]
[f:[1, 2] r:[4, 3]]
[f:[1, 2] r:[5, 4, 3]]
[f:[2] r:[5, 4, 3]]
[f:[3, 4, 5] r:[]]
```

Finally, following are the important parts of the code for the queue class. For brevity, some elements have been left out here; the complete code is part of the download for the book. Most of the elements have been described in this chapter.

```
public sealed class Queue<T> {
  private readonly List<T> f, r;

  // ... some constructor code cut

  public static Queue<T> Snoc(Queue<T> q, T e) {
    return CheckBalance(new Queue<T>(q.f, q.r.Cons(e)));
  }

  public Queue<T> Snoc(T e) {
    return Snoc(this, e);
```

```
    }

    private static Queue<T> CheckBalance(Queue<T> q) {
      if (q.f.IsEmpty)
        return new Queue<T>(new List<T>(Functional.Reverse(q.r)), List<T>.Empty);
      else
        return q;
    }

    public T Head {
      get {
        return f.Head;
      }
    }

    public Queue<T> Tail {
      get {
        return CheckBalance(new Queue<T>(f.Tail, r));
      }
    }

    public override string ToString( ) {
      return String.Format("[f:{0} r:{1}]", f, r);
    }
  }
```

Unbalanced Binary Tree

Like the list, an unbalanced binary tree is probably one of the types every programmer has written at one point, as part of algorithm 101. Also like the list, a persistent implementation of this type is in some ways significantly different from an imperative one.

By now you already know many of the basic ideas of persistent data types, so the tree structure as well as the simple insertion algorithm aren't going to contain any surprises:

Available for download on Wrox.com

```
public sealed class UnbalancedBinaryTree<T> : IEnumerable<T> {
  private readonly bool isEmpty;
  public bool IsEmpty { get { return isEmpty; } }

  private readonly UnbalancedBinaryTree<T> left;
  public UnbalancedBinaryTree<T> Left {
    get {
      return left;
    }
  }
  private readonly UnbalancedBinaryTree<T> right;
  public UnbalancedBinaryTree<T> Right {
    get {
      return right;
    }
  }
  private readonly T value;
  public T Value {
```

```
      get {
        return value;
      }
  }
  public static readonly UnbalancedBinaryTree<T> Empty =
    new UnbalancedBinaryTree<T>( );
  public UnbalancedBinaryTree( ) {
    isEmpty = true;
  }

  public UnbalancedBinaryTree(UnbalancedBinaryTree<T> left,
    T value, UnbalancedBinaryTree<T> right) {
    this.left = left;
    this.right = right;
    this.value = value;
  }

  public static UnbalancedBinaryTree<T> Insert(T value,
    UnbalancedBinaryTree<T> tree) {
    if (tree.IsEmpty) {
      return new UnbalancedBinaryTree<T>(Empty, value, Empty);
    }
    else {
      int compareResult = Comparer<T>.Default.Compare(value, tree.Value);
      if (compareResult < 0)
        return new UnbalancedBinaryTree<T>(
          Insert(value, tree.Left),
          tree.Value,
          tree.Right);
      else if (compareResult > 0)
        return new UnbalancedBinaryTree<T>(
          tree.Left,
          tree.Value,
          Insert(value, tree.Right));
      else
        return tree;
    }
  }
  public UnbalancedBinaryTree<T> Insert(T value) {
    return UnbalancedBinaryTree<T>.Insert(value, this);
  }
  ...
}
```

code snippet UnbalancedBinaryTree.cs

An interesting thing to observe in this simple example is that the .NET type system doesn't allow you to put a useful constraint on the type used with the tree. There is a logical constraint: only those types that can be compared using the Comparer<T> standard mechanism are going to work. But Comparer<T> tries at least two different interfaces to do its job: IComparable<T> and IComparable. It is impossible to put a constraint on the class that says "type T must implement either IComparable<T> or IComparable."

Even if a type supports comparison with Comparer<T>, that doesn't provide for great flexibility. When using data structures to store ordered data, it is a regular requirement to sort these according to a certain algorithm. Therefore the implementation of comparison logic on the basis of classes and interfaces is often not enough. Being able to pass in a delegate to perform the comparison would make much more sense, and the .NET Framework has a few different such delegates declared by default. But the generic comparison mechanism as supplied by Comparer<T>.Default doesn't provide any help — to create a generic class with flexible options for comparisons, you have to write quite a lot of code yourself to cover all the possibilities.

Because there are at least generic and non-generic variations of the IComparable interface to consider, it is practically impossible to use generic constraints with the UnbalancedBinaryTree<T> class. These shortcomings of the type system and the framework itself make a big difference compared to those of the typed functional languages that have a very strong type system (Haskell, for example).

Finally, using the UnbalancedBinaryTree<T> is very simple; it has the same functional API as the queue and the list before it. Here are a few lines of code for illustration:

```
var tree = FCSColl::UnbalancedBinaryTree<int>.Empty;
tree = tree.Insert(10);
tree = tree.Insert(5);
tree = tree.Insert(15);
tree = tree.Insert(1);
tree = tree.Insert(10);
Console.WriteLine(tree);
```

As you can see, the value 10 is inserted twice. The tree is implemented as a Set collection type, so it doesn't actually store a second value that is equal to one already in the collection. Therefore, the output from the last line is this:

```
[1, 5, 10, 15]
```

Red/Black Tree

The final example for persistent container data structures is a red/black tree implementation. This may not be something you've tried yet. It is based on a more complicated algorithm, which is interesting to see in a functional implementation.

How does the red/black tree work? Imagine each node in a usual binary search tree to have a color in addition to the value and left and right members that tree nodes usually have. The color can be either red or black. There are a number of rules that define how the nodes are colored, and which color combinations are allowed when looking at a parent node and its children. During insertion there is a balancing operation, which performs rotations on certain node combinations if it finds that the insertion operation violated one or more of the rules.

The point of this rather complicated mechanism is to balance the tree so that its depth is as small as possible for the number of items it contains. A tree of little depth can be searched faster than one of great depth, so the red/black tree optimizes access time using its color algorithm. The algorithm itself is well documented in computer science literature, as well as resources like Wikipedia.

The insertion function of the tree looks like this:

```
public static RedBlackTree<T> Insert(T value, RedBlackTree<T> tree) {
  Func<RedBlackTree<T>, RedBlackTree<T>> ins = null;
  ins = t => {
    if (t.IsEmpty)
      return new RedBlackTree<T>(Color.Red, Empty, value, Empty);
    var compareResult = Comparer<T>.Default.Compare(value, t.Value);
    if (compareResult < 0)
      return Balance(t.NodeColor, ins(t.Left), t.Value, t.Right);
    else if (compareResult > 0)
      return Balance(t.NodeColor, t.Left, t.Value, ins(t.Right));
    else
      return t;
  };

  var insResult = ins(tree);
  return new RedBlackTree<T>(Color.Black, insResult.Left,
    insResult.Value, insResult.Right);
}
```

This `Insert` function is quite close to that of the `UnbalancedBinaryTree`. One difference is that the `Balance` helper function is called in the right places. A second one is that internal recursion is used, which allows the final step of the function to be a "repainting" of the return tree as a black node. By using a nested delegate for the insertion step, the algorithm takes advantage of closures for the value; without closures, the value would have to be passed in as another parameter, which isn't desirable for simplicity of the recursion.

Here's the `Balance` function:

Available for
download on
Wrox.com

```
private static RedBlackTree<T> Balance(Color nodeColor,
  RedBlackTree<T> left, T value, RedBlackTree<T> right) {
  if (nodeColor == RedBlackTree<T>.Color.Black) {
    if (!(left.IsEmpty) &&
      left.NodeColor == RedBlackTree<T>.Color.Red &&
      !(left.Left.IsEmpty) &&
      left.Left.NodeColor == RedBlackTree<T>.Color.Red)
      return new RedBlackTree<T>(Color.Red,
        new RedBlackTree<T>(Color.Black,
          left.Left.Left, left.Left.Value, left.Left.Right),
        left.Value,
        new RedBlackTree<T>(Color.Black,
          left.Right, value, right));
    if (!(left.IsEmpty) &&
      left.NodeColor == RedBlackTree<T>.Color.Red &&
      !(left.Right.IsEmpty) &&
      left.Right.NodeColor == RedBlackTree<T>.Color.Red)
      return new RedBlackTree<T>(Color.Red,
        new RedBlackTree<T>(Color.Black,
          left.Left, left.Value, left.Right.Left),
        left.Right.Value,
        new RedBlackTree<T>(Color.Black,
          left.Right.Right, value, right));
```

```
        if (!(right.IsEmpty) &&
          right.NodeColor == RedBlackTree<T>.Color.Red &&
          !(right.Left.IsEmpty) &&
          right.Left.NodeColor == RedBlackTree<T>.Color.Red)
          return new RedBlackTree<T>(Color.Red,
            new RedBlackTree<T>(Color.Black,
              left, value, right.Left.Left),
            right.Left.Value,
            new RedBlackTree<T>(Color.Black,
              right.Left.Right, right.Value, right.Right));
        if (!(right.IsEmpty) &&
          right.NodeColor == RedBlackTree<T>.Color.Red &&
          !(right.Right.IsEmpty) &&
          right.Right.NodeColor == RedBlackTree<T>.Color.Red)
          return new RedBlackTree<T>(Color.Red,
            new RedBlackTree<T>(Color.Black,
              left, value, right.Left),
            right.Value,
            new RedBlackTree<T>(Color.Black,
              right.Right.Left, right.Right.Value, right.Right.Right));
    }

    return new RedBlackTree<T>(nodeColor, left, value, right);

}
```

code snippet RedBlackTree.cs

This is a quite impressive piece of code, which performs all the right operations to make sure that the red/black tree rules are no longer violated. However, the main reason why it is included here is to compare it to the implementation of the same balancing algorithm in Haskell:

```
balance B (T R (T R a x b) y c) z d = T R (T B a x b) y (T B c z d)
balance B (T R a x (T R b y c)) z d = T R (T B a x b) y (T B c z d)
balance B a x (T R (T R b y c) z d) = T R (T B a x b) y (T B c z d)
balance B a x (T R b y (T R c z d)) = T R (T B a x b) y (T B c z d)
balance color a x b = T color a x b
```

This is a very interesting example of how syntactic elements in functional languages are extremely concise and expressive. These five lines of Haskell code do exactly the same as the preceding C# code. It would go beyond the scope of this book to explain this in any more detail. The Haskell code is taken from Okasaki's book *Purely Functional Data Structures* — a highly recommended read if you are interested in more functional data structures and their implementations in functional languages!

Utilizing the RedBlackTree<T> in C# is the same as using the UnbalancedBinaryTree<T>:

```
var tree = FCSColl::RedBlackTree<int>.Empty;
tree = tree.Insert(10);
tree = tree.Insert(5);
tree = tree.Insert(15);
tree = tree.Insert(1);
```

```
tree = tree.Insert(10);
Console.WriteLine(tree);
```

The output in this class has been written to provide some debugging information about the colors of nodes as well. Here it is:

```
[B [B [R Empty] 1 [R Empty]] 5 [B [R Empty] 10 [R [R Empty] 15 [R Empty]]]]
```

ALTERNATIVES TO PERSISTENT DATA TYPES

This chapter has described immutable data and persistent types as a good solution to problems resulting from parallelization efforts. This is indeed a common scenario that leads developers to persistent data types. The APIs introduced by the types in this chapter also have a nicely functional feel about them, and the advantages in debugging and testing as well as general maintainability of persistent types are hard to describe in written text. It is strongly recommended that you try the approaches that were outlined because there's nothing like first-hand experience to understand how persistent types make many algorithms so much easier!

Nevertheless, the chapter shouldn't end without mentioning that for the purpose of parallelization there are other, mutable, collection types that can be considered. The .NET Framework, since the inclusion of the Parallel Extensions for .NET (short PFX) in version 4.0, contains a few such types. They can be found in the System.Collections.Concurrent namespace.

These types differ from collection types in old .NET versions because they implement thread safety in different ways. The history of this is actually interesting: in .NET 1.0, collections had the means to be thread-safe, through the Synchronized property. The pattern was not a good one, though, because it meant that the entire collection would always be locked whenever it was being accessed from one thread .NET 2.0 introduced all sorts of new collection types, which were generically typed. This was a great success with developers, but the problem was that these types had been implemented without any support for thread-safety! In .NET 4.0, matters have finally improved, and the System.Collections.Concurrent namespace has a few collection types that are both thread-safe and generically typed, and they employ much cleverer algorithms for thread-safety than their .NET 1.0 counterparts, thereby reducing the overhead of using them.

Some of the new classes are thread-safe through locking, but they use more specialized access control mechanisms than the .NET 1.0 collections did. This subject was mentioned earlier; it means that the collections are optimized for specific use cases, which are detailed in Microsoft's documentation. You should understand how a given collection type performs synchronization before you use it, at least if your code is in any way performance sensitive.

There are currently two types of collections that use yet another mechanism for synchronization. They utilize a class called Interlocked (in the System.Threading namespace since old .NET 1.0 days), which can take advantage of certain CPU-level features of modern computers, to implement very basic operations on variables in a way that is atomic. The operations that can be performed in this manner are restricted to a certain set, including incrementing and decrementing values as well as changing a variable of basic type, like a pointer or an integer, from one value to another. On the basis of this functionality it is possible to implement so-called lock-less algorithms. This is another big research area and you have a chance to dip into it with the `Interlocked` class as well as the new .NET 4.0 collection classes.

SUMMARY

You have seen various applications of immutable, persistent data types in this chapter, small ones and large ones. Some of the approaches derived from immutable data in functional environments are easily usable in C#, others are a bit more complex. More than many other individual disciplines, working with immutable data is something that often shows its strengths only after you've tried it out yourself. Fortunately that's easy to do: Most programmers regularly work with data that doesn't or can't change, but they never make the steps to formalize that fact. The next time you find yourself in that situation, consider using the techniques outlined in this chapter and see for yourself.

17

Monads

WHAT'S IN THIS CHAPTER?

➤ What's in a typeclass

➤ What's in a monad

➤ Two sample monads

➤ Why LINQ doesn't do it for monads

Monads are a construct that is very interesting, mentioned frequently when people discuss functional programming, and forms the basis of many mechanisms found in functional languages. Haskell especially uses monads a lot, and it has been said that you need to understand monads to understand Haskell. Whether that's true or not, Haskell is a language that surfaces the monad as a first class construct, which makes it particularly simple to explain what they are. You will find some Haskell examples in this chapter, and even without knowing Haskell, these should be easy enough to follow.

Monads are interesting because once you understand their nature, you will find that many APIs you use today, even in C#, can be understood and represented as monads. Unfortunately, mainstream imperative languages like C# haven't made the step to a formal definition of monad mechanisms. Current .NET and C# implementations of monadic patterns are typically quite loose, and the lack of the kind of special syntax provided in Haskell, or even in F#, means that the code that utilizes monadic APIs remains quite verbose.

Before getting started with the real explanations, my editors insist I try for a basic definition of monads. Here's my best try: A monad is a description of a particular class of types that can be grouped by a certain commonality of their behavior, coupled with feature implementations related to the class. Across types belonging to the class, you can chain operations on instances of those types, with the monad providing a "side channel" for information not contained directly in the types. A formal declaration of Monad itself, such as provided in Haskell (but unfortunately impossible in C#), allows for generalized handling of these already very abstract concepts.

WHAT'S IN A TYPECLASS?

Monads are an advanced abstraction mechanism, and the abstraction in Haskell is based on the idea of *typeclasses* (typeclasses, not type classes). Typeclasses are an abstraction that C# and many other object oriented languages don't have. Look at the following examples to understand what they do.

Say you have your own data type — a discriminated union in Haskell, very similar to an enum in .NET:

```
data Food = Pasta | Pizza | Chips
```

You also have a function that can check whether two given values of type Food are considered equal:

```
isEqualFood :: Food -> Food -> Bool
isEqualFood Pasta Pasta = True
isEqualFood Pizza Pizza = True
isEqualFood Chips Chips = True
isEqualFood _ _ = False
```

The variations of the function declare the three special cases explicitly in which the two given parameters are the same — in these cases the result is True. In all other cases, denoted by the use of the wildcard operator _, the result is False.

Using the function on a Haskell console at this stage would render these results:

```
Main> isEqualFood Pizza Chips
False
Main> isEqualFood Pizza Pizza
True
Main>
```

Of course, a check for equality of two values is something you want to be able to do with most data types. In other words, there is a group, a class of types, for which comparing for equality makes sense. In Haskell, a typeclass can be used to describe that class of types. Here's how a typeclass for the purpose of equality comparison could be written:

```
class MyEq a where
  isEqual :: a -> a -> Bool
  isEqual x y = not (isNotEqual x y)

  isNotEqual :: a -> a -> Bool
  isNotEqual x y = not (isEqual x y)
```

The typeclass declares that there should be two functions called isEqual and isNotEqual. Each of these functions takes two parameters of type a (this is generic notation in Haskell; it's like talking about type T in C#) and returns a Bool. The typeclass also does something it can optionally do: it implements both functions. As you can see, they are both implemented in terms of the other, so with this implementation alone, none of them would actually work. The advantage of using such a default implementation pattern is that a programmer who implements the typeclass for a particular type (as you will see later) has a choice of implementing just one of the two functions and the other one will then work automatically.

With the preceding declaration alone, the typeclass already makes its functions available. You can't call them yet because there are no instances:

```
Main> isEqual Pizza Pizza

<interactive>:1:0:
    No instance for (MyEq Food)
      arising from a use of `isEqual' at <interactive>:1:0-18
    Possible fix: add an instance declaration for (MyEq Food)
    In the expression: isEqual Pizza Pizza
    In the definition of `it': it = isEqual Pizza Pizza
Main>
```

It is possible, however, to see the type of the isEqual function:

```
Main> :type isEqual
isEqual :: (MyEq a) => a -> a -> Bool
Main>
```

You need to create instances of a typeclass for specific types to declare "this type is now among those which can do what is required by this typeclass" — in this case, perform equality comparisons. Here's a typeclass instance of MyEq, for the type Food:

```
instance MyEq Food where
  isEqual Pasta Pasta = True
  isEqual Pizza Pizza = True
  isEqual Chips Chips = True
  isEqual _ _ = False
```

In fact, because you already have the function isEqualFood, which performs equality comparisons for the Food data type, you could just refer to that function in the typeclass instance:

```
instance MyEq Food where
  isEqual = isEqualFood
```

Now that the instance exists, it is possible to compare values of type Food through the MyEq typeclass, using isEqual instead of isEqualFood:

```
ain> isEqual Pizza Chips
False
Main> isEqual Pizza Pizza
True
Main>
```

It is also possible to create typeclass instances of MyEq for other types, including standard types:

```
instance MyEq Bool where
  isEqual True True = True
```

```
    isEqual False False = True
    isEqual _ _ = False

Main> isEqual True True
True
Main> isEqual True False
False
Main>
```

For equality comparison, Haskell already has a typeclass, which is called `Eq`. It is very similar to `MyEq`, with the major exception that the comparison function itself is not called `isEqual`, instead it is called `(==)`. The operator `==` itself is an infix function in Haskell, declared by the typeclass `Eq`. In the same way, lots of standard behavior is described in typeclasses.

Up to this point, you might associate typeclasses with two constructs from the object oriented world: interfaces and abstract base classes. In reality there are many differences.

It is correct that typeclasses, similar to interfaces, can declare a number of functions that need to be available for the typeclass to be satisfied. However, interfaces can't contain implementation code. Abstract base classes can contain code and specify implementation requirements at the same time, but a data type that fulfils the contract defined by an abstract base class must be derived from that base class.

As the example `MyEq` instance for the `Bool` type has shown, typeclass instances can be created outside of, and totally independent from, the type to which they apply. There are three clearly separated tasks in fully implementing a type with typeclass support:

1. Obtain a type — create it, or perhaps you've already got it.

2. Decide on a typeclass, that is, a behavior you think this type should support — again, perhaps you need to create that typeclass, but you can just use one somebody else has already created.

3. Create a typeclass instance that defines how, with the help of which functions, the type is going to satisfy the requirements of the typeclass.

The freedom resulting from the separation of these three steps is one of the most important reasons for the power of typeclasses.

Another reason is that the type inference mechanisms in the Haskell compiler can use typeclasses to infer, instead of actual types. For instance, here's a simple add function in Haskell, and its inferred type information from the console:

```
add x y = x + y

...

Main> :type add
add :: Num a => a -> a -> a
Main>
```

The type information indicates that the type a, which is the type of both arguments as well as the return value for the add function, has a constraint: it needs to be a member of the typeclass Num. In other words, it needs to be part of the class of types that support the requirements of the Num typeclass. The reason for this is that Haskell finds the function (+), the infix operator, defined in the typeclass Num, so it infers that the types used as arguments to that function must be members of Num.

As a result of this, it's possible to use the add function with various different types:

```
Main> add 10 20
30
Main> add 7.6 3.9
11.5
```

That isn't possible in .NET because every variable must have a known type on the CLR level. Of course that type can be an interface, but interfaces can't implement operators, and they are also not inferred in the same way, automatically.

WHAT'S IN A MONAD?

In Haskell, Monad is a typeclass. Here's what it looks like:

```
class Monad m where
  (>>=) :: m a -> (a -> m b) -> m b
  return :: a -> m a
```

Granted, at a glance this doesn't explain much. But the important thing is to recognize that a monad *is* a particular typeclass, in other words, Monad describes a particular class of types. It is the class of types that support the two rather cryptic functions (>>=) (this is usually pronounced "bind") and return.

To illustrate the requirements that are declared by the Monad typeclass, here's an implementation of a C# interface with a very similar set of two functions:

```
public interface IMonad<A> {
  IMonad<A> Return(A val);
  IMonad<b> Bind<b>(Func<A, IMonad<b>> g);
}
```

That looks much simpler! The Return function takes a value of type A and returns an IMonad<A>. It wraps the value in the monad, so to speak. The Bind function takes a delegate as an argument, which can receive a value of type A and returns an IMonad<B>. Bind itself also returns an IMonad<B>. In reality this interface is usually not used because the formalization it provides is regarded as too strict. For example, the process of wrapping a value in a monad, as described earlier by the Return function, might be implemented as a constructor call in object oriented C#. The two functions also could be implemented as static methods, perhaps extension methods, elsewhere, instead of being instance methods in the type itself.

To summarize the theoretical part: a monad is an abstraction of a certain system, consisting of some sort of a data encapsulation (hence the wrapping of A in IMonad<A>), and a declared set of functions that work with that particular data.

WHY DO A WHOLE ABSTRACTION?

As usual, concrete examples of the abstraction will help you understand why an abstraction makes sense. In Haskell there's a monad called Maybe, which will be the subject of the first example. Consider this code:

```
var tree = new FCSColl::UnbalancedBinaryTree<string>( );
tree = tree.Insert("Paul");
tree = tree.Insert("Adam");
tree = tree.Insert("Bernie");
tree = tree.Insert("Willy");
tree = tree.Insert("Suzie");
Console.WriteLine(tree);
```

This instantiates an immutable tree with a few string values. You could now try to access those values by following the path along the tree branches:

```
Console.WriteLine(tree.Left.Left.Left.Value);
```

The problem is that this is unsafe. In the example, the structure of the tree would be such that the third Left evaluation throws an exception because there's no branch to follow at that point. To be on the safe side, you'd have to write a much more verbose algorithm:

```
static string GetThirdLeftChild(FCSColl::UnbalancedBinaryTree<string> tree) {
  if (tree != null) {
    if (tree.Left != null) {
      if (tree.Left.Left != null) {
        if (tree.Left.Left.Left != null) {
          return tree.Left.Left.Left.Value;
        }
        else {
          return "No such child";
        }
      }
      else {
        return "No such child";
      }
    }
    else {
      return "No such child";
    }
  }
  else {
    return "No such child";
  }
}
```

Following is a little helper class called `Maybe<T>`. It's is rather similar to the type `Option<T>` in Chapter 15, although without all the bells and whistles.

```
public class Maybe<T> {
  public static readonly Maybe<T> Empty = new Maybe<T>( );
  private readonly T val;
  public T Value { get { return val; } }
  private readonly bool isEmpty;
  public bool IsEmpty { get { return isEmpty; } }
  public bool HasValue { get { return !isEmpty; } }

  public Maybe(T val) {
    this.val = val;
  }

  private Maybe( ) {
    this.isEmpty = true;
  }
}
```

The class encapsulates a simple value, and allows you to state that there is no actual value associated with an instance of `Maybe<T>`. With the help of this extension method, it can be made easier to use:

```
public static class MaybeHelpers {
  public static Maybe<T> ToMaybe<T>(this T val) {
    return new Maybe<T>(val);
  }
}
```

As a result, you could implement the helper function that retrieves the "third left child" like this:

```
static Maybe<string> GetMaybeThirdLeftChild(FCSColl::UnbalancedBinaryTree<string>
tree) {
  if (tree != null) {
    if (tree.Left != null) {
      if (tree.Left.Left != null) {
        if (tree.Left.Left.Left != null) {
          return tree.Left.Left.Left.Value.ToMaybe( );
        }
        else {
          return Maybe<string>.Empty;
        }
      }
      else {
        return Maybe<string>.Empty;
      }
    }
    else {
      return Maybe<string>.Empty;
    }
  }
}
```

```
    else {
      return Maybe<string>.Empty;
    }
  }
```

Given the declaration of the `Maybe<T>` type or the `Option<T>` type, this is probably what most programmers imagine at first. This implementation doesn't gain much — the main difference is that there's now a standard value to say "the item could not be retrieved," and of course you could have done that with null as well. The algorithm itself is still just as complex as before.

With the `Monad` declaration in mind, add this method to the `Maybe<T>` class:

```
public Maybe<R> Bind<R>(Func<T, Maybe<R>> g) {
  return IsEmpty ? Maybe<R>.Empty : g(Value);
}
```

The signature here is the same as in the earlier hypothetical `IMonad<T>` interface. For simplicity, the name `Bind` has been kept, but the method could be called anything you like. The important thing is that the functionality of `Bind` is provided for the type `Maybe<T>`. There's also already a `Return` implementation for `Maybe<T>`, in the form of the constructor: `public Maybe(T val)`. So the type `Maybe<T>` satisfies the requirements of the Haskell monad typeclass now.

The implementation of `Bind` is quite simple in this case. If the current `Maybe<T>` instance is empty, an empty value is returned immediately. Otherwise, the delegate is called with the current value, and the return value from the delegate is then returned.

Following is the next implementation of the method that retrieves the "third left child" from the tree. This time it uses `Bind` to chain operations together:

```
static Maybe<FCSColl::UnbalancedBinaryTree<string>>
  GetMonadicThirdLeftChild(FCSColl::UnbalancedBinaryTree<string> tree) {
  return tree.ToNotNullMaybe().
    Bind(t => t.Left.ToNotNullMaybe( )).
    Bind(t => t.Left.ToNotNullMaybe( )).
    Bind(t => t.Left.ToNotNullMaybe( ));
}
```

There's also one more utility function being used. Added as an extension method to the `MaybeHelpers` class, here it is:

```
public static Maybe<T> ToNotNullMaybe<T>(this T val) where T : class {
  return val != null ? val.ToMaybe( ) : Maybe<T>.Empty;
}
```

`ToNotNullMaybe<T>` is very simple: it works only with reference types, and if a given value is null, it returns an empty `Maybe<T>`, otherwise it returns a `Maybe<T>` encapsulating the value. With the help of this utility function, the nested checks of the variables `tree`, `tree.Left`, `tree.Left.Left`, and so on become clean steps in a schema based on repeated applications of the `Bind` function. Each step gets the result from the previous step passed in, and each step is responsible only for one simple check, which happens to be implemented by the `ToNotNullMaybe` function. Here's a second example of calling this API, which actually finds a value in the tree:

```
var bernie =
  tree.ToNotNullMaybe( ).
    Bind(t => t.Left.ToNotNullMaybe( )).
    Bind(t => t.Right.ToNotNullMaybe( ));
Console.WriteLine(bernie.HasValue ? bernie.Value.Value : "No Bernie found");
```

Take a step back and think about it. The monad abstraction is that a data type should exist that wraps other data, and that there should be functions declared that can perform (a) the wrapping itself, and (b) the binding, that is, chaining together of operations on the data type. For the `Maybe<T>` type, binding is implemented according to a simple rule: if the chain returns an empty value at some point, further steps in the chain are ignored and an empty value is returned instead. `Maybe<T>` has now become a monad.

A SECOND MONAD: LOGGING

Haskell uses monads for a lot of things, but the basic reason is one important thing: in Haskell, functions are always free from side effects. As a result, all functions that logically do anything apart from the things allowed by functional programming (basically calculate a result based on their arguments and return it) must encode the results of whatever they did in their return values. The notion of monads revolves around the idea of having wrappers of data, chained together in a type-safe manner. Those wrappers usually store information in addition to the data itself — like the `IsEmpty` flag in the case of the `Maybe` monad.

One situation where programmers find themselves wanting to create side effects is the debug scenario in which information needs to be written out by a function that is otherwise functionally pure. How do you allow such a function to return not just its actual return value, but also some debug output? Why, with a monad of course!

Here is an implementation for the class `Logger<T>`, which is a monad:

Available for download on Wrox.com

```
public class Logger<T> {
  private readonly FCSColl::List<string> outputLines;

  private readonly T val;
  public T Value { get { return val; } }

  public Logger(T val, FCSColl::List<string> outputLines) {
    this.val = val;
    this.outputLines = outputLines;
  }

  public Logger(T val, string message) :
    this(val, new FCSColl::List<string>(message)) { }
  public Logger(T val) : this(val, FCSColl::List<string>.Empty) { }

  public string LogOutput( ) {
```

```
        var builder = new StringBuilder( );
        foreach (string outputLine in outputLines)
          builder.AppendLine(outputLine);
        return builder.ToString( );
      }

      public Logger<R> Bind<R>(Func<T, Logger<R>> g) {
        var r = g(val);
        return new Logger<R>(r.Value, outputLines.Append(r.outputLines));
      }
    }
```

code snippet Logger.cs

There are also three helper methods for `Logger`:

```
public static class LoggerHelpers {
  public static Logger<T> ToLogger<T>(this T val) {
    return new Logger<T>(val);
  }

  public static Logger<T> ToLogger<T>(this T val, string message) {
    return new Logger<T>(val, message);
  }

  public static Logger<T> ToLogger<T>(this T val, string format, params object[] args) {
    return new Logger<T>(val, String.Format(format, args));
  }
}
```

`Logger` implementation is straightforward. Like the `Maybe` monad, it stores a computation value, but extends the information by adding its own management information. In the case of `Logger`, this is a list of output lines. `Logger` has the capability to construct a complete text from these output lines, which happens when logging needs to take place. Finally, the `Bind` method is simple: call the delegate that represents the next function in the chain. Append the resulting log output to the log output that has been accumulated up to this point, and return a new `Logger` instance with the return value from the chained function and the combined log output list.

Here's an example of using the `Logger` monad:

```
private static void Logger( ) {
  var orders = new List<Order> {
    new Order{ Date =new DateTime(2010,6,3), Value = 29.9m},
    new Order{ Date =new DateTime(2010,6,3), Value = 18.6m},
    new Order{ Date =new DateTime(2010,6,4), Value = 119.99m},
    new Order{ Date =new DateTime(2010,7,1), Value = 3.99m},
    new Order{ Date =new DateTime(2010,7,2), Value = 47.62m},
    new Order{ Date =new DateTime(2010,7,3), Value = 99.99m}
  };

  var average =
    orders.ToLogger("Starting with a list of {0} orders", orders.Count()).
```

```
        Bind(l => Functional.Filter(o => o.Date >= new DateTime(2010, 7, 1), l).ToLogger(
            "Got list with {0} items, filtering...", l.Count())).
        Bind(l => l.Average(o => o.Value).ToLogger(
            "Calculating average for list with remaining {0} items...", l.Count()));

    Console.WriteLine("Result: " + average.Value);

    Console.WriteLine( "-------- Log Output:");
    Console.Write(average.LogOutput( ));
}
```

Starting with a list of `Order` objects, the sequence of steps calls `Bind` twice to execute first a filtering operation using `Functional.Filter` and second, the LINQ `Average` function to calculate the average order value after the date of July 1, 2010. Each of the steps calls `ToLogger()` with some information, which gets stored away for later evaluation with the help of the Logger Monad. The accumulated output is retrieved later from the `LogOutput` function — clearly separated in the demo code from the process of retrieving the actual result of the calculation. Here's the output from the demo code:

```
Result: 50.5333333333333333333333333333
-------- Log Output:
Starting with a list of 6 orders
Got list with 6 items, filtering...
Calculating average for list with remaining 3 items...
```

SYNTACTIC SUGAR

It would certainly be possible to make the `Logger` API a bit nicer. For a start, you could try to think of a better name for the `Bind` operation. When designing monads, it's always advantageous to name the functions so they make sense within the context of what the monad does. `Bind` is just a generic name that is rarely meaningful.

On the other hand, it is unfortunately not possible to change the semantics of the API in C# — you will always have to chain calls like in the sample, pass in lambdas, and so on — things that not every programmer may find easy to read or write.

When it comes to applying monads to everyday situations, this is where languages like Haskell and even F# have big advantages, because they have special syntax. In Haskell, a chain is built using the >>= operator mentioned before, which results in a sequence that is a little easier to understand. What's more, there is also special de-sugaring support for a simple block construct: write a sequence of commands within a block encapsulated with `do{...}`, and the compiler inserts the >>= calls automatically to create the chain. F# offers the same with its workflow syntax. Both languages also have a lot of variants of the described mechanisms for added flexibility and ease of use.

In C#, such de-sugaring syntax exists only in one place, which is LINQ. The compiler understands the LINQ expression syntax and translates it into calls to extension methods (more about the details of this in Chapter 21). The C# language specification describes the query expression pattern, which summarizes all the methods that are used by the de-sugaring process performed by the compiler on behalf of LINQ. This is as close as C# gets to typeclasses, and the de-sugaring is not extensible.

BINDING WITH SELECTMANY?

Check out the various functions made available to LINQ by the `System.Linq.Enumerable` class and you might notice a particular overload of the `SelectMany` method:

```
public static IEnumerable<TResult> SelectMany<TSource, TResult>(
    this IEnumerable<TSource> source, Func<TSource, IEnumerable<TResult>> selector);
```

`SelectMany` is one of the methods specified in the query expression pattern, but this is not that particular overload. In fact, this overload is not documented as being used by the de-sugaring at all. You are free to call it yourself, but the compiler won't do it for you. The overload is interesting because it has the exact same signature as the monad `Bind`, assuming that your monad is called `IEnumerable`.

The following lines of code implement an operation that takes two `Maybe<int>` values and tries to add them — of course this will only work if both values are not empty:

```
var result1 = 5.ToMaybe( ).
    Bind<int>(v => Maybe<int>.Empty.Bind<int>(v2 => (v + v2).ToMaybe( )));
```

A `SelectMany` implementation with the `Bind` signature can be added easily to the `MaybeHelpers` class:

```
public static Maybe<R> SelectMany<T, R>(this Maybe<T> m, Func<T, Maybe<R>> g) {
    return m.Bind(g);
}
```

As a result, it is now possible to use `SelectMany` instead of `Bind`, like this:

```
var result2 = 5.ToMaybe( ).SelectMany<int, int>(
  v => Maybe<int>.Empty.SelectMany<int, int>(
    v2 => (v + v2).ToMaybe( )));
Console.WriteLine("Result 2: " +
  (result2.HasValue ? result2.Value.ToString( ) : "None"));
```

This would be great if LINQ was going to translate a query expression into calls to this `SelectMany` overload. Unfortunately, as mentioned previously, that doesn't happen. But here's a `SelectMany` implementation with a different signature, which can also be implemented for the `Maybe` monad:

```
public static Maybe<R> SelectMany<T, TCollection, R>(
      this Maybe<T> source,
      Func<T, Maybe<TCollection>> collectionSelector,
      Func<T, TCollection, R> resultSelector) {
  if (source.IsEmpty)
    return Maybe<R>.Empty;
```

```
    var x = source.Bind(collectionSelector);
    if (x.IsEmpty)
      return Maybe<R>.Empty;
    var r = resultSelector(source.Value, x.Value);
    return r.ToMaybe( );
}
```

The important difference is that this is an overload used by the de-sugaring process, in the case where your query expression uses two `from` clauses. Like in this code:

```
var result3 =
  from x in 5.ToMaybe( )
  from y in Maybe<int>.Empty
  select (x + y);
Console.WriteLine("Result 3: " +
  (result3.HasValue ? result3.Value.ToString( ) : "None"));

var result4 =
  from x in Maybe<int>.Empty
  from y in 5.ToMaybe( )
  select (x + y);
Console.WriteLine("Result 4: " +
  (result4.HasValue ? result4.Value.ToString( ) : "None"));

var result5 =
  from x in 5.ToMaybe( )
  from y in 7.ToMaybe( )
  select (x + y);
Console.WriteLine("Result 5: " +
  (result5.HasValue ? result5.Value.ToString( ) : "None"));
```

Each of these blocks executes one addition operation, which works with `Maybe<int>` values. The first two return `Maybe<int>.Empty`, the final one returns a `Maybe<int>` with value 12. By adapting the monad pattern implementation to the mechanisms implemented by LINQ, you can make use of the standard de-sugaring process to an extent.

This doesn't take you very far. The syntax implemented for LINQ was constructed to be intuitive for the use case of querying data, and the keywords were selected to be close to SQL. This syntax doesn't lend itself particularly well to more generalized monads, and even in the demo it is a stretch. In other cases it doesn't make sense to try to squeeze a given monad into the mold given by LINQ.

SUMMARY

Monads are an interesting topic, and this chapter gave you an understanding of what they are and how they are relevant. The fact remains that C# doesn't lend itself well to programming with monads — some concepts can be adopted, but for many purposes monads are cumbersome to use. Nevertheless, I made the decision to include this chapter because monads are such an important idea in functional programming, and the basic understanding you have gained will be useful to any further research you may do in this area.

PART IV

Putting Functional Programming into Action

18

Integrating Functional Programming Approaches

WHAT'S IN THIS CHAPTER?

➤ Functional approaches in refactoring

➤ Writing new code

➤ Finding Likely Candidates for Functional Programming

With all the technical background sorted out in the previous parts of this book, one important challenge remains: applying all those ideas to the everyday scenarios that you face in your work.

This is somewhat similar to learning a new programming language. All programmers have done it before. The first step is to try to remember some of the unfamiliar syntax constructs, so they come readily to mind when a particular element is called for while writing code. The second step is to start thinking the way that new language works. Sometimes different languages have different philosophies. A particular solution that you can come up with quickly may work, but at the same time it may be very different from the solution a more experienced programmer of the same language would choose. In extreme cases of course, languages can differ so drastically that without the right mindset it is impossible to achieve any meaningful results.

Applying functional programming ideas to C# seems easy at first because it isn't necessary to learn the syntactical basics of a new language. The elements of the language, the tools, are familiar, so you can focus on the philosophy alone. It seems like this should be half the work, but in reality that's not always true. The problem is that there's always a way out; the fallback of the old, familiar approaches is always available. It's a temptation, and there's nothing there to enforce discipline. Those extreme cases of unfamiliar languages have that one big advantage: when you start working with them, you can only either keep going until you have that mental breakthrough you're looking for, or you can drop them. There's no in-between.

With functional programming in C#, there's a lot of in between. In fact, in between is often the name of the game. The C# language and the .NET platform are a hybrid world today, and sticking to one true path is never going to deliver optimal results.

You need to decide how you want to write code for each little part, module, and unit, and you need to revisit your decisions again and again to confirm you're doing the right thing. The advantage of hybrid platforms is that they give you flexibility. They allow you to choose and adjust your tools so you can do the best job possible. At the same time, these characteristics are also the greatest disadvantages of hybrid platforms. If you're not prepared to make an informed decision, you are losing the flexibility advantage!

REFACTORING

A very large part of all the code that programmers work on exists already. Even on the .NET platform, code has been written now for almost ten years. More importantly, a large part of the code that was written in the C# language isn't really new code. It's new in that it was written from scratch in C#, but it was following the exact same ideas that the programmers used before they started writing C# code. These are the basic ideas of object oriented systems, patterns ranging from simple class hierarchy structures to enterprise-level multitier data exchange, ideas that were favored on platforms like MFC, Java, Delphi, and many others.

Refactoring — that is, the process of making structural code changes to promote reuse and maintainability — is a necessity for many reasons. Every programmer refactors continually, which can be a healthy evolutionary process that leads to better software quality over time. Modern software development methodologies such as Agile approaches favor refactoring as a prescribed technique to be used during the development cycle. "Red, Green, Refactor" is sometimes called the mantra of test-driven development (TDD).

The core of refactoring is the idea of making changes to existing code without changing the outcome of that code. You can look at this from far away or close up, and the definition may change a bit. While you are refactoring the content of a single method, for example, the outcome you're aiming not to change may be the return type and value of the method. On the other hand, you can also refactor a larger system, in which case the mesh of single methods and their return types and values may well be subject to change. Whatever you do, you need to make sure that your goal of leaving the outcome unchanged is reached, which usually involves automated testing on many different levels.

This book won't cover any more about refactoring in general. There are many publications available about that topic. In the context of functional programming ideas in C#, the important points are these:

➤   You refactor anyway.

➤   Refactoring is a well-defined idea with associated techniques that make it a safe practice.

➤   Refactoring is the perfect vehicle for you to start applying functional ideas selectively to particular parts of your code while making sure nothing is broken.

The sample solution for this chapter contains two separate example projects, which demonstrate some aspects of refactoring existing code. One of the projects is an abstract implementation of a small business application use case, the other is an implementation of a Mandelbrot fractal calculation algorithm, to represent a more scientific scenario. Both examples have several stages, which are represented in different projects so you can follow along step by step.

List Filtering with a Windows Forms UI

The first stage of the first example can be found in the aptly named project ShowFilteredListUgly, contained in the solution folder Show Filtered List. Run the project and it comes up with a Windows Forms user interface that displays a list of data — just names in this case — in a list box. The form includes an edit field in which you can enter a string to filter the list.

For simplicity, the code for this example is contained entirely in the file `Form1.cs`, the code-behind file for the visual Form-derived class. The first few lines below the constructor declaration declare a few class-level fields:

```
Person[] people;
const int maxPeople = 10;
Person[] displayPeople;
int displayCount;
```

Arrays are used to store the source data itself as well as a list of those people who are presently (according to the current filter settings) visible in the UI. A constant value is defined for the maximum number of people to be contained in the source array, and a variable for the number of people currently visible.

Moving along, the `InitData` function creates some test data in the people array, and a `ResetDisplayPeople` function initializes the `displayPeople` to the same basic state:

```
private void InitData( ) {
  people = new Person[maxPeople];
  people[0] = new Person { Name = "Anna" };
  people[1] = new Person { Name = "Chris" };
  people[2] = new Person { Name = "Willy" };
  people[3] = new Person { Name = "Hugh" };
  people[4] = new Person { Name = "Steve" };
  people[5] = new Person { Name = "Betty" };
  people[6] = new Person { Name = "Carla" };
  people[7] = new Person { Name = "John" };
  people[8] = new Person { Name = "Pete" };
  people[9] = new Person { Name = "Susan" };
  displayPeople = new Person[maxPeople];
  ResetDisplayPeople( );
}

private void ResetDisplayPeople( ) {
  displayCount = people.Length;
  for (int i = 0; i < displayCount; i++)
    displayPeople[i] = people[i];
}
```

The next method, `UpdateUI`, makes the elements from the `displayPeople` array visible in the UI by creating the corresponding items in the list box.

```
private void UpdateUI( ) {
  DisplayListBox.Items.Clear( );
  for (int i = 0; i < displayCount; i++)
    DisplayListBox.Items.Add(displayPeople[i]);
}
```

The logic that's executed when the user clicks the filtering button is implemented in the event handler for the button click event:

```
private void button1_Click(object sender, EventArgs e) {
  string filter = FilterTextBox.Text;
  if (filter != null && filter != "")
    FilterData(filter);
  else
    ResetDisplayPeople( );
  UpdateUI( );
}
```

And finally there's one method that implements the filtering logic itself:

```
private void FilterData(string filter) {
  int filteredCount = 0;
  for (int i = 0; i < maxPeople; i++)
    if (people[i].Name.Contains(filter))
      displayPeople[filteredCount++] = people[i];
  displayCount = filteredCount;
}
```

Each of these methods is very straightforward and doesn't require further explanation.

Of course there are several reasons why this little application seems a bit peculiar at first glance. The most striking ones are probably the use of arrays for data storage, and the fact that data seems to be copied around quite a bit. The latter is a consequence of the decision not to use data binding.

These implementation details may strike you as a bit outdated on the .NET platform, but that doesn't make them all too uncommon. Most programmers have probably written code like this at one time or another, and depending on the platforms and languages you work with, you may well write code today without thinking twice about it. The decision to go with arrays instead of List<T> and to do without data binding was made to focus on the exact algorithms at the core of this application. After all, an array is basically a low-level representation of a block of data somewhere in computer memory, and any other higher level API still needs to store the same data in the same memory. Data binding is a nice API to automate the process of transferring data to and from the UI, but in the end the list box in this example is a Windows control and it needs its elements created at some point, whether that happens with the help of automatic data binding or not.

The real focus of this example should be on the business logic algorithm, and as a consequence of that, on the choice of data storage location. The business logic is implemented in the `FilterData` method. Checking for a string to be contained in another string is, of course, one of the easiest possible scenarios, but it is representative of any real-world filtering operation you may perform in your own applications. This example filters for names with an "a" in them while your application may be filtering for those customers who are in the top 10 percent of the list of customers who spent at least a million dollars last year for services related to category C contracts. The point is that it doesn't matter what you're filtering for — there are reasonable assumptions that the filtering operation can be quite complex and that it might have to deal with large numbers of objects.

For these reasons, it would be good to be able to consider parallelizing the implementation of `FilterData`. Unfortunately, this is almost impossible without major changes to the structure of the code. The main problem in the current implementation is the data storage, specifically with those class-level fields for `displayPeople` and `displayCount`.

The `people` array and the `maxPeople` constant aren't so important because they are regarded as read-only by the algorithm. Of course it would be possible to change the read/write array for an immutable `List<T>` implementation as shown in Chapter 16 — that would easily eliminate issues around data changes in this list.

`displayPeople` and `displayCount` are the main issues in this implementation. The `FilterData` algorithm changes both these variables, and what's worse, they need to be kept in sync. Any change to `FilterData` that would execute the actual business logic in parallel multiple times would also break the synchronization between `displayPeople` and `displayCount`.

In addition, there is at least one other place in the class where these values are also changed: the `ResetDisplayPeople` method. This is one more point that has to be synchronized when parallelization is considered. As a result, if no changes were to be made to the algorithmic structure of the program, you'd have to place locks around all pieces of code that make changes to `displayPeople` and `displayCount`.

These days there are all sorts of fancy locks, which may allow certain types of access to run in parallel, while other access types are being blocked. The weight of locking is also being reduced. But the fact remains that locking is an enemy of parallelization. Any type of lock restricts the degree of parallelization you can achieve in your code, because at its core a lock says "here is a piece of code that can't be run in parallel."

There are probably algorithms in the world that cannot be implemented without locking, and there are certainly those that can be implemented more easily with the help of locks, or are actually more efficient when implemented that way, at least in certain runtime environments. But the goal has to be to try to live without locks as much as possible because a high degree of potential parallelization is beneficial.

Remember one of the core ideas of functional programming: the pure function. A pure function is a nicely self-contained element that isn't supposed to do much, if anything, outside its own scope. It is a perfect building block for parallelizable systems. In stage 1, the sample application neglects the principles of pure functions entirely because important data elements are stored in a place where they can be accessed and changed arbitrarily by all methods in the class.

The second stage of the sample application, ShowFilteredListBetter, differs from stage 1 in several ways. At the top of `Form1.cs`, the data storage now looks like this:

```
List<Person> people;
```

This is not an immutable `List<T>` in the stage 2 implementation, although it could be. It is simply a more commonly used representation of a data source today. In addition to this change away from the array type, all the other variables and constants are gone — they aren't needed anymore.

You could argue that this still leaves you with a class-level field for data storage, and you would be correct. There are two reasons that this is presented as an intermediary stage: first, it can be worked around by making the data read-only, and second, the steps required to get rid of the field come with their own drawbacks. This introduces a very important concept in the world of hybrid paradigm programming: compromising, and deciding when and where to compromise.

There is more compromise in the rest of the stage 2 implementation. The new implementation of the `UpdateUI` method is another example:

```
private void UpdateUI( ) {
  DisplayListBox.DataSource =
    GetFilteredList(GetFilterString( ));
}
```

Data binding is now being used, by setting the `DataSource` property of the list box element to the list of potentially filtered objects. This reduces the process of pushing data into the UI for visualization to an atomic operation, from the perspective of this application. Of course the operation is not really atomic and in a fully parallel scenario you might have to deal with the expectation that `UpdateUI` gets called twice, or that the `DataSource` property is otherwise set to a different value at the same time. It is also clear that the method is not pure, since it performs a write access to data outside its own scope. But this is the sort of compromise you need to be prepared to make. After all, you are working on top of the inherently object-oriented .NET Framework. You could, theoretically, make a decision to ignore all APIs that are in the way of function purity, but chances are you'd be better off not working with the .NET Framework at all in that case.

The same kind of compromise is made in the method `GetFilterString`:

```
string GetFilterString( ) {
  string value = FilterTextBox.Text;
  return String.IsNullOrEmpty(value) ?
    null : value;
}
```

If you were prepared to define function purity as an analog scale, and taking the cooperation with existing .NET/WinForms APIs into account, you could say that these functions are as pure as they're going to get.

Less compromise is required in the function that performs the data filtering. Here it is:

```
private List<Person> GetFilteredList(string filter) {
  return filter == null ? people :
    (from p in people
     where p.Name.Contains(filter)
     select p).ToList( );
}
```

The loop algorithm from stage 1 has been replaced with a simple LINQ expression. This removes the need for any local variables, and will eventually enable you to apply parallelization through PLINQ (Parallel Language Integrated Query).

The only element that is in the way of function purity here is the people list, which was discussed earlier. Again, `people` could be made immutable, and then the function could reasonably be described as pure. This is the place where purity counts the most because this is the function that implements the business logic, that part of the algorithm that you are trying to parallelize.

Stage 3 of the sample is called ShowFilteredListEvenBetter. The most important change in this stage is the implementation of `InitData`:

```
private void InitData(List<Person> data) {
  Action updateUI = delegate {
    DisplayListBox.DataSource =
      GetFilteredList(data, GetFilterString( ));
  };
  FilterButton.Click += delegate { updateUI( ); };
  updateUI( );
}
```

The data is now passed in as a parameter, which is the most realistic scenario anyway (in previous stages, the data was always generated for testing purposes). Now look closely at what happens to the data in the function: the variable data, which stores the one existing reference to the list that's going to be shown in the UI, is used in the call to `GetFilteredList` inside the anonymous function `updateUI`. That function is roughly the same as the `UpdateUI` method in the previous stage, but it is now created dynamically during initialization. It is then used to hook up the button click event, which had been a separate handler method, and finally it is called once — just like before.

The reason for this structural step is that it helps remove the class field `people`. In all the previous stages, there was always information available to any method in the class because that information was stored in a field on the class level. This time, the source list reference is passed into `InitData` and then passed on to `GetFilteredList`, but not stored anywhere else. The compiler recognizes that the data element is going to be needed when the anonymous function is called later, so it creates a closure and thereby keeps the data element around, accessible only to the one function that actually requires that access.

 Chapter 6 covers the basics on closures.

The second change in stage 3 is the implementation of `GetFilteredData`:

```
private static List<Person> GetFilteredList(List<Person> source, string filter) {
  return filter == null ? source :
    (from p in source
```

```
      where p.Name.Contains(filter)
      select p).ToList( );
}
```

These last two changes have been introduced in their own stage for a reason. These are obviously important changes because they get rid of the one remaining semi-public data element in the application, thereby enabling the important business logic function to be entirely pure. The problem with the change to the `InitData` implementation is that it disables some of the common mechanisms used in the development of Windows Forms applications — usually you create event handlers for Windows Forms applications by using Visual Studio design time support. To take advantage of the closure mechanisms, you need to create the handler manually instead. This may or may not matter greatly to you — in many larger business applications, a UI is often created from code for automation reasons, so that this is just a minor change to the code. On the other hand, if the loss of the Visual Studio designer functionality is significant to you, you may be better off keeping an immutable source list around as a field on the class level. Again, it's all about compromise.

The final stage in the sequence of business application scenarios is the project ShowFilteredListParallel, which has just one minor difference compared to stage 3. The implementation of the `GetFilteredList` function has been changed to this:

```
private static List<Person> GetFilteredList(List<Person> source, string filter) {
   return filter == null ? source :
     (from p in source.AsParallel()
      where p.Name.Contains(filter)
      select p).ToList( );
}
```

The difference is the addition of the call to `AsParallel` to the source list. `AsParallel` is an extension method made available by the Parallel Extensions to the .NET Framework (PFX), which are officially available on .NET since framework version 4.0. The particular block of features that `AsParallel` belongs in is called Parallel LINQ, or PLINQ, and it provides declarative data parallelism. The method `AsParallel` takes an `IEnumerable` as a parameter and returns an `IParallelEnumerable`, which changes the function mapping for the LINQ expression and executes the LINQ query using the parallelization support from PFX. An elegant solution, no question — but made possible only by the careful structural work that lead to a functionally pure business logic implementation in `GetFilteredList`!

Calculating Mandelbrot Fractals

The starting point for the next example is a project called ReallyImperative in the solution folder Mandelbrot. In contrast to the previous section, this example is about an algorithm. It is more on the scientific side of computing, thereby covering the second major area where computer programs get written in mainstream industries today.

The algorithm calculates the Mandelbrot set, named after Benoit B. Mandelbrot, who studied and described the set. The set can be used to display colorful images with a fractal — that is, repetitive at different resolutions — character. Calculating the set for display of a certain image involves running an iteration for each image pixel and finding out whether the iteration tends towards a certain value or whether it is unbounded. Depending on the outcome, colors for the image are then assigned.

The demo project is once more a Windows Forms application, and all the code is initially contained in Form1.cs. At the top of the class, there are a few helper methods and fields:

Available for download on Wrox.com

```csharp
private void InitColors( ) {
  colors = new Color[COLOR_COUNT];
  colors[0] = Color.White;
  colors[1] = Color.FromArgb(0, 0, 25);
  colors[2] = Color.FromArgb(0, 0, 50);
  colors[3] = Color.FromArgb(0, 0, 75);
  colors[4] = Color.FromArgb(0, 0, 100);
  colors[5] = Color.FromArgb(0, 0, 125);
  colors[6] = Color.FromArgb(0, 0, 150);
  colors[7] = Color.FromArgb(0, 0, 175);
  colors[8] = Color.FromArgb(0, 0, 200);
  colors[9] = Color.FromArgb(0, 0, 255);
}

Color[] colors;
const int COLOR_COUNT = 10;

private void DrawButton_Click(object sender, EventArgs e) {
  waitEvent = new ManualResetEvent(false);
  ThreadPool.RegisterWaitForSingleObject(waitEvent, CalculationDone,
    null, -1, true);
  lastLine = 0;
  Thread thread = new Thread(CalculateImage);
  thread.Start( );
  InvalidateTimer.Start( );
}

private void CalculationDone(object irrelevant, bool timedOut) {
  InvalidateTimer.Stop( );
  panel.Invalidate( );
}

ManualResetEvent waitEvent;
```

code snippet ReallyImperative\Form1.cs

The method InitColors and the two fields Colors and COLOR_COUNT provide for the mapping of calculation results to colors. This is done using an array of colors and pre-computed values, and this part of the algorithm is going to remain in place until the end.

DrawButton_Click is where the image calculation process is triggered, as a reaction to a click on the Draw button in the UI. Don't be fooled by the mention of the Thread type in that method. The calculations in this first stage of the example are not multithreaded. The threads are only used to provide concurrent updates of the drawing in the UI while the calculation proceeds.

The method `CalculateImage` is the most interesting part of the code. After a few lines of initial calculations, there are two nested loops for the rows and columns of the target image, and then a third nested loop that performs the iteration necessary for the Mandelbrot algorithm. There are locks being used for coordination of the parallel process of updating the image during calculation, as well as many temporary variables that are modified all over the place. This function may not look elegant, but it is quite typical for an imperative, state-driven algorithm implementation. And with 43 lines, counting the color mapping code and all the lines with curly braces, it isn't even really a very long function:

Available for
download on
Wrox.com

```
private void CalculateImage() {
  int width = panel.Width;
  int height = panel.Height;
  image = new Bitmap(width, height);
  const int MAX_ITERATION = 1000;

  double xstart = -2.1;
  double ystart = -1.3;
  double xend = 1.0;
  double yend = 1.3;

  double xstep = (xend - xstart) / width;
  double ystep = (yend - ystart) / height;

  double y = ystart;

  for (int py = 0; py < height; py++) {
    lock (lineLock) {
      currentLine = py;
    }
    double x = xstart;

    for (int px = 0; px < width; px++) {
      double tx = 0;
      double ty = 0;
      int iteration = 0;

      while (((tx * tx + ty * ty) < (2*2)) &&
        iteration < MAX_ITERATION) {
        double xtemp = tx * tx - ty * ty + x;
        ty = 2 * tx * ty + y;
        tx = xtemp;
        iteration++;
      }

      Color color;

      if (iteration == MAX_ITERATION) {
        color = Color.Black;
      }
      else {
        int cind = iteration % COLOR_COUNT;
```

```
      color = colors[cind];
    }

    lock (imageLock) {
      image.SetPixel(px, py, color);
    }

    x += xstep;
  }
  y += ystep;
}

waitEvent.Set( );
}
```

code snippet ReallyImperative\Form1.cs

The idea of parallelizing the algorithm is obvious, since the code performs the same steps, namely the `while` loop roughly in the middle of the method, for each pixel. At the same time, the structure of the implementation, with all those loops and temporary variables, makes it very hard to imagine at a glance how such parallelization might work. The logic of state changes is so complex that it takes a while to read the code and understand what each variable contains at a given point in time, and when and how it changes. Without that understanding, it is impossible to even think about making major changes to the structure. Don't worry if the details of the algorithm look complicated; the structure is more important to make the point: Imperative algorithms are often hard to parallelize due to the way they use loops and variables to implement continuous state change.

For the second stage of this example, the code has been structured differently, and for purposes of easy reuse it has also been extracted into its own assembly. There is a project contained in the solution by the name of NicelyFunctional, which shows the easiest and most straightforward way of using the newly structured code.

Just like before, there is an event handler method `DrawButton_Click` in `Form1.cs`. This is it:

```
private void DrawButton_Click(object sender, EventArgs e) {
  int width = panel.Width;
  int height = panel.Height;
  double xstart = -2.1;
  double xend = 1.0;
  double ystart = -1.3;
  double yend = 1.3;

  Point startPoint = new Point(0, 0);
  var results = Calculator.CalcArea(width, height,
    new CalcInfo(xstart, (xend - xstart) / width,
      ystart, (yend - ystart) / height));
  var image = Calculator.CalcImage(results, startPoint, width, height);
  paintImage = image;
  panel.Invalidate( );
}
```

Parts of the code you should recognize — the first few lines perform the same initialization of the mathematical variables that was previously contained in the method `CalculateImage`. After that, things change. There are only two function calls, to functions in a static class called `Calculator`. `CalcArea` receives some width and height information as well as an encapsulation of the mathematical values, and it delivers results. The return type of `CalcArea` is `IEnumerable<PointResult>`, in other words, a lazy enumeration of result values. The second function call, to `CalcImage`, takes those results and converts them into an image representation, which is then made visible in the UI.

For clarity, this implementation of the application doesn't have any threaded UI update functionality or similar gimmicks. It just shows how the new functional Mandelbrot calculation API needs to be used. That API itself is contained in the project FunctionalMandelbrot in the solution.

The file `Calculator.cs` in that project has the implementation of those functions you saw being used a moment ago. This is `Calculator.CalcArea`:

```
public static IEnumerable<PointResult> CalcArea(int width, int height,
  CalcInfo calcInfo) {
  var points = PointSequence(width, height);
  return Functional.Map(p => CalcPoint(p, calcInfo), points);
}
```

Given width and height, as well as the `CalcInfo` math values, `CalcArea` generates a sequence of points and then uses the `Map` function to call `CalcPoint` for each element from the points sequence, returning a sequence of results from that call. Here is `PointSequence`:

```
public static IEnumerable<Point> PointSequence(int width, int height) {
  for (int y = 0; y < height; y++)
    for (int x = 0; x < width; x++)
      yield return new Point(x, y);
}
```

This function uses loops to generate a sequence of points representing all the pixels in the area defined by width and height. There are several other implementation variants that come to mind for this function, including using the general `Sequence` function introduced in Chapter 13, or replacing the loops with recursion.

A decision has been made specifically against using `Sequence` in this case, because it is not optimal in C# in this scenario. `Sequence` is written to calculate each value from the previous one. Here is its implementation again:

```
public static IEnumerable<T> Sequence<T>(Func<T, T> getNext, T startVal,
  Func<T, bool> endReached) {
  if (getNext == null)
    yield break;
  yield return startVal;
  T val = startVal;
  while (endReached == null || !endReached(val)) {
    val = getNext(val);
    yield return val;
  }
}
```

There are separate delegates being used to calculate the next value and to find out whether any particular value represents the end of the sequence. For comparison, here is an implementation of the PointSequence function based on Sequence:

```
public static IEnumerable<Point> PointSequenceUsingSequenceFunction(int width,
  int height) {
  return Functional.Sequence<Point>(
    p =>
      p.X < width - 1 ?
        new Point(p.X + 1, p.Y) :
        p.Y < height - 1 ?
          new Point(0, p.Y + 1) :
          Point.Empty,
    new Point(0, 0),
    p => p.X == width - 1 && p.Y == height - 1);
}
```

This could be written more verbosely by replacing the ternary expressions with if clauses and then, necessarily, the expression body lambda expression with a statement body implementation. The fact remains that this algorithm for sequence generation is represented more elegantly with the help of the imperative loop constructs.

Here is also a theoretical implementation of PointSequence using recursion:

```
public static IEnumerable<Point> TheoreticalPointSequenceWithRecursion(int width,
  int height, int x, int y) {
  if (x < width && y < height)
    yield return new Point(x, y);
  if (x < width - 1)
    return TheoreticalPointSequenceWithRecursion(width, height, x + 1, y);
  else if (x < height - 1)
    return TheoreticalPointSequenceWithRecursion(width, height, 0, y + 1);
}
```

This implementation is just for comparison purposes. It doesn't work, and there are two reasons why. The more obvious one is the potential length of the sequence being generated, coupled with a lack of tail call optimization support in C#. The sequence can easily be several hundreds of thousands of items long, and that is much more than what can be handled gracefully without tail recursion.

The second reason is that this function isn't even valid in C# because it uses yield return and return in the same function. The C# compiler doesn't accept this. As a result, each of the two return lines would have to be replaced with a foreach loop that gets the result from the recursive call, iterates over it, and yield returns each single value.

```
foreach (var p in TheoreticalPointSequenceWithRecursion(width, height, x + 1, y))
  yield return p;
```

 Sequence *is covered in Chapter 13,* Map *in Chapter 12, and iterators and* yield return *in Chapter 5.*

Of course, this approach makes tail recursion impossible because each return value has to be handled separately right after it has been returned. Theoretically it would be possible for the C# compiler to unravel all this and convert it into a single working iterator, but there is no support for this.

As a final note on the topic of the `PointSequence` implementation, it is possible to create such a sequence using ranges (either those described in Chapter 13, or even the ones returned by `Enumerable.Range`) and `Functional.Map` or the `Select` method of LINQ. The discussion here isn't meant to be exhaustive — as always, there are many ways of doing the same thing.

Returning to the `CalcArea` implementation, the second function used there is `CalcPoint`. Here it is:

```
private static PointResult CalcPoint(Point point, CalcInfo calcInfo) {
  var iterations = Iterator(calcInfo.XStart + point.X * calcInfo.XStep,
    calcInfo.YStart + point.Y * calcInfo.YStep);
  return new PointResult(point, ColorFromIterations(iterations));
}
```

This function is simple. It uses the `Iterator` function to calculate the mathematical result for the given point, then calls `ColorFromIterations` to map the result to a color, and returns a nicely packaged block of result information in a `PointResult` instance.

`Iterator` is the final interesting function in this class:

```
private static int Iterator(double x, double y) {
  double tx = 0, ty = 0;
  int iteration = 0;
  while ((tx * tx + ty * ty) < (2 * 2) &&
    iteration < MAX_ITERATION) {
    double ttx = tx * tx - ty * ty + x;
    ty = 2 * tx * ty + y;
    tx = ttx;
    iteration++;
  }
  return iteration;
}
```

You will recognize this piece of code from the initial example; it corresponds exactly to the inner loop used there. In the refactoring efforts on this project, the choice was made to stop at this point and leave the per-point calculation in its original format. That means that the loop in this function is the smallest element that can be parallelized (in the sense that several loops, for different x and y values, can run in parallel, not different iterations of the same loop). This is a conscious decision because with parallelization it is not just important to achieve the largest possible number of chunks. It is also important to keep the size of each chunk to a certain minimum because at some point the overhead through generation and management of a huge number of chunks of work can grow too large if the work done in each chunk is comparatively insignificant. Finally, even if the decision hadn't been made to define one pixel as the smallest unit to consider for parallelization, I would have noticed next that in the iteration itself, each run depends on the previous run — it's not called an iteration for nothing!

There are possible variations to this implementation, but similar to the earlier discussion, they don't seem to be beneficial. Recursion is, once more, an alternative that might turn out useful in a language with tail call optimization support — especially since there's just one loop here instead of two nested ones. The other variation would be to implement the function Iterator as an actual iterator in the C# sense of the word. But an iterator in .NET is meant and expected to return something to a different flow of control on each iteration — in other languages, the same mechanism is referred to as a generator, which seems to capture the idea of .NET iterators a little better. In this case there is no value to return after each run of the loop, and constructing such a value artificially would mean creating an unneeded result object for each iteration run. Because this loop runs once for each pixel in the target image, at a depth of several hundred as a low guess of the average iterations, that would mean perhaps 240 million unneeded result objects for an image of 800x600 points and MAX_ITERATION=1000.

At the end of this summary of the functions that are involved with the newly structured calculation algorithm, a lot has been said about compromises and decisions for and against certain implementation patterns. One thing hasn't been said yet: all these functions are almost entirely pure, with the one exception being the use of a mutable array for the color mapping step. This is of course the perfect basis for parallelization of the algorithm, because it is now possible to execute arbitrary numbers of parallel control flows without any potential collisions.

The sample solution for this chapter contains a frontend implementation called ManualConcurrent, which uses the approach of splitting the target image into blocks and managing them in jobs for parallel calculation with the help of the FunctionalMandelbrot library. This implementation is called Manual because it uses basic .NET Thread objects for the parallelization work and handles the jobs in custom data structures. This is an approach that can be used on .NET versions 2.0 (the implementation makes heavy use of generics) and later.

In .NET 4.0, the availability of the Parallel Extensions takes away a lot of the technical work associated with creating and managing threads, their runtime behavior and return values. The project FunctionalMandelbrotParallel is a slightly changed version of FunctionalMandelbrot, which makes use of the Parallel Extensions for concurrent calculation. Only a single important change has been made in this version, in the function CalcArea:

```
public static void CalcArea(int width, int height, CalcInfo calcInfo,
  Action<PointResult> resultReceiver) {
  var points = PointSequence(width, height);

  Parallel.ForEach(points, p => {
    var pointResult = CalcPoint(p, calcInfo);
    resultReceiver(pointResult);
  });
}
```

One change is the new resultReceiver delegate that is used to push the results right into a separate execution path once they have been calculated. But the more relevant element is the replacement of the Map function call with a call into Parallel.ForEach. Similar to the last step in the List Filtering example, this is a single change for a feature of the Parallel Extensions. In this case, Parallel.ForEach is used to iterate over the points sequence and call into CalcPoint for each of them.

As a result, each point is handled as a separate `Task` object in the Parallel Extensions, which makes for extremely granular parallelization.

In both cases of the Refactoring examples, functional ideas and in some cases techniques were used to change structural aspects of the algorithms to the point where the functionality delivered by the Parallel Extensions can be deployed through one simple change. Don't forget that this is an example, though! There are plenty of other reasons why the restructured code is just overall better than the original one: Whether you parallelize or not, you will benefit from greater stability and maintainability, easier application of tests, easier debugging, and probably other consequences, if you apply similar restructuring steps to your own code.

WRITING NEW CODE

When writing new code, you have the opportunity to make structural decisions up front, and you can define the discipline you would like to use for certain cases. Here are several ideas for guidelines you may find useful. The rest of this section will discuss these choices in some more depth.

➤ Keep methods static if possible.

➤ Prefer anonymous functions over named ones.

➤ Prefer higher order functions over manual algorithm implementation.

➤ Prefer immutable data.

➤ Watch behavior implementation in classes.

Use Static Methods

Static methods is one of the basic ideas worth considering as a general guideline. It is supported by many object oriented programmers, and from a functional point of view, functions can be made static most of the time. Any pure function can be made static.

In object oriented programming, a commonly discussed question is how to handle method parameters when the values received by the method as parameters are ones that are already available in the class. Consider this rough outline of a class:

```
public class DataThing {
  private int field1;
  private int field2;
  ...
  private string field13;

  public void DoSomethingWithFields1And5() {
    // doing something that involves fields 1 and 5
  }

  public int CalculateWithFields() {
    // use all or several of the fields in the class to perform some
    // calculation and return the result
  }
}
```

The class has a number of private fields and two methods, both of which are meant to use at least some of the fields to do their job. Both the methods are written to not take any parameters, which is possible because the methods have access to the data directly, being members of the class.

Someone usually asks, "Shouldn't we perhaps pass in the values, which are needed in a particular function, as parameters? That would enable us, for instance, to consider calling this function from multiple threads."

If you think about it logically, you will find that there are really only two possible answers. Answer one is that you don't care about any potential multithreading, which means you are fine accessing the fields in the class directly. Of course the syntax is much less verbose if you don't have to enumerate all the field names in each method signature.

Answer two is that multithreading is, or may become in the future, important to you. In that case, you should always pass in all the values needed by a particular function as parameters so that each execution of the function is self-contained. You might come very close to making the function pure by performing this step.

There are other similar considerations. For instance, maintainability can be improved by listing the parameters explicitly because it is then obvious at a glance which values are needed by a particular function.

Here's an important point, though. It can make sense to vary this decision for different functions. For example, in this piece of sample code there's a function that uses only two of the field values, and a second one that is described as using lots of them. The decision to introduce parameters for the two-value function is perhaps easier than for the other one, and if it so happens that the idea of multithreading makes much more sense for whatever the two-value function does, then it might seem sensible to be flexible.

A certain way to create new confusion is to go only half way. You might be surprised, but it happens all the time: a few values, sometimes a rather arbitrary selection, are passed in as parameters, while some others are simply accessed directly. Of course there's a reason behind this. For instance, a public method that needs some values from the class instance it lives in gets additional information supplied from the outside. That is understandable, but it's still a useful recommendation to have stricter guidelines than that.

Some may argue that the idea of always passing around all parameters means you're not exploiting the ideas of object orientation as much as you could. That may in fact be true, but then perhaps it is because object orientation concepts don't give as much consideration to issues of parallel execution as they should. In the end, parallelization isn't the only thing to consider when deciding about the handling of parameters, variables, fields, and static versus instance methods, but it should be an important part of your considerations. You may find that sometimes you don't have to keep it in mind at all, but you should always make that decision consciously.

Finally, a guideline to recommend: when you have written a method that does not require access to any field in the class it lives in, make it static! That's like putting a label on the function to say, "I intend that this function shall not access fields in the class." The typical argument against this is that you might change your mind about it later — there's nothing wrong with that, but at least you're going to give some conscious thought to it once you've made the method static.

Prefer Anonymous Methods Over Named Ones

The anonymous method preference guideline is not about deciding when an anonymous method or a named method *can* be used. That is a separate consideration that can be answered strictly on technical terms. For example, an anonymous method can't be reused in the object oriented sense, through overloading or calls from derived classes, it can't be generic, etc. On the other hand, named methods don't have support for closures.

This guideline is about situations where both types of functions could be used from a technical point of view. This guideline says, if a method is only used locally, it should be declared locally as well. That's the same thing everybody accepts easily when talking about data. That's why it's possible in C# to declare local const values. The idea is not to move something into a larger namespace, the class level, without the proven need to do so.

The downside of this idea is that C# syntax doesn't make the decision easy. Declaring functions locally requires the use of either delegate types, which need to be declared somewhere separately (they can't be declared locally in a method), or standard delegate types, which are very flexible, but also result in complex syntax.

To illustrate, here are two implementations of classes for prime number calculations. They use the same algorithms, but are implemented using an anonymous internal helper function for the functional case, and a method for the imperative case.

Available for download on Wrox.com

```
public class PrimeCalculatorImperative {
  public bool IsPrime(int v) {
    for (int d = 2; d <= v / 2; d++)
      if (v % d == 0)
        return false;
    return true;
  }

  public List<int> GetPrimes(int max) {
    var result = new List<int>();
    for (int v = 3; v <= max; v++) {
      if (IsPrime(v))
        result.Add(v);
    }
    return result;
  }
}

public static class PrimeCalculatorFunctional {
  public static IEnumerable<int> GetPrimes() {
    Func<int, bool> isPrime = v => {
      for (int d = 2; d <= v / 2; d++)
        if (v % d == 0)
          return false;
        return true;
    };

    for (int v = 3; true; v++)
```

```
        if (isPrime(v))
          yield return v;
    }
  }
```

code snippet PreferAnonymousMethods/Program.cs

There are a few other differences: the "functional" implementation (called that to distinguish from the "imperative" implementation – it's certainly not very functional in its inner workings) uses a static function, and it is implemented as an iterator. You can see the difference the anonymous function makes to the implementation — it becomes clear that isPrime is only used from inside GetPrimes, but the syntactical downside is the use of the Func<...> delegate type to store the reference for the function.

Prefer Higher Order Functions over Manual Algorithm Implementation

The advantages of higher order functions overlap with those of many other techniques that are commonly used in object oriented programming. For example, the Template Method Pattern is a design approach in which a base class is used to implement part of an algorithm, leaving certain details to a separate method (or several of them), which is typically abstract in the base class and implemented only in more specific derived classes. That description fits the ideas of higher order functions just as well.

Generally speaking, higher order functions use a form of injection to execute a template algorithm with the details being filled in by separate functions. The advantage is that the higher order function itself defines a sort of pattern, which can be recognized and understood more easily than an explicit implementation of the algorithm. Consider these two implementations of a function that sums up values from a list:

```
private static void SumIntsImperative(IEnumerable<int> ints) {
  int result = 0;
  foreach (int v in ints)
    result += v;
  Console.WriteLine(result);
}

private static void SumIntsFunctional(IEnumerable<int> ints) {
  var result = Functional.FoldL((s, v) => s + v, 0, ints);
  Console.WriteLine(result);
}
```

The imperative function requires you to look at the loop instruction as well as the calculation instruction. This is a simple example, of course, and you're going to see very quickly what's happening. But the functional example with its application of Fold makes this even easier — you see the word Fold, have one look at the aggregation instruction, and you're done. By the way: the use of foreach in the imperative example has very much the same purpose as the higher order functions.

It is a simplification of vastly more complex looping constructs like `for` itself, and it helps you understand the code without having to look in all too many places.

Here is a second example for some inline code:

```
var ints = new int[] { 1, 2, 8, 93 };

var squaredInts1 = new int[ints.Length];
for (int i = 0; i < ints.Length; i++)
  squaredInts1[i] = ints[i] * ints[i];

var squaredInts2 =
  Functional.Map(x => x * x, ints).ToList( );

var squaredInts3 =
  (from x in ints
   select x * x).ToList( );
```

In this example, both the `squaredInts2` and the `squaredInts3` calculations are done functionally, while `squaredInts1` is calculated imperatively. The added complexity of the array handling and the elements of the `for` loop is baffling compared to the simplicity of the other two samples.

What are the downsides of preferring higher order functions? There are not many — issues like the complexity of the syntax and the deficiencies of type inference in C# have been mentioned before — but it is important to see that the advantages of the patterns offered by higher order functions are useful only if everybody who needs to work with the code understands the functions being used and knows their patterns well. This is especially true for higher order functions you create yourself, which are new to the reader and generally likely to work on a slightly lower level of abstraction than the well-known `Map`, `Filter`, and `Fold` functions.

 Chapters 3 and 12 describe basic and advanced use cases of higher order functions.

Prefer Immutable Data

The topic of immutable data has been discussed in much detail in Chapter 16, but is it a good idea to make it a guideline? There are certain usability issues with immutable data in C#, at least for the single-object cases. Some technologies in .NET also rely on data being mutable, or at least they offer a lot more functionality if data can be changed. For instance, data binding in conjunction with complex and highly interactive visual UI controls in WinForms, WPF, or Silverlight loses a lot of its appeal when data is immutable.

Nevertheless, the guideline says "*prefer* immutable data," and beyond the considerations around gain or loss of functionality and practicality, it is still worthwhile keeping data mutability in mind as a potential problem, and working around it whenever you can.

If you want to use immutable data as a guideline, remember that C# doesn't have much language support for it. This means, among other things, that your co-workers aren't necessarily aware of your intentions about a block of data in your code. It's important to have a certain discipline about this and possibly to create a naming convention or similar to avoid misunderstandings. Remember, it's easy enough for you to make variables read-only, or to implement functions in a pure style. The compiler provides little bits of help, like the `readonly` keyword. But only discipline and communication will help prevent your coworkers from accidentally undoing your efforts.

Finally, for scenarios of parallelization, immutable data structures can be very useful; in such cases, this guideline can be recommended wholeheartedly.

Watch Behavior Implementation in Classes

In programming languages with more of a focus on functional elements than C# has to offer, there are often special data "container" types that allow flexible storage of complex data, but don't always implement any of their own behavior. Of course, object orientation's aim is to implement all behavior in classes, but you still have a choice to make: to what extent you are going to combine data storage and behavior implementation.

It is important to realize that the question of how to handle data storage and data flow is the important point when it comes to discussions about object orientation versus functional programming. Using only static methods in C# doesn't make your program functional automatically, just like wrapping all your variables in classes doesn't make you an object oriented programmer. The choice you really have is between two programming paradigms, each of them fully workable on its own — mixing and matching is allowed, but take great care in doing so!

The guideline is stated carefully (watch behavior implementation in classes) and is not meant to contradict the ideas of object orientation. Your choice may depend on what your driving factor for the adoption of functional programming is. For parallelization, for example, the problem is that any class you view as a black box of data with associated behavior will not allow any intrinsic parallelization. This may or may not be a problem for you — you can see that these choices are very subjective. Your perspective may be that the degree of encapsulation afforded by a black box is just what you want. Your perspective may in fact be different for different parts of your code, for modules of your application, or certainly from one project to the next.

The guideline is meant to help you remember that there is a choice here, and that going for one or the other extreme, or indeed anywhere in between, is perfectly fine if your circumstances warrant it — and if you've made a conscious decision about it.

FINDING LIKELY CANDIDATES FOR FUNCTIONAL PROGRAMMING

This is a question that users of Microsoft's new F# language have to deal with all the time: where in your architecture are the places where it makes sense to use F#? Opinions on this vary wildly — some people think it should be restricted to certain science-intensive parts of the code, whereas others like to stress that F# is a general purpose programming language just like others on .NET. Questions of tooling are important in the area of F# as well, because Visual Studio support for things like UI designers isn't available so far.

Shades of Grey

In C#, and perhaps in F#, the question really needs to be what disciplines to use for particular areas of your code, or how strictly to adhere to certain ideas. These considerations are not new, but perhaps more attention must be paid in these days of hybrid languages and programming environments.

In the past, a consideration might have been about typing. Generally, C# aims to be a strictly typed language, and with the advent of generics this focus became even more pronounced. Nevertheless, there are situations when it seems like a good idea to work with an untyped list of objects, perhaps as implemented by the `ArrayList` type. In .NET 4.0 times, this may overlap with scenarios where the use of dynamic programming features, or even direct interfacing with DLR (Dynamic Language Runtime) is considered.

With functional programming, you need to make similar decisions. Object orientation and functional programming are not enemies, but sometimes they are at cross purposes. Object orientation tries to encapsulate behavior, often together with its related data. Functional programming doesn't say this is wrong, but if, for instance, functional programming is used as a means to facilitate parallelization, a very strong encapsulation pattern may be in the way of that.

Classes and objects are generally very useful to model real-world information. Think of a business scenario — there are customers and projects and employees and invoices. These are often concrete "things" with certain properties. Object orientation suggests that these elements should have their own behavior. Perhaps the `Invoice` class knows how to `Send` an instance of itself to somebody, or the `Project` can `MarkCompleted` itself.

It seems to make sense to encapsulate all the little bits of information, which make up a `Project` in their entirety, in a class. But the real-world analogy breaks with the inclusion of behavior. After all, in the real world it's not the project that marks itself completed, it's a separate person who does this. It's not the invoice that sends itself out, and it's certainly not the `Employee` that `Promotes` herself. These are actions that are carried out from outside the object in reality.

For that reason, encapsulation is often handled quite flexibly when it comes to business logic implementation of any significant size. You might introduce an additional helper class, which contains all the logic implementations for "things that can be done with a `Customer`." This is a cleaner approach as well because it provides a good location for the related "things that can be done with collections of `Customers`" as well as "things that can be done with `Customers` and `Projects`."

Imagine this scenario:

```
public enum Position {
  Worker,
  Suit,
  BigBoss
}

public class Customer {
  public string Name { get; set; }
```

```
      public Position Position { get; set; }
    }

    public static class CustomerLogic {
      public static void Promote(this Customer customer) {
        switch (customer.Position) {
          case  Position.Worker:
            customer.Position = Position.Suit;
            break;
          case Position.Suit:
            customer.Position = Position.BigBoss;
            break;
        }
      }
    }
  }
```

This is an implementation of business logic in a separate class. This even looks rather functional, with the `Promote` method being static. Calling the `Promote` method is just as easy as if the method lived inside the `Customer` class because the use of the `this` keyword makes it an extension method.

Some people may argue that `Promote` belongs inside the `Customer` class, because its purpose is to modify a field inside the `Customer` class. But then, what about this implementation, which is even functionally pure:

```
  public static Customer PromotePure(this Customer customer) {
    switch (customer.Position) {
      case Position.Worker:
        return new Customer { Name = customer.Name, Position = Position.Suit };
      case Position.Suit:
        return new Customer { Name = customer.Name, Position = Position.BigBoss };
    }
  }
```

This uses the principles of immutable data to create a new `Customer` instance that differs in part from the original one. It doesn't modify anything inside the original `Customer`. So where does it belong?

This chapter (this book in fact) can't give you the definitive answers about the best placement of business logic code. In reality, there are probably no such perfect answers. But many programmers today choose to keep business logic implementation outside the classes that store the data, for many different reasons. No matter why that decision is made in the first place, it is very much compatible with the ideas of functional programming.

The decision to "do functional programming" is not one between black and white.

Using What's There

There are situations where decisions about the particular style of programming to be used come more easily: when the code that is being written must interface with code that has already been written. This may be code written by others on the same project, but it can also apply to the code that has been written for the programming platform you are working on. The .NET Framework has been written as an object oriented framework, and often it's the easiest to be object oriented as well if you need to interact with it directly. And interact you will, because otherwise why are you using it?

Everything in the .NET Framework is a class, very few things are immutable, and very few functions are pure. Parts of the framework are made for extensibility, and the technical mechanisms that were chosen are those supplied by object orientation: classes you can derive from, interfaces you can implement. In C# there's no way to implement an interface functionally, so the feature set of the language defines the approach you will have to take. ("Implementing the interface" refers to the C# technique of doing so — adding all the relevant members to a class, or using explicit implementation syntax — not to the implementation of the individual members themselves.)

On the other hand, there are parts of the framework that implement APIs that are inherently functional. An example of that are Web requests. Web requests are in themselves stateless. They don't necessarily have the requirement of being implemented in a pure way, but on a low level, a Web request closely resembles a function call. Newer developments on the Microsoft platform, like ASP.NET MVC, make this more obvious.

Systems like ASP.NET Web Forms put a thick layer on top of the basic HTTP request system, implementing complex state preservation and automated state recovery and the page and control rendering cycles. But even in this complex framework, there are still places where you need to write pieces of code that are very functional in nature: take a few parameters and return something that will be used as part of the output.

SUMMARY

There is a prejudice among programmers, especially those who have never programmed anything in functional languages, that 99% of the time you are going to use functional programming ideas in scientific scenarios. And because those same programmers tend to work on typical business application scenarios more than on other types of development, they conclude that functional ideas are not interesting to themselves.

It is hard to argue with that mindset, and it is hard to come up with examples that just happen to fit what any particular programmer does in her daily work. There are lots of examples out there, as well as in the previous chapters, but you have to keep an open mind and think about them creatively. LINQ was recently mentioned to me as proof that functional programming is of great practical use. That is certainly true, but in reality LINQ is just a package full of old ideas in a brilliant shiny new wrapper — it's great and you just have to like it, but it can also be used as proof of how great things can sometimes be neglected by many, for a long time.

The last section of this chapter has tried to apply some broad considerations to common topics of object orientation in business application scenarios.

To apply functional programming requires thinking outside the box, assuming your box is object orientation. Functional programming isn't always the best thing to do, but neither is any other approach.

19

The MapReduce Pattern

WHAT'S IN THIS CHAPTER?

➤ A simple MapReduce implementation

➤ Abstracting the problem

The idea of MapReduce was proposed by Google in 1994. Google has since received a (much criticized) software patent for it, and the technology has been implemented in a number of open source and commercial libraries and products.

MapReduce is a framework that allows parallel execution of the steps required to perform potentially complex computations over possibly very large sets of data. Any number of physical or logical nodes can be involved in the process, and the approach can be used for parallelization on just one physical machine. Keep in mind the rather large amounts of data! The algorithms implemented with MapReduce are not usually very complex, so the overhead of the implementation pattern and the backend infrastructure make it worthwhile only if the benefit of parallelization comes largely from the data volume.

The basic concept is simple to describe, and Google uses the canonical example of counting word occurrences in text. There are two steps for this, Map and Reduce:

1. The Map step splits the text into a list of words. MapReduce generally works with key/value pairs, so examples usually use a data type for this with a pair of the word and a 1 (one).

2. For each unique key in the list of pairs, the Reduce step is executed, given the key (in the word counting example, that's the word itself) and a list of values (again, in the example, that's a list of 1s, with as many items as there were words found). The Reduce step then accumulates the data and returns a result.

There are a lot of variables in the basic description. One of the interesting aspects of any real-world implementation is that of data exchange. Obviously, there is a block of data to handle in the beginning. Before Map can be executed, the data needs to be split up and the chunks made available to a number of parallel Map processes, which may be running on different physical machines. It is probable that the Map implementation itself must still be able to work with a whole list of texts instead of just one — not a big difference, but important nevertheless — in which case it will simply iterate over its input and process the individual elements one by one.

Next, there is really a step missing between 1 and 2: grouping the data from all Map processes by their keys. That can only be done after all Maps have run through, so it is of consequence to the parallelization implementation of a MapReduce engine.

Finally, the Reduce step can be implemented in different ways. You may have noticed already that these Map and Reduce functions, previously called "steps," have only passing similarity to the generic ones that have been discussed at length in this book. Once more, with Reduce it's about the data. A pure functional implementation of Reduce just returns a single value (which may be a list in itself, of course). But the point of MapReduce is to run many Reduce steps in parallel, and so the results need to be persisted somewhere, accumulated into an overall result set, and so on.

IMPLEMENTING MAPREDUCE

The example in this chapter will break things down to the point where standard Map and Reduce functions from FCSlib can be used. There is no automatic parallelization going on, but because you know the functions are all functionally pure, they could be parallelized easily enough if all the issues of data exchange, distributed node management, and so forth are solved.

The first sample counts words, so it starts with a piece of text:

```
const string hamlet = @"Though yet of Hamlet our dear brother's death
The memory be green, and that it us befitted
To bear our hearts in grief and our whole kingdom
To be contracted in one brow of woe,
...
To business with the king, more than the scope
Of these delated articles allow.
Farewell, and let your haste commend your duty.";
```

Step 1 is the mapping of data:

```
var pairs = Functional.Collect(
  text => Functional.Map(
    word => Tuple.Create(word, 1),
    text.Split(new[] { " ", Environment.NewLine },
      StringSplitOptions.RemoveEmptyEntries)),
  new[] { hamlet });
```

There are two different Map calls here, so things are a bit confusing. The outer one is called Collect, which is an extension of the standard Map function: it assumes that each iteration of the source list produces not just a single element of output, but a list of items, and so it concatenates all the resulting sublists into one whole result before returning it. The function `Collect` and the helper `Concat`, which make this possible together, are here:

```
public static IEnumerable<T> Concat<T>(IEnumerable<IEnumerable<T>> sequences) {
  foreach (IEnumerable<T> sequence in sequences)
    foreach (T item in sequence)
      yield return item;
}

public static IEnumerable<R> Collect<T, R>(Converter<T, IEnumerable<R>> converter,
  IEnumerable<T> list) {
  var listOfLists = Map(converter, list);
  return Concat(listOfLists);
}
```

 If you're using LINQ functions, the `Collect` *functionality is available under the name* `SelectMany`.

That outer `Collect` call is the important mapping step of the MapReduce processing pipeline. The second parameter it takes is a sequence of inputs. In this case, there's just one element in the sequence, which is the Hamlet text. The function that `Collect` gets passed in as its first parameter is the calculation formula that is specific to the operation being performed right now by `MapReduce`. It takes one of the input elements and converts it into a list of key/value pairs. In the example, this is done by using the standard `String.Split` function to split the text into words on whitespace boundaries, and then using an inner `Map` call to combine each word in a tuple with the number 1. As a result of this and the outer `Collect` call, the variable pairs is now a list of tuples containing words from all text blocks that have been passed in, and the number 1 in the second value items.

Next is the intermediate grouping operation. With the help of a special data structure (to make things a bit more readable) as well as a new helper function, this is what it looks like:

```
var groups = Group(pair => pair.Item1, pairs);
```

Here's the data structure and the helper function:

```
public class Group<TKey, TValue> {
  public Group(TKey key) {
    this.key = key;
  }

  private TKey key;
  public TKey Key {
    get {
      return key;
    }
  }

  private List<TValue> values = new List<TValue>( );
```

```
    public List<TValue> Values {
      get {
        return values;
      }
    }
  }

  static IEnumerable<Group<TKey, TValue>> Group<TKey, TValue>(
    Converter<TValue, TKey> extractor, IEnumerable<TValue> list) {
    var dict = new Dictionary<TKey, Group<TKey, TValue>>( );
    foreach (TValue val in list) {
      var key = extractor(val);
      if (!dict.ContainsKey(key))
        dict[key] = new Group<TKey, TValue>(key);
      dict[key].Values.Add(val);
    }
    return dict.Values;
  }
```

The implementation is quite specific for the purpose at hand and shouldn't be regarded as the best possible grouping approach (that isn't to say that there's a best possible grouping approach out there; as usual in programming, "the best" is a very volatile concept). There are several things noteworthy about it:

➤ The Group data structure has a mutable Values list. You could replace this with either an immutable data structure (which would mean that the property of the Group would then have to change), or with an IEnumerable sequence. The latter could end up in a very nice interface, but internally it wouldn't be that elegant, since for performance reasons it would be necessary to create additional wrapper data structures. In other words, there are other options depending on your preferences, but none of them comes without certain complications.

➤ The Group function uses a helper dictionary to facilitate fast lookups by the group keys. This introduces a certain degree of overhead on the storage side, but seems like a tradeoff that's worthwhile to keep things working smoothly for large numbers of items. This is another area where implementation choices are subjective.

➤ Before grouping is performed, an extraction function is executed to retrieve the element from the source data that will be used as a key. It would extend flexibility by a great margin to have a exchangeable comparer as well as this extractor — right now, grouping only works for key types that are supported by a standard equality comparison as used by the Dictionary type.

Regardless of the implementation details, the result is a list of groups that each has a key (the word) and a list of values (lots of 1s). The final step is the per-group reduction, which looks like this:

```
var results = Functional.Map(
  g => Tuple.Create(g.Key,
    Functional.FoldL((r, v) => r + v.Item2, 0, g.Values)),
  groups);
```

The Reduce step itself is really just about the parameters given to the Functional.FoldL function, in this case summing up of all values. Each per-group result is then wrapped in a tuple together with the key value from the group, and the list of these tuples is the result of the overall operation. In the sample, a final block of code is used to output the word counting results for the piece of Hamlet:

```
foreach (var t in results)
   Console.WriteLine("{0}: {1}", t.Item1, t.Item2);
```

Now that the steps are all in place, the whole process can be abstracted out into a helper function:

```
static IEnumerable<Tuple<TKey, TReduceResult>>
  MapReduce<TKey, TValue, TReduceInput, TReduceResult>(
  Converter<TValue, IEnumerable<Tuple<TKey, TReduceInput>>> mapStep,
  Func<TReduceResult, Tuple<TKey, TReduceInput>, TReduceResult> reduceStep,
  TReduceResult reduceStartVal,
  IEnumerable<TValue> list) {
  var pairs = Functional.Collect<TValue, Tuple<TKey, TReduceInput>>(
    mapStep, list);
  var groups = Group(pair => pair.Item1, pairs);
  return Functional.Map(
    g => Tuple.Create(g.Key,
      Functional.FoldL(reduceStep, reduceStartVal, g.Values)), groups);
}
```

The functionality stays the same — don't be confused by the various generic type variables; you should easily recognize the steps described earlier. Type inference does a good job in this case, and the entire word counting operation now boils down to this:

```
var newResults =
  MapReduce(
    text => Functional.Map(
      word => Tuple.Create(word, 1),
      text.Split(new[] { " ", Environment.NewLine },
        StringSplitOptions.RemoveEmptyEntries)),
    (r, v) => r + v.Item2, 0,
    new[] { hamlet });
```

In spite of a certain usefulness, the function MapReduce has not been made a part of FCSlib. There is value in the pattern of MapReduce alone, but it has been hinted before that a certain infrastructure is necessary to be able to apply it easily to any given problem, and to benefit from parallelization as well. It wouldn't be too hard to make a few more steps in that direction, but a complete engine with all the necessary data pipelining is outside the scope of this book.

ABSTRACTING THE PROBLEM

Having a MapReduce engine available doesn't solve any problems automatically. An important step is to abstract any given problem in such a way that it fits the pattern. Another consideration is of making the executable code for a given problem available to the engine together with the data — but again, this is beyond the scope of this book, and the implementation details of the engine you use obviously influence this greatly.

Most programmers remember when they were new to the art of computer programming, and abstraction was, at that time, something that came hard to many. You have some information, you want something out of it, but how do you get there? What steps are needed to reach the goal? You learned how to think within the system, whichever system you worked with. An object oriented programmer learns to model things in classes, shaping elements and things that interact with one another. A functional programmer evaluates the order in which certain results, and thereby calculations, depend upon one another.

With MapReduce, the process is the same, but the system works differently. It is probably closer to functional programming, but the firm requirement to implement everything in only two formalized steps still seems restrictive. Experts claim that the family of problems that can be solved with the help of MapReduce is extremely large, and there's the benefit of hiding away all the details of parallelization — every implementation of a problem solution that adheres to the pattern will automatically be parallelized by the engine.

For example, consider a structure of data initialized like this:

```
static List<Order> InitOrders( ) {
  return new List<Order> {
    new Order {
      Name = "Customer 1 Order",
      Lines = new List<OrderLine> {
        new OrderLine{ ProductName = "Rubber Chicken", ProductPrice=8.95m,
          Count=5},
        new OrderLine{ ProductName = "Pulley", ProductPrice=0.99m, Count=5 }
      }
    },
    new Order {
      Name = "Customer 2 Order",
      Lines = new List<OrderLine> {
        new OrderLine{ ProductName = "Canister of Grog", ProductPrice=13.99m,
          Count=10}
      }
    }
  };
}
```

This type of data structure may be returned from a relational database, or you might have in-memory objects to work with. Calculating some summaries over this data with the help of `MapReduce` is easy enough:

```
var orderValues = MapReduce(
  o => Functional.Map(
    ol => Tuple.Create(o.Name, ol.ProductPrice * ol.Count), o.Lines),
  (r, t) => r + t.Item2, 0m,
```

```
    orders);

    foreach (var result in orderValues)
      Console.WriteLine("Order: {0}, Value: {1}", result.Item1, result.Item2);

    var orderLineCounts = MapReduce(
      o => Functional.Map(ol => Tuple.Create(o.Name, 1), o.Lines),
      (r, t) => r + 1, 0,
      orders);

    foreach (var result in orderLineCounts)
      Console.WriteLine("Order: {0}, Lines: {1}", result.Item1, result.Item2);
```

The hard part is arriving at the answers. There is no golden bullet solution — you need to understand the steps of the process, be aware what they do, what they can do, what structure of data they use as input, and the structure of data they generate. Generally, Map can take any unstructured data and split it up, while Reduce summarizes things. It is often easiest to start from the desired output: a list of result tuples with per-order summary values in this example. From there, the chain of thought could be to have a list of per-order groups as the input to Reduce, which means that the output from Map needs to be a flat list of items that have the order info as the key and some sort of a value that can be used by Reduce to do the summary work.

In their original paper on MapReduce, the Google authors describe a few other examples, including a distributed grep (searching lines of text for certain expressions) and a sorting program. They also outline performance characteristics of these implementations, which are impressive. They all have one thing in common, though, which is that they run simple algorithms against large amounts of data — another hint at the importance of infrastructure beyond the MapReduce pattern itself.

A more complex example for MapReduce has been shown already in Chapter 18. The functional implementation of the Mandelbrot algorithm breaks everything down to an API with two calls that need to be made in sequence: CalcArea and CalcImage. Here are those functions:

```
    public static IEnumerable<PointResult> CalcArea(int width, int height,
      CalcInfo calcInfo) {
      var points = PointSequence(width, height);
      return Functional.Map(p => CalcPoint(p, calcInfo), points);
    }

    public static Image CalcImage(IEnumerable<PointResult> results, Point start,
      int width, int height) {
      return Functional.FoldL<PointResult, Bitmap>(
        (r, v) => {
          r.SetPixel(v.Point.X, v.Point.Y, v.Color);
          return r;
        },
        new Bitmap(width, height),
        results);
    }
```

As you can see, `CalcArea`, which is called first, contains a `Map` call over a sequence of values, while `CalcImage` consists entirely of a single `FoldL` call. Map and reduce, nothing more — and with the complex calculations going on during `Map`, and the use of `FoldL` to construct an image, this is certainly also an interesting example for the applicability of this pattern. Caveat: the particular way the image object is handled in this example would not translate easily to a real MapReduce engine, where there has to be cleaner coordination between the parallel-running tasks involved in `Reduce`, when it comes to data storage.

SUMMARY

This chapter is intended to provide some food for thought. The MapReduce pattern is a great abstraction of an enormously large family of algorithms, and the thought processes its designers went through can provide an interesting basis for your own developments. Provide your own pluggable algorithmic extensibility for your applications on the basis of MapReduce. Utilize one of the public services that make parallelized MapReduce infrastructure available at a fee. The pattern is even valuable as a learning tool: Structuring your algorithms to fit the static requirements of MapReduce may seem easier to you than fitting together arbitrary pieces from the complete functional toolset. For some pointers at existing implementations of MapReduce, see Chapter 21.

20

Applied Functional Modularization

WHAT'S IN THIS CHAPTER?

➤   A functional approach to running SQL queries

Many of the chapters that describe particular techniques of functional programming have had their own illustrative examples, practical things to do with those techniques. The nature of the techniques makes it somewhat complicated to come up with examples that are useful and meaningful to most readers — it's almost like describing the `for` statement in C# and trying to list all the things you can practically do with it. There are so many different possibilities that it seems more worthwhile to stay with basic, generic examples that apply to the widest possible family of scenarios.

Nevertheless, this chapter provides an example for the use of functional modularization techniques to achieve something practical. Hopefully it will serve as additional food for thought, to give your own creativity another push.

EXECUTING SQL CODE FROM AN APPLICATION

The example deals with the simple scenario of executing some SQL code from an application — to generate some default data, for instance. You may find code like this in many applications:

Available for download on Wrox.com

```
static void FillDatabase( ) {
  using(var conn = new SqlCeConnection(DBCONNSTR)) {
    conn.Open( );
    try {
      using (var trans = conn.BeginTransaction( )) {
```

```
        ExecuteSQL(trans, "create table people(id int, name ntext)");
        trans.Commit( );
    }

    using (var trans = conn.BeginTransaction( )) {
        ExecuteSQL(trans, "insert into people(id, name) values(1, 'Harry')");
        ExecuteSQL(trans, "insert into people(id, name) values(2, 'Jane')");
        ExecuteSQL(trans, "insert into people(id, name) values(3, 'Willy')");
        ExecuteSQL(trans, "insert into people(id, name) values(4, 'Susan')");
        ExecuteSQL(trans, "insert into people(id, name) values(5, 'Bill')");
        ExecuteSQL(trans, "insert into people(id, name) values(6, 'Jennifer')");
        ExecuteSQL(trans, "insert into people(id, name) values(7, 'John')");
        ExecuteSQL(trans, "insert into people(id, name) values(8, 'Anna')");
        ExecuteSQL(trans, "insert into people(id, name) values(9, 'Bob')");
        ExecuteSQL(trans, "insert into people(id, name) values(10, 'Mary')");

        trans.Commit( );
    }
}
finally {
    conn.Close( );
}
}
}
```

Code snippet Program.cs

Many programmers would probably find this a bit unclean, and they would consider refactoring the code to create a utility method to execute the insert into statements given just the parameters for the transaction, the id, and the name of the record being created. This is generally the same abstraction you might get for free by using a data layer framework of some description, or possibly an object/relational mapping toolkit.

From the perspective of functional programming, it makes sense to keep one thing in mind when performing a simple refactoring like this: new members shouldn't be introduced on a scope larger than the function itself, unless they benefit not only the function being refactored but also others. In other words, while you know that you're using a helper function several times during the data initialization process, you don't know at this point that any other piece of code in your application would benefit from the same helper. Consider modularizing within your own scope instead of going beyond it.

As a result of these considerations, you might want to rewrite the code like this:

Available for
download on
Wrox.com

```
static void FillDatabase2( ) {
    using (var conn = new SqlCeConnection(DBCONNSTR)) {
        conn.Open( );
        try {
            using (var trans = conn.BeginTransaction( )) {
                ExecuteSQL(trans, "create table people(id int, name ntext)");
                trans.Commit( );
            }

            using (var trans = conn.BeginTransaction( )) {
```

```
              Action<SqlCeTransaction, int, string> exec = (transaction, id, name) =>
                ExecuteSQL(transaction, String.Format(
                  "insert into people(id, name) values({0}, '{1}')", id, name));
              exec(trans, 1, "Harry");
              exec(trans, 2, "Jane");
              exec(trans, 3, "Willy");
              exec(trans, 4, "Susan");
              exec(trans, 5, "Bill");
              exec(trans, 6, "Jennifer");
              exec(trans, 7, "John");
              exec(trans, 8, "Anna");
              exec(trans, 9, "Bob");
              exec(trans, 10, "Mary");

              trans.Commit( );
            }
          }
          finally {
            conn.Close( );
          }
        }
      }
```

Code snippet Program.cs

There's now a helper function being constructed as a simple lambda expression, implemented exactly as outlined before. Modularization happens on a functional level, so that the precise implementation you need at this point is made reusable but the outer scope is not extended or potentially polluted by your change.

REWRITING THE FUNCTION WITH PARTIAL APPLICATION AND PRECOMPUTATION IN MIND

This doesn't look like the end of the line, however. The individual calls to your newly created function are still somewhat redundant, because they accept the trans argument on each line. Again, from the functional programming perspective, partial application and precomputation come to mind, and maybe you find yourself rewriting your function like this:

Available for download on Wrox.com

```
static void FillDatabase3( ) {
  using (var conn = new SqlCeConnection(DBCONNSTR)) {
    conn.Open( );
    try {
      using (var trans = conn.BeginTransaction( )) {
        ExecuteSQL(trans, "create table people(id int, name ntext)");
        trans.Commit( );
      }

      using (var trans = conn.BeginTransaction( )) {
        var exec = (
          (Func<SqlCeTransaction, Func<int, Action<string>>>)
```

```
          (transaction => id => name =>
            ExecuteSQL(transaction, String.Format(
              "insert into people(id, name) values({0}, '{1}')", id, name))))
            (trans);

        exec(1)("Harry");
        exec(2)("Jane");
        exec(3)("Willy");
        exec(4)("Susan");
        exec(5)("Bill");
        exec(6)("Jennifer");
        exec(7)("John");
        exec(8)("Anna");
        exec(9)("Bob");
        exec(10)("Mary");

        trans.Commit( );
      }
    }
    finally {
      conn.Close( );
    }
  }
}
```

Code snippet Program.cs

This time, the lambda function is created in curried format and the `trans` parameter is then partially applied. Unfortunately it is necessary to put an explicit cast in place for this to be accepted by the C# compiler because of the deficiencies in the type inference system previously discussed, and it is even necessary to mention explicitly the type `SqlCeTransaction`, although the final result function `exec` doesn't have a parameter of this type anymore. The compiler also insists on very clear use of parentheses.

This example has been included as a possible evolutionary step, although it is not a step that should really be made at this point. It shows how easy it is to "overshoot your target," in that the full currying of the `exec` helper function resulted in a complex signature and complicated individual calls. Instead, here's a final suggestion that makes more sense:

Available for download on Wrox.com

```
static void FillDatabase4( ) {
  using (var conn = new SqlCeConnection(DBCONNSTR)) {
    conn.Open( );
    try {
      using (var trans = conn.BeginTransaction( )) {
        ExecuteSQL(trans, "create table people(id int, name ntext)");
        trans.Commit( );
      }

      using (var trans = conn.BeginTransaction( )) {
        Action<int, string> exec = (id, name) =>
            ExecuteSQL(trans, String.Format(
```

```
                    "insert into people(id, name) values({0}, '{1}')", id, name));

        exec(1, "Harry");
        exec(2, "Jane");
        exec(3, "Willy");
        exec(4, "Susan");
        exec(5, "Bill");
        exec(6, "Jennifer");
        exec(7, "John");
        exec(8, "Anna");
        exec(9, "Bob");
        exec(10, "Mary");

        trans.Commit( );
      }
    }
    finally {
      conn.Close( );
    }
  }
}
```

Code snippet Program.cs

There are several advantages to this simpler approach. First, it's short — the shortest of the options mentioned. Second, it doesn't use curried format, which simplifies the call syntax in C#. Third, it uses a closure directly to keep the transaction parameter available. The previous example went a step too far when it came to that parameter — because the function is only for reuse locally, there's no need to have a transaction parameter in the first place.

Overall, an interesting example of functional modularization in a form that can be applied to everyday coding.

SUMMARY

The functional techniques shown in this chapter are especially interesting because they are in a "sweet spot" that makes them applicable to many everyday scenarios. The syntax these techniques use is not as esoteric as some more extreme scenarios tend to use, and there is no major algorithmic rethinking required either. You can find applications for such techniques in any program code.

21

Existing Projects Using Functional Techniques

WHAT'S IN THIS CHAPTER?

➤ The .NET Framework

➤ LINQ

➤ MapReduce implementations

➤ NUnit

Functional programming is not theoretical. It exists; it is out there. It is interesting how polarizing any discussion about these facts is. There are those programmers who think it's obvious how exciting functional programming is, and all their friends do it. There are also those who have hardly ever met somebody who does functional programming, and who think it's rather academic and doesn't apply to their work. Of course, there are many somewhere in between these extremes.

As programmers on the .NET platform, you don't need to be shown places where classes and objects live. To provide a more complete overall perspective, this chapter attempts to point out some of the more popular places where functions are important.

THE .NET FRAMEWORK

Since its first versions, the .NET Framework and its languages have had certain influences from functional programming. From the outside it's hard to judge whether somebody from the Framework team came up with the idea of creating a `System.Delegate` type, or whether that was set in motion by the language teams. However, this happened before the first version of the .NET Framework became publicly available, and it is a great improvement over the loosely typed function pointers available in many other, usually older, object oriented languages. In the same way, some patterns were implemented in a functional fashion from the get-go.

The `IEnumerable` and `IEnumerator` interfaces provide one example of a framework feature that allows for all the lazy evaluation goodness of sequences in functional languages, although the first version of C# only implemented the reading of such sequences with the `foreach` keyword. Programmers had to wait for C# 2.0 if they wanted an easy way to construct such sequences themselves, but when it came in the shape of iterators, it was another feature reminiscent of the approaches found in functional languages.

.NET version 2.0 was a larger release in terms of new framework features in the realm of functional approaches. Iterators, as mentioned, are a language feature. Generics, which are not strictly a framework feature but are of the type system, were introduced. Of course Framework support is required for generics — in the form of changes to the Reflection type information classes, for instance. Generics also had major influence on the Framework and can probably be described as the most important feature to come to the .NET platform after version 1.0.

Generics *is a term typically used in object oriented programming, and as such it is said to have been introduced first by the Ada programming language. But it goes back to the more general idea of type polymorphism, more specifically parametric polymorphism, which has been a staple of functional programming languages since the introduction of ML, and later influenced the designers of Ada. In .NET, generics were introduced at the initiative of Don Syme, who is also the architect and designer of the F# language.*

Version 2.0 was an important one for functional programming in C# because anonymous methods were introduced. These are entirely a language feature, a strategy employed by Microsoft language teams quite a lot over the years. Introducing features on the language level makes it easier for them because they don't have to go through the process of agreeing with several other teams on more general changes and additions to the Framework or even the CLR.

A final interesting framework nugget in version 2.0 came in the form of a few methods on the `Array` and `List<T>` classes. `ConvertAll<T>` and `FindAll<T>` were the first standard framework implementations of `Map` and `Fold`, however crippled, because they worked only on the specific types they were implemented in. There was also `ForEach<T>`, which worked like a typical `Apply` function.

With packages like Windows Presentation Foundation (WPF), Windows Communication Foundation (WCF), Workflow Foundation (WF), and others, lots of new functionality was introduced to .NET in version 3.0. These platforms remain largely imperative in their architecture, which may be sensible given the nature of their applications involving user interaction and communication layers.

Version 3.5 was the next major step for functional ideas on .NET. The largest new block of framework functionality in that version was LINQ, and you can find the details on that in the next section of this chapter. Much of the LINQ functionality goes back to framework support, and there's a layer of language features on top, which makes the APIs much easier to use in C#. This includes features such as lambda expressions, expression trees, and extension methods.

Most recently, in .NET version 4.0, there is new functionally oriented functionality in the Parallel Extensions (PFX), which are also mentioned later in this chapter. Some of their syntax is based on higher order functions, and some on mechanisms of lazy evaluation. Functional purity is a great target if you would like to work with PFX easily.

Overall, there is quite a list of elements of the .NET Framework that have a functional nature or were at least visibly influenced by functional ideas. But .NET is meant to be largely a language agnostic platform, and the languages do most of the grunt work to implement their own paradigms. The central framework of functionality is often reason for compromises in the languages, but the functionality that has been introduced in C# over the years, as well as the official support for new languages like F#, show that .NET is at least open to a wide spectrum of different language paradigms.

LINQ

LINQ is a functional API that is largely pure. It was introduced in .NET version 3.5, with Visual Studio 2008 and C# 3.0. Many of the new language features in C# 3.0 were originally introduced to support LINQ, and creative programmers have found many other applications since then. An in-depth look at LINQ is quite telling when trying to assess Microsoft's position regarding functional programming in the "old" .NET languages (that is, leaving F# out of the equation).

LINQ to Objects

Many different features on both the language and the framework level play together for the experience provided by LINQ to Objects. The term LINQ to Objects usually describes the part of LINQ that works entirely within your application, that is, with native .NET objects as opposed to data that is queried from elsewhere. The latter scenario is also discussed later in this section, but for now the focus is what you can do with objects alone.

A very simple example of a LINQ query is this:

```
var values = new[] { 1, 2, 3, 4, 5, 6, 7, 8 };
var valuesGreater5 =
  from v in values
  where v > 5
  select v;
```

Starting from a simple array of integer values, the query selects those values that are greater than 5. It's important to understand that the query expression itself is just syntactic sugar, which is translated by the C# compiler into method calls. The API of LINQ is therefore language agnostic, and it could even be used from a .NET language that doesn't have any special LINQ syntax. Here's an equivalent of the preceding code, without using the LINQ Expression feature of C# 3.0:

```
var values = new[] { 1, 2, 3, 4, 5, 6, 7, 8 };
var valuesGreater5 =
  values.Where(v => v > 5).Select(v => v);
```

Where and Select are extension methods being called, threading through the values array, filtering, and then selecting. The Select call is not strictly necessary, and the compiler doesn't really generate it; it was just left in for completeness' sake. Of course the functionality itself could be written without LINQ — with the help of the Filter function as introduced in Chapter 12, for instance:

```
var values = new[] { 1, 2, 3, 4, 5, 6, 7, 8 };
var valuesGreater5 =
  Functional.Filter(v => v > 5, values);
```

If you really want the Select, the function Functional.Map() does the same thing:

```
var people = new[] {
  new Person() { Name = "Harry", Age = 22 },
  new Person() { Name = "Jodie", Age = 35 },
  new Person() { Name = "William", Age = 56 },
  new Person() { Name = "Susan", Age = 41 }
};

var agesGreater40 =
  from p in people
  where p.Age > 40
  select p.Age;

// or with Extension Methods
var agesGreater40_2 =
  people.Where(p => p.Age > 40).Select(p => p.Age);

// or with Functional
var agesGreater40_3 =
  Functional.Map(p => p.Age, Functional.Filter(p => p.Age > 40, people));
```

You know how Functional.Map() and Functional.Filter() work, their implementations were discussed in Chapter 12 in some detail. The LINQ functions Where() and Select() work the same way, with one important difference: they are extension methods, which allows you to use them in that nice chained way. This makes the API appear monadic in nature — the chaining of operations on a particular type is a monadic idea.

It is unfortunate that Microsoft decided to allow extension methods only with their first argument specifying the type that is being extended. The Functional functions don't have the collection itself as their first argument, to facilitate easier reuse for currying and partial application, which means they can't be used as extension methods in this case.

Looking at the extension method version of the preceding LINQ code, you notice that there are lambda expressions being passed to the Where() and Select() functions. These lambdas get constructed by the compiler automatically based on the criteria used in the LINQ expression. Finally, the compiler needs to be able to find the helper methods that make LINQ work, and these live in a class called Enumerable in the namespace System.Linq. As the following table shows, there are many other extension methods defined in that class, not all of which have a corresponding keyword on the language side of LINQ.

ENUMERABLE FUNCTION	LANGUAGE INTEGRATED
Aggregate	
All	
Any	
Average	
Contains	
Count	
Distinct	
GroupBy	group… by
GroupJoin	
Intersect	
Join	join… on
Max	
Min	
OrderBy	orderby
OrderByDescending	orderby… descending
Reverse	
Select	select
SelectMany	select
Skip	
Sum	
Take	
ThenBy	
Union	
Where	where

On the basis of a slightly more complex data class, here is an example that uses a combination of sorting, grouping, and selecting:

```
public class CountryInfo {
  public CountryInfo(string name, int areaKM2, int population) {
    this.Name = name;
```

```
      this.AreaKM2 = areaKM2;
      this.Population = population;
    }
  public string Name { get; set; }
  public int AreaKM2 { get; set; }
  public int Population { get; set; }

  public override string ToString( ) {
    return String.Format("Country: {0}, Area km^2: {1}, Population: {2}",
      Name, AreaKM2, Population);
  }
}


...

var list = new CountryInfoList( );

var groupList =
  from info in list
  orderby info.Population
  group info by info.Population / 1000000
    into g
    select new {
      Group = g,
      PopulationGroup = g.Key,
      MaxPopulation = g.Max(info => info.Population)
    };

var groupList_2 =
  list.
  OrderBy(i => i.Population).
  GroupBy(i => i.Population / 1000000).
  Select(g => new {
    Group = g,
    PopulationGroup = g.Key,
    MaxPopulation = g.Max(info => info.Population)
  });
```

The example uses yet another C# 3.0 language feature: anonymous types. These were introduced to cover query scenarios that require projection. Projection is used to create a result set from one or more sources, where the result set combines pieces of information that are not available in the same shape from the source. Grouping is one example of this, and joining is another:

```
var countries = new CountryInfoList( );
var people = new CountryPerson[] {
    new CountryPerson {Name = "Bert Bott", Country="Brazil"},
    new CountryPerson {Name = "Jill Jones", Country = "Cameroon"}
  };

var joinedList =
  from person in people
  join country in countries
  on person.Country equals country.Name
  select new {
```

```
        Name = person.Name,
        Country = person.Country,
        Population = country.Population
    };

var joinedList_2 =
    people.Join(countries, p => p.Country, c => c.Name,
        (p, c) => new {
            Name = p.Name,
            Country = p.Country,
            Population = c.Population
        });
```

Anonymous types are also persistent data types, in the sense discussed in Chapter 16 about immutable data. Unfortunately they are restricted to quite specific use cases because they have no name, but they are yet another piece in the puzzle of LINQ.

LINQ to Objects is a very well-constructed system. The functions that implement the querying features are all functionally pure, and modeled after the higher order functions many functional environments have provided for a long time. They use lambda expressions as a means of abstraction, which helps to make them entirely type agnostic. The functions build heavily on the support for iterators in the .NET interfaces `IEnumerable<T>` and `IEnumerator<T>` as well as the C# 2.0 iterator features.

With the help of the extension method feature, chains can be built — functional languages often provide special chaining syntax support, and monads go in the same direction. Finally, features like anonymous types and the `var` keyword work together to add projection functionality that programmers are familiar with when writing queries.

LINQ to a Query Backend

Expression trees (the basics of which were discussed in Chapter 7) provide an understanding of "code as data." An interesting aspect of their implementation in C# is the fact that a caller doesn't know, or care, whether an expression he's passing in to another function is stored as an executable expression or as an expression tree. Take a look at this piece of code:

```
namespace Compiled {
  public static class IntExtensionsCompiled {
    public static int Mangle(this int value, Func<int, int> mangler) {
      return mangler(value);
    }
  }
}
```

This is an extension method that takes a lambda expression and calls it on the value. You can use it like this:

```
namespace ManglerDemo {
  using Compiled;

  public class ManglerTesterCompiled {
```

```
    public static void ShowIt( ) {
      int val = 42;

      // result will be 42*42 here
      int result = val.Mangle(x => x * x);
      Console.WriteLine(result);
    }
  }
}
```

The extension method `Mangle` could just as well be implemented like this:

```
namespace Expressions {
  public static class IntExtensionsExpressions {
    public static int Mangle(this int value, Expression<Func<int, int>> mangler) {
      // let's mangle the mangler before we do anything with it
      // -- just because we can
      Func<int, int> mangledMangler =
        Expression.Lambda<Func<int, int>>(
          Expression.Add(mangler.Body, Expression.Constant(23)),
          mangler.Parameters).Compile( );
      return mangledMangler(value);
    }
  }
}
```

In this case, the variable that accepts the delegate is of type `Expression<Func<int, int>>` instead of just `Func<int, int>`. This instructs the C# compiler to receive and store the argument as an expression tree instead of a compiled delegate. As a result, the expression can be analyzed and even modified before it is eventually executed.

What is the caller going to look like in this case? Like this:

```
namespace ManglerDemo {
  using Expressions;

  public class ManglerTesterExpressions {
    public static void ShowIt( ) {
      int val = 42;

      // result will be 42*42 + 23 here - but
      // my own code is exactly the same as before!!
      int result = val.Mangle(x => x * x);
      Console.WriteLine(result);
    }
  }
}
```

This is almost exactly the same as before. The only difference is that the `using` line pulls in the namespace `Expressions` instead of `Compiled`. That's sufficient for the resolution mechanisms to find a different extension method called `Mangle`, which even has a slightly different parameter type. From the caller side, this is invisible, and so is the fact that the delegate that is passed in is changed before it is executed.

In the case of LINQ, this fact is used for an interesting purpose. It allows the LINQ infrastructure to take a delegate, which was passed in to those LINQ methods you saw early in this chapter — `Where()`, `Select()`, `GroupBy()`, and so on — and pass it into a process of parsing and translating the expression. It is perfectly possible that the expression never gets executed in its literal form, but instead it is translated into a different language to make its execution more efficient.

This is, in a nutshell, what LINQ does to execute queries you write in C# code as SQL queries on the database server. Because the system is based on interfaces that you can implement in your own types, it is extensible, and there are now lots of independent LINQ providers that allow you to query all sorts of data stores through LINQ — third-party ORM tools, for example, but also data sources like Amazon or Twitter.

Parallelization

With the inclusion of the Parallel Extensions (PFX) in .NET 4.0, LINQ has become a great example of how easy parallelization can be with a purely functional API. There is a helper function, `AsParallel()`, which converts an `IEnumerable<T>` into an object called `ParallelQuery<T>`. The effect of this is that a different set of extension methods applies to the object after the conversion, in this case those from the class `ParallelEnumerable`. These extension methods have the same names as the ones shown earlier in the `Enumerable` class, so that once more the calling code looks the same as before. But the methods work differently in that they automatically partition the source sequence and run several parallel `Task`s instead of just one sequential one. This feature is known as PLINQ, or Parallel LINQ.

 PFX uses clever algorithms to figure out how Task instances are eventually parallelized — or in fact, if they are parallelized at all — on any given hardware. PLINQ doesn't influence this directly; it just interfaces with the PFX infrastructure by running Tasks.

For example, here's some code for an iterator:

```
static IEnumerable<int> GetValues( ) {
  int i = 0;
  while (i < 20) {
    Console.WriteLine("({0}) Returning {1}", Task.CurrentId, i);
    yield return i++;
  }
}
```

The output line includes a value retrieved from the PFX infrastructure, the ID of the currently executing task. (This is a value of type `int?`; it is `null` when the code is not running in a `Task` instance.) Here's a normal LINQ call to calculate the sum of the values from the iterator, and its output:

```
Console.WriteLine(GetValues( ).Sum( ));

() Returning 0
```

```
() Returning 1
() Returning 2
() Returning 3
() Returning 4
() Returning 5
() Returning 6
() Returning 7
() Returning 8
() Returning 9
() Returning 10
() Returning 11
() Returning 12
() Returning 13
() Returning 14
() Returning 15
() Returning 16
() Returning 17
() Returning 18
() Returning 19
190
```

By modifying the calling code to include a call to `AsParallel()`, the result becomes this:

```
Console.WriteLine(GetValues( ).AsParallel().Sum( ));
```

```
(1) Returning 0
(1) Returning 1
(1) Returning 2
(2) Returning 3
(1) Returning 4
(2) Returning 5
(2) Returning 6
(2) Returning 7
(1) Returning 8
(1) Returning 9
(1) Returning 10
(1) Returning 11
(1) Returning 12
(1) Returning 13
(1) Returning 14
(1) Returning 15
(1) Returning 16
(1) Returning 17
(1) Returning 18
(1) Returning 19
190
```

Note the values in parentheses at the start of the lines — these are the task IDs. The precise sequence of the output is quite random and you get different sequences with every test run. But it is clear that the values are no longer sequentially retrieved by one running process, but instead by two different ones. The result remains the same. By creating an algorithm implementation based on pure functions and other functional paradigms, it has become possible to parallelize quickly and easily, using just a minor change in one single location.

GOOGLE MAPREDUCE AND ITS IMPLEMENTATIONS

The MapReduce pattern, described in Chapter 19, was invented by Google, and a U.S. software patent was issued for it in January 2010.

There are many different implementations of MapReduce in use today, employed in and usable from a variety of programming languages. The MapReduce pattern is just a part of the whole infrastructure required in order to benefit from the distributed computing idea behind the approach. There are complex implementations that provide the required data storage mechanisms, specialized languages to construct MapReduce solutions, and all the infrastructure to deploy such solutions to clusters of machines that execute the calculations, access the data, and construct and persist the resulting information.

One popular complex implementation is called Hadoop. Created by Doug Cutting, Hadoop is now an open source project coordinated by the Apache Software Foundation. It's written in Java and has seen great investment by commercial users such as Yahoo! It is, or was at one point, the basis of systems run by Amazon, Facebook, Microsoft, and many others.

Through Amazon Web Services, a platform for Amazon's Elastic Compute Cloud (EC2) services, you can access a system called Amazon Elastic MapReduce. Based on Hadoop, it takes its data out off Amazon's S3 storage system and uses EC2 machine instances to build the cluster on which MapReduce job flows are executed. These job flows can interact with either Hive or Pig — more infrastructure, as well as language support, related to the Hadoop project — or they can be implemented as streaming job flows, which can utilize a number of different programming languages.

The documentation pages on Elastic MapReduce don't list C# or .NET as supported for the purpose of creating job flows. But it has been suggested in the Amazon forums that installing Mono via a bootstrap action should be possible. As a result, it may be possible to utilize the Amazon MapReduce engine as a .NET programmer, but it will require some effort at this time.

On Microsoft platforms, there has been talk for a while of Hadoop becoming available to users of Microsoft's own cloud computing platform, Windows Azure. Microsoft has been using Hadoop as the basis of its Bing search engine, so this seems like a possibility, although Microsoft's strategies are not entirely clear in this area. Currently it looks more likely that it will push forward a research project named Dryad, which uses different approaches to Google MapReduce, but with similar purposes, and it already has a LINQ binding, making it very easy to translate LINQ queries into Dryad processes. It is even possible to implement the MapReduce pattern on the basis of Dryad very easily through the use of LINQ. And with the help of AppFabric services, many Azure developers have built their own processing environments for the MapReduce pattern.

Outside of Microsoft, there are several third-party products that make MapReduce available to the .NET programmer. MongoDB, for example, is an open-source document database system with great .NET bindings that uses MapReduce patterns for aggregation implementation. MongoDB has built-in support for the MapReduce pattern, which is normally controlled by JavaScript functions. The C# driver, however, can generate these functions automatically, based on LINQ queries executed against the database. MongoDB also has a feature called sharding, which allows horizontal scaling of the MongoDB infrastructure to a large number of machines, and any MapReduce algorithms can automatically distribute across all shards.

MySpace Qizmt is an open source system that implements MapReduce, which can be readily installed on your own machine or machines. Qizmt is reasonably well documented in a wiki and getting started with your own C#-written MapReduce "jobs" is straightforward. Unfortunately the project status is a little unclear: At the time of writing, the latest public download (which is called an alpha version) is from February 2010.

Numerous other products, some of them commercial, exist in the .NET space that make MapReduce an option for C# developers. Depending on your needs, it makes sense to consider implementing the pattern yourself. In the case where your needs don't involve any infrastructure outside of the machine where the code executes, MapReduce still offers a simple and widely accepted pattern for the implementation of parallel data algorithms.

Curiously, Google doesn't provide access to a MapReduce service similar to the Amazon offering. In the cloud computing space, Google has its own offering called App Engine. There are independent projects that implement MapReduce for this platform, but nothing official from Google. It has also become known that Google has moved on from MapReduce for the indexing needs of its Web search engine. MapReduce is not a golden bullet, and Google's decision is purely requirements based. For extensible, parallelizable, infrastructure-backed systems that perform data and compute intensive tasks, MapReduce can be a great solution.

NUNIT

You're probably familiar with the unit-testing framework NUnit, the .NET variant of the original Java-based JUnit. Just in case you don't do unit testing at all (and you should, of course!), here's how NUnit can be used to implement a test:

```
public static class Calculator {
  public static int Add (int a, int b) {
    return a + b;
  }
}

...

[TestFixture]
public class Tests {
  [Test]
  internal void AddTest1( ) {
    Assert.AreEqual(20 + 10, Calculator.Add(20, 10));
  }
}
```

Using a *test runner*, a program that loads the assembly with the tests inside and executes all the methods marked with the attributes, you can now execute the tests against your implemented functionality. When a test fails, the Assert.AreEqual() method (or one of the other methods in the Assert class) throws an exception, and the test runner outputs information about the test that has failed and the exception it has caught.

For quite a while now, NUnit has had a fluent API in addition to the standard one. Here's how you can rewrite the preceding test with that fluent API:

```
[Test]
public void AddTest1f( ) {
  Assert.That(Calculator.Add(20, 10),
    Is.EqualTo(10 + 20));
}
```

The idea of fluent APIs is that the user of the API can chain together calls to various API functions. These APIs are quite hard to write because of the complex interactions that are possible between the return values and parameters of all the functions involved. Here are a few more examples:

```
public static class DataSource {
  public static string GetValue( ) {
    return "Some String";
  }

  public static IEnumerable<string> GetData( ) {
    yield return "First string";
    yield return "Second string";
    yield return "Another string";
    yield return "One final string";
  }
}

...

[Test]
public void ValueTest1f( ) {
  Assert.That(DataSource.GetValue( ),
    Is.Not.Null.
    And.StartsWith("S").
    And.Not.EqualTo("Something else"));
}

[Test]
public void DataTest1f( ) {
  Assert.That(DataSource.GetData( ).ToList( ),
    Has.Count.GreaterThan(0).
        And.Some.Matches<string>(v => v.StartsWith("O")));
}
```

As you can see, the NUnit API takes great care to allow the user to compose its parts in order to form a sentence that describes the conditions that are being checked: "Assert that <my value> is not null, and starts with S, and [is] not equal to 'Something else.'" It is great to be able to write unit tests this way!

From a functional point of view, the interesting thing about the API structure of NUnit is that it is based on lots of functionally pure methods and properties. There are a few exceptions, some of them rather severe, and it isn't quite clear whether the authors of that API had functional ideas in mind when they created it. But their structure obviously tended in the functional direction whether they planned it or not.

The following piece of code deconstructs the fluent calls in the last example test into several steps:

```
[Test]
public void DataTest1( ) {
  var step1 = new ConstraintExpression( );
  var step2 = step1.Append(new PropOperator("Count"));
  var step3 = step2.Append(new GreaterThanConstraint(0));

  var step4 = step3.And;
  var step5 = step4.Append(new SomeOperator( ));
  var step6 = step5.Append(new PredicateConstraint<string>(v => v.StartsWith("O")));

  Assert.That(DataSource.GetData( ).ToList( ), step6);
}
```

The resulting structure should immediately remind you of something: the code that uses immutable collection data structures, like those discussed in Chapter 16. A chain is being built of constraints (these are the building blocks of the filter that NUnit uses to check the correctness of the test result), and the Append function returns a new instance. Well, that's what it looks like!

In reality, things are a bit different than they look. The rather odd-looking step4 gives it away a bit because it makes it clear that this is not a simple hierarchical tree of condition testing expressions, like you may have thought. Instead, a class called ConstraintBuilder is used under the covers, and through some clever redirection each of the chained Append calls adds an element to just one ConstraintBuilder instance. In most cases, Append only returns a reference to the same constraint that was passed in. In the case of step4, the And property accesses the ConstraintBuilder instance directly in order to deal with the operator.

In spite of the non-functional decisions that were made in places, the API remains widely functionally pure. The vast majority of the hundreds of utility functions that make up the API contain only a single return statement each and are free of side effects. NUnit is certainly not a product that is going to require parallel execution (on this level!), but the study of the source code is recommended if you would like to see how functional purity is achieved naturally through clever architecture — or the other way, how clever architecture leads directly to functional purity.

It is interesting to note that some of the functions of the NUnit API return the same object they were passed — it might be modified, but it is still the same object. For instance, if you check the sequence from the preceding example carefully, you will find that the step5 variable refers to the same object as step4. A function that works this way can't be considered functionally pure (and I said there were exceptions to the theme in NUnit), and this issue provides an opportunity to point out that the call interface of a function doesn't allow conclusions about its inner working in the C# environment, where most objects are mutable.

SUMMARY

Many real-world projects utilize functional approaches today. This chapter has shed some light on a few interesting ones, but the list is by no means exhaustive and expanding all the time. The ideas demonstrated in this book show that while C# is not a language with a primary focus on functional programming, it can still be used productively with the paradigm in mind. You've got the toolset — go out explore!

INDEX

F

R.C.L.

SEP. 2011

G